LOCKJAW

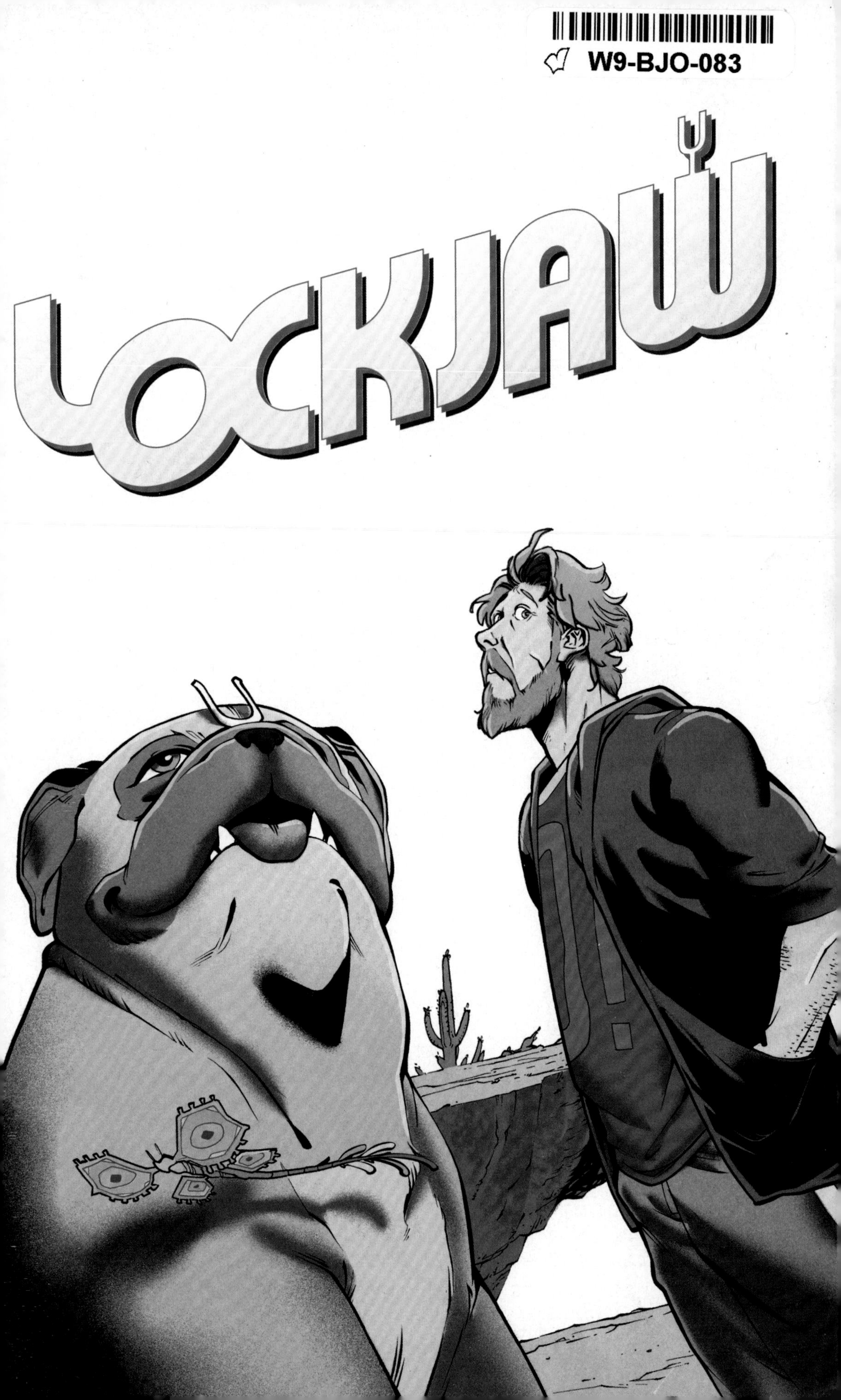

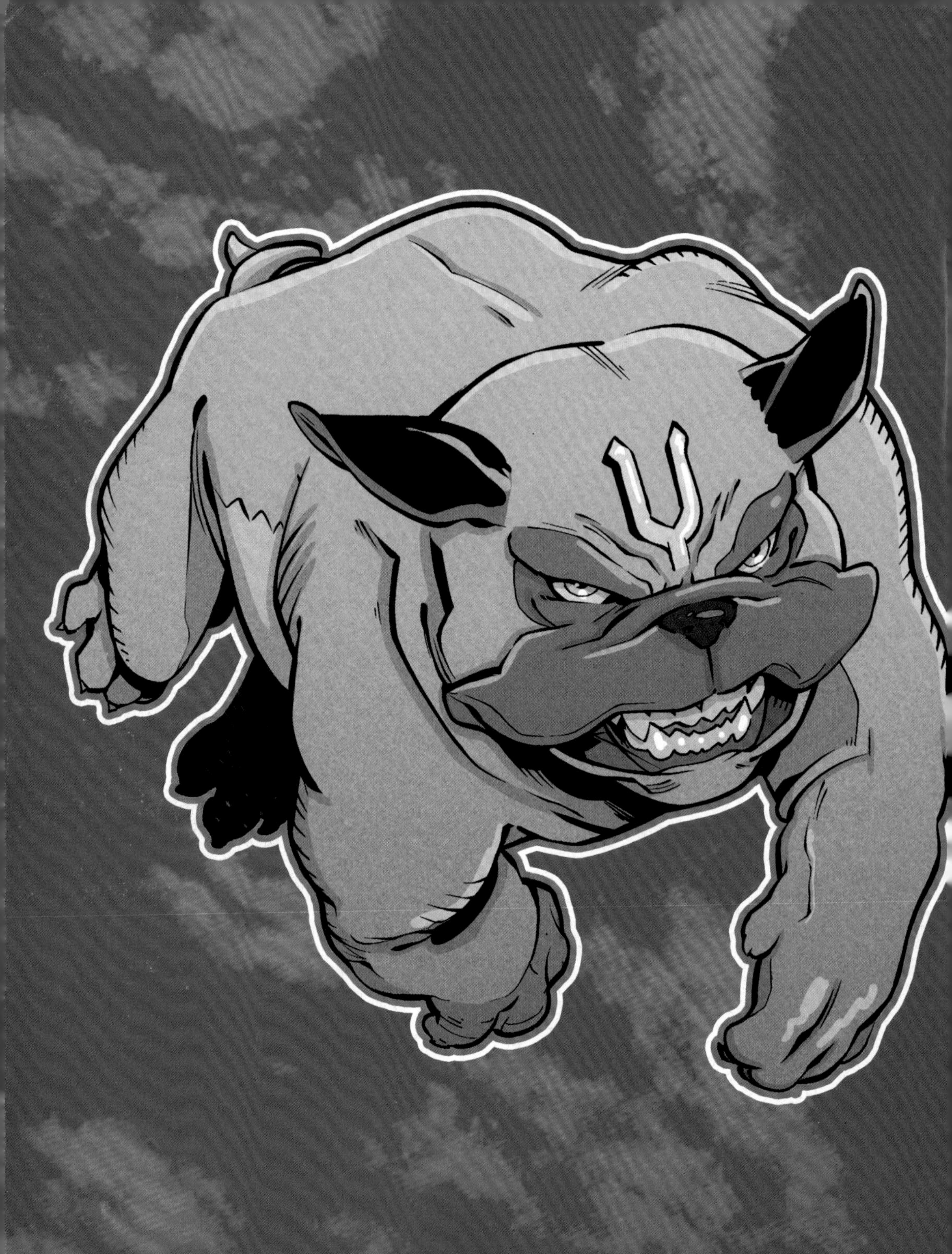

COLLECTION EDITOR **JENNIFER GRÜNWALD** · ASSISTANT EDITOR **CAITLIN O'CONNELL**
ASSOCIATE MANAGING EDITOR **KATERI WOODY** · EDITOR, SPECIAL PROJECTS **MARK D. BEAZLEY**
VP PRODUCTION & SPECIAL PROJECTS **JEFF YOUNGQUIST** · SVP PRINT, SALES & MARKETING **DAVID GABRIEL**
BOOK DESIGNER **JAY BOWEN**

EDITOR IN CHIEF **C.B. CEBULSKI** · CHIEF CREATIVE OFFICER **JOE QUESADA**
PRESIDENT **DAN BUCKLEY** · EXECUTIVE PRODUCER **ALAN FINE**

LOCKJAW: WHO'S A GOOD BOY? Contains material originally published in magazine form as LOCKJAW #1-4, THE THING #4, GIRL COMICS #2, ORIGINAL SINS #1 and INHUMANS: ONCE AND FUTURE KINGS #1-5. First printing 2018. ISBN 978-1-302-91252-9. Published by MARVEL WORLDWIDE, INC., a subsidiary of MARVEL ENTERTAINMENT, LLC. OFFICE OF PUBLICATION: 135 West 50th Street, New York, NY 10020.

Printed in Canada. DAN BUCKLEY, President, Marvel Entertainment; JOHN NEE, Publisher; JOE QUESADA, Chief Creative Officer; TOM BREVOORT, SVP of Publishing; DAVID BOGART, SVP of Business Affairs & Operations, Publishing & Partnership; DAVID GABRIEL, SVP of Sales & Marketing, Publishing; JEFF YOUNGQUIST, VP of Production & Special Projects; DAN CARR, Executive Director of Publishing Technology; ALEX MORALES, Director of Publishing Operations; DAN EDINGTON, Managing Editor; SUSAN CRESPI, Production Manager; STAN LEE, Chairman Emeritus. For information regarding advertising in Marvel Comics or on Marvel.com, please contact Vit DeBellis, Custom Solutions & Integrated Advertising Manager, at vdebellis@marvel.com. For Marvel subscription inquiries, please call 888-511-5480. **Manufactured between 6/29/2018 and 7/31/2018 by SOLISCO PRINTERS, SCOTT, QC, CANADA.**

10 9 8 7 6 5 4 3 2 1

LOCKJAW
WHO'S A GOOD BOY?

DANIEL KIBBLESMITH

WRITER

CARLOS VILLA

PENCILER

ROBERTO POGGI

INKER

CHRIS O'HALLORAN

COLORIST

VC's CLAYTON COWLES

LETTERER

ED McGUINNESS & **MATTHEW WILSON** (#1),
KRIS ANKA & **MATTHEW WILSON** (#2),
DAVID NAKAYAMA (#3) AND **ULISES FARINAS** & **RYAN HILL** (#4)

COVER ART

GUSTAVO DUARTE

LOGO

SARAH BRUNSTAD

ASSOCIATE EDITOR

WIL MOSS

EDITOR

LOCKJAW CREATED BY **STAN LEE** & **JACK KIRBY**

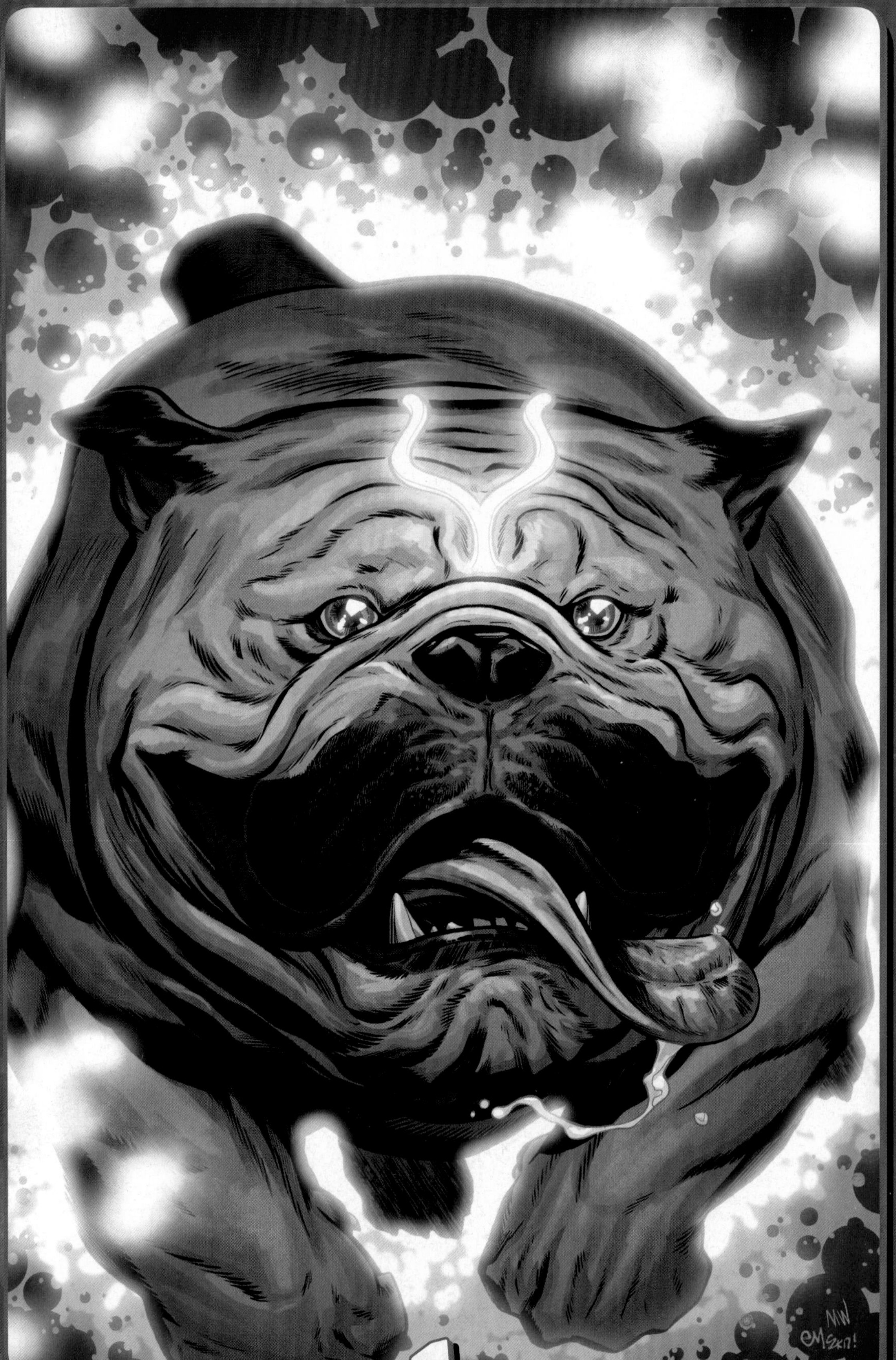
1

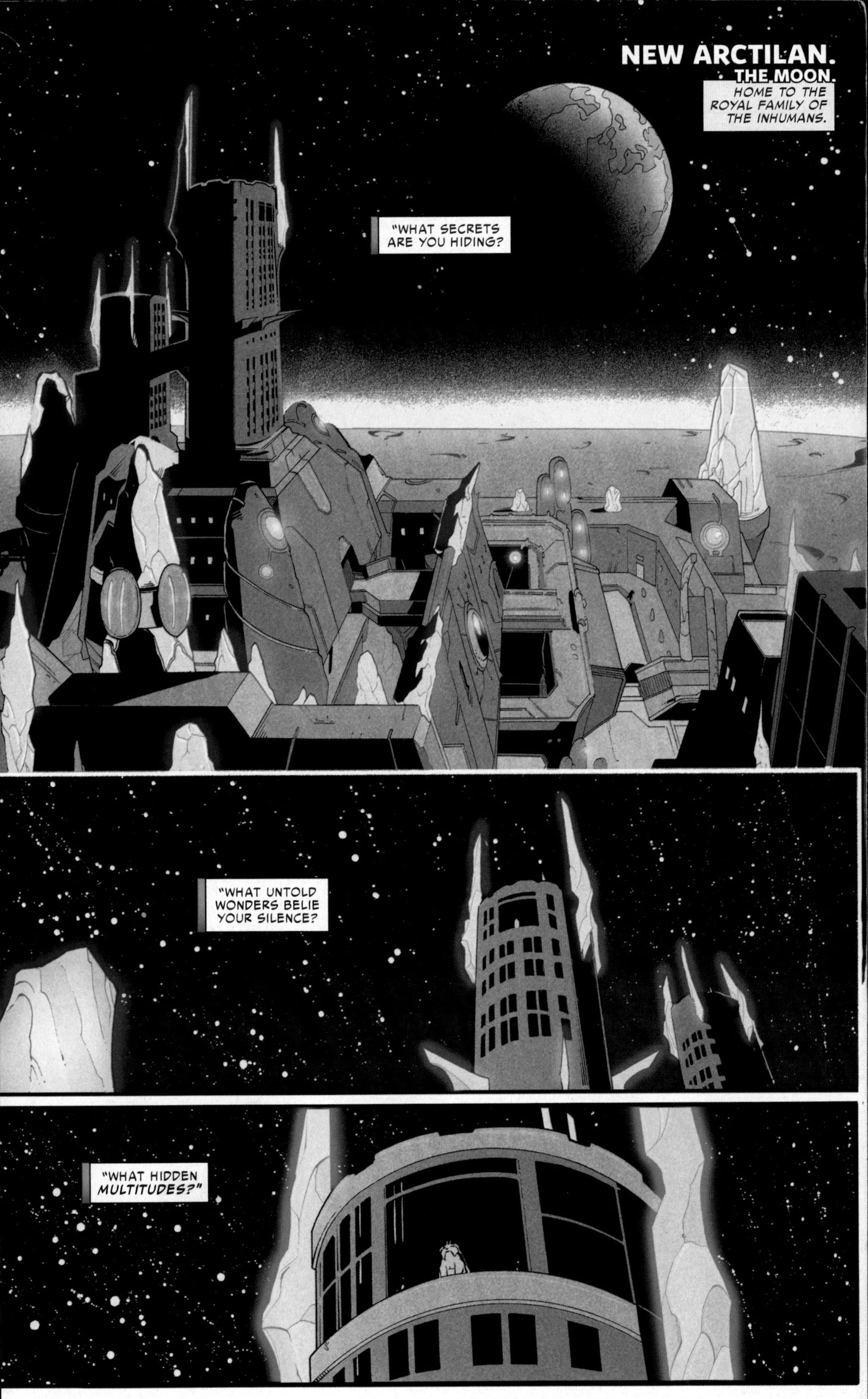
NEW ARCTILAN.
THE MOON.
HOME TO THE ROYAL FAMILY OF THE INHUMANS.
"WHAT SECRETS ARE YOU HIDING?
"WHAT UNTOLD WONDERS BELIE YOUR SILENCE?
"WHAT HIDDEN *MULTITUDES?*"

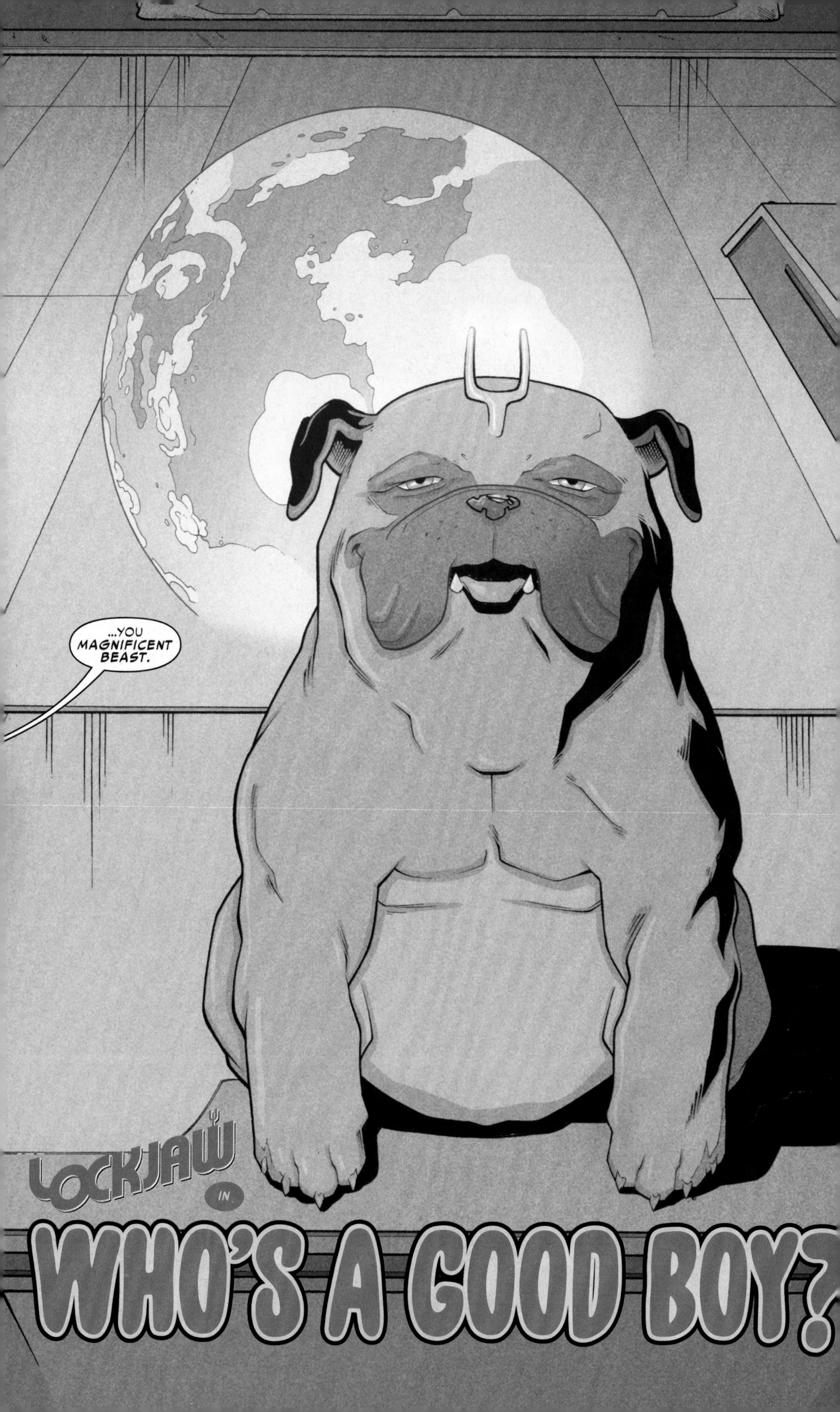
...YOU MAGNIFICENT BEAST.
LOCKJAW IN
WHO'S A GOOD BOY?

PREVIOUSLY

LOCKJAW IS A GIANT TELEPORTING BULLDOG BORN OF INHUMAN EXPERIMENTS ON CANINES. HIS POWERS ALLOW HIM TO TRAVEL AND CARRY OTHERS THOUSANDS OF MILES AND EVEN ACROSS DIMENSIONS. HE IS A LOYAL COMPANION OF THE INHUMAN ROYAL FAMILY, ESPECIALLY KING BLACK BOLT, WITH WHOM LOCKJAW SPENT MUCH OF HIS PUPPYHOOD. EVEN BLACK BOLT, HOWEVER, KNOWS LITTLE OF LOCKJAW'S ORIGINAL FAMILY.

AND SOMETIMES,
A DOG'S GOTTA STRIKE OUT ON HIS OWN.

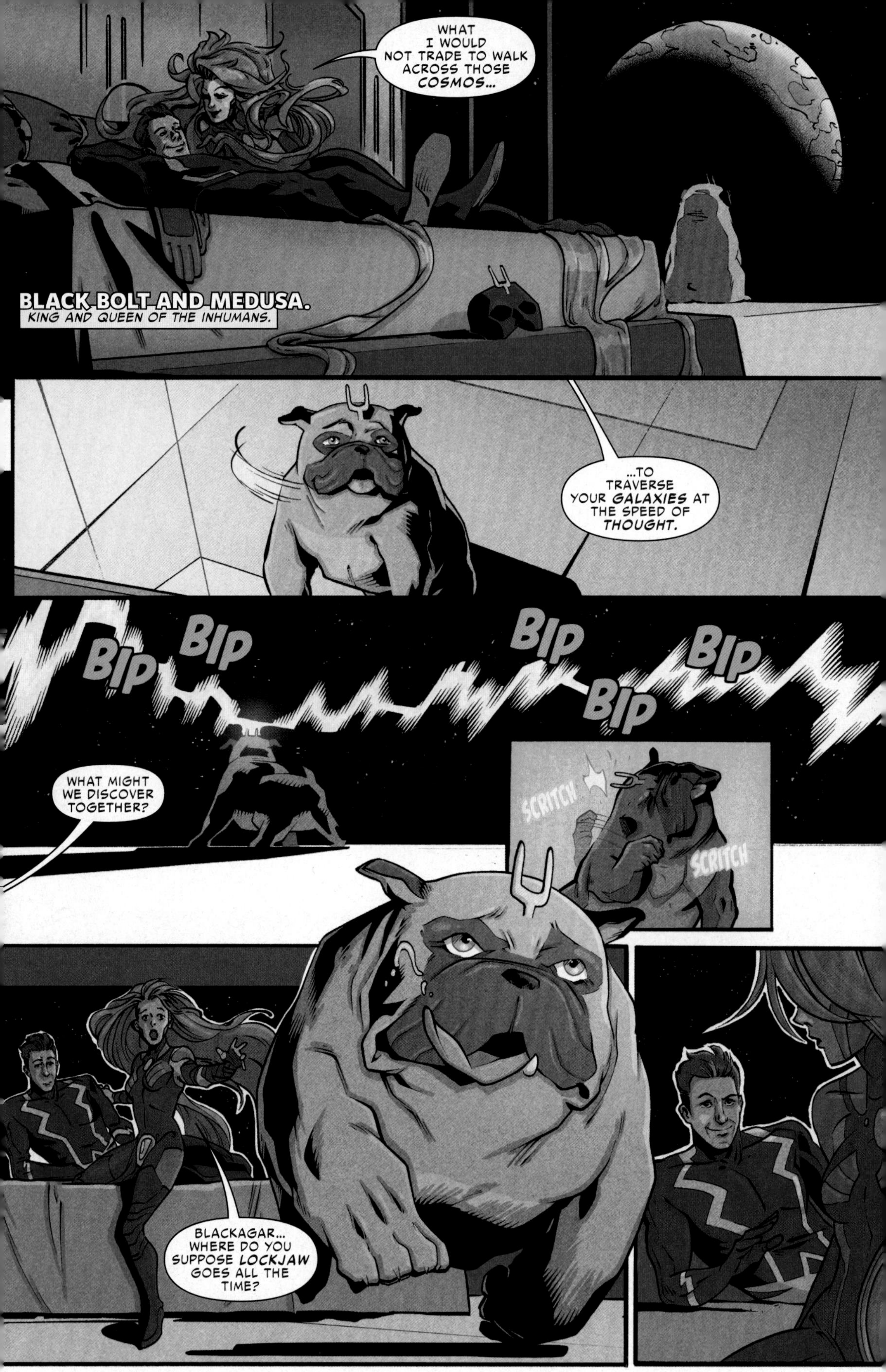

WHAT I WOULD NOT TRADE TO WALK ACROSS THOSE COSMOS...
BLACK BOLT AND MEDUSA.
KING AND QUEEN OF THE INHUMANS.
...TO TRAVERSE YOUR GALAXIES AT THE SPEED OF THOUGHT.
BIP BIP BIP BIP BIP
WHAT MIGHT WE DISCOVER TOGETHER?
SCRITCH
SCRITCH
BLACKAGAR... WHERE DO YOU SUPPOSE LOCKJAW GOES ALL THE TIME?

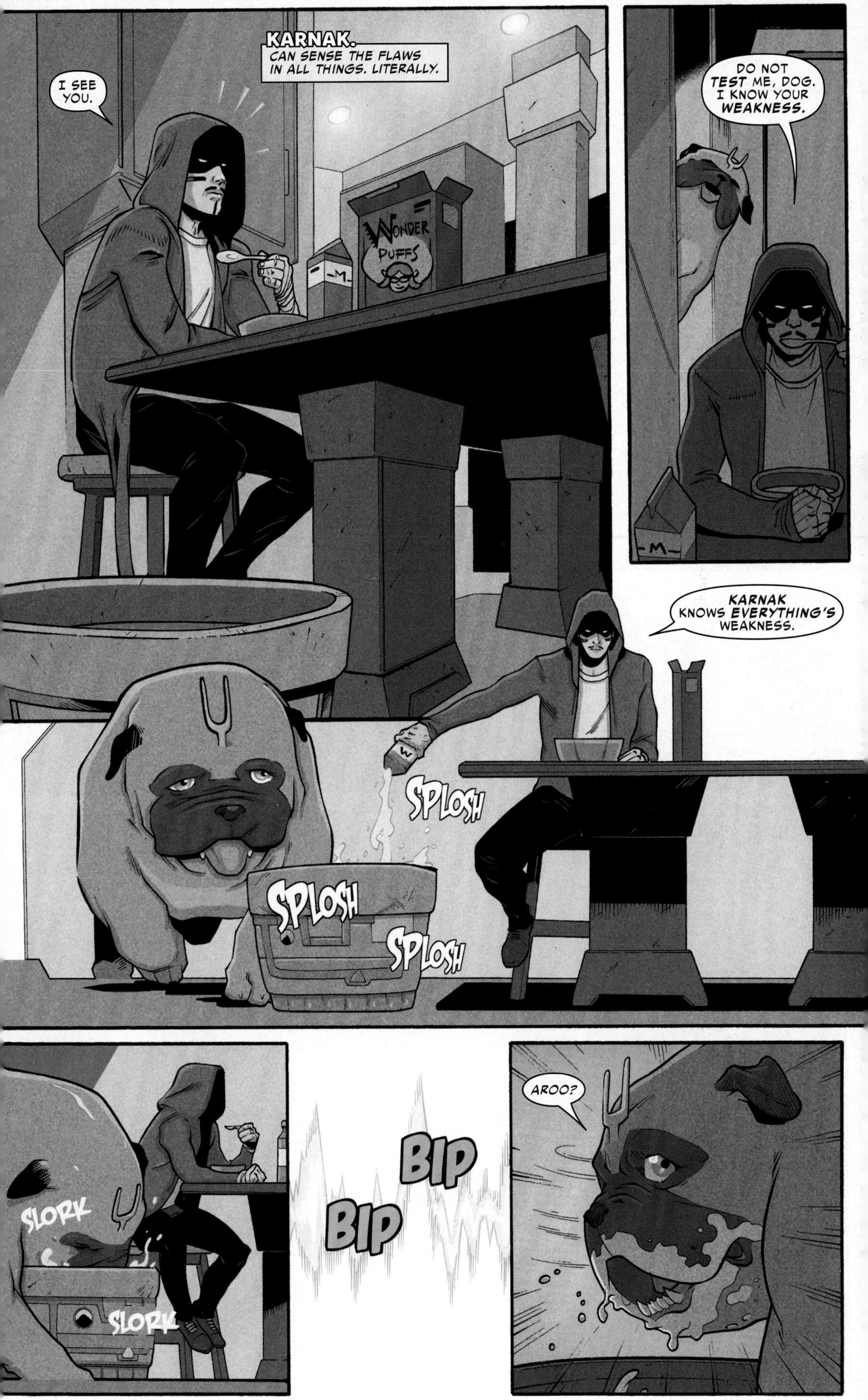
KARNAK.
CAN SENSE THE FLAWS IN ALL THINGS. LITERALLY.
I SEE YOU.
WONDER PUFFS
DO NOT TEST ME, DOG. I KNOW YOUR WEAKNESS.
KARNAK KNOWS EVERYTHING'S WEAKNESS.
SPLOSH
SPLOSH
SPLOSH
SLORK
SLORK
BIP
BIP
AROO?

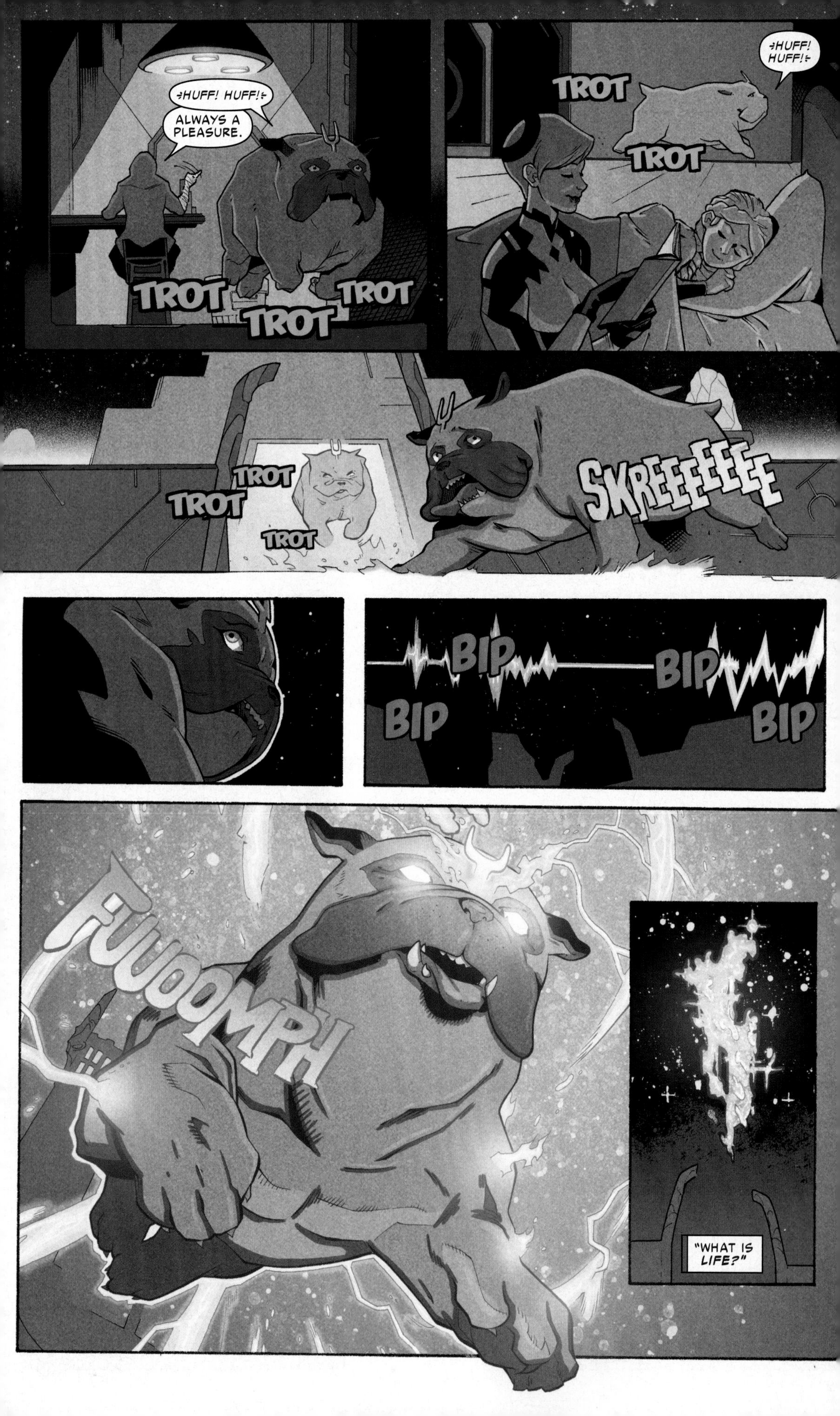

HUFF! HUFF!
ALWAYS A PLEASURE.
TROT
TROT
TROT
TROT
HUFF! HUFF!
TROT
TROT
TROT
TROT
SKREEEEEEE
BIP
BIP
BIP
BIP
FUUOOMPH
"WHAT IS LIFE?"

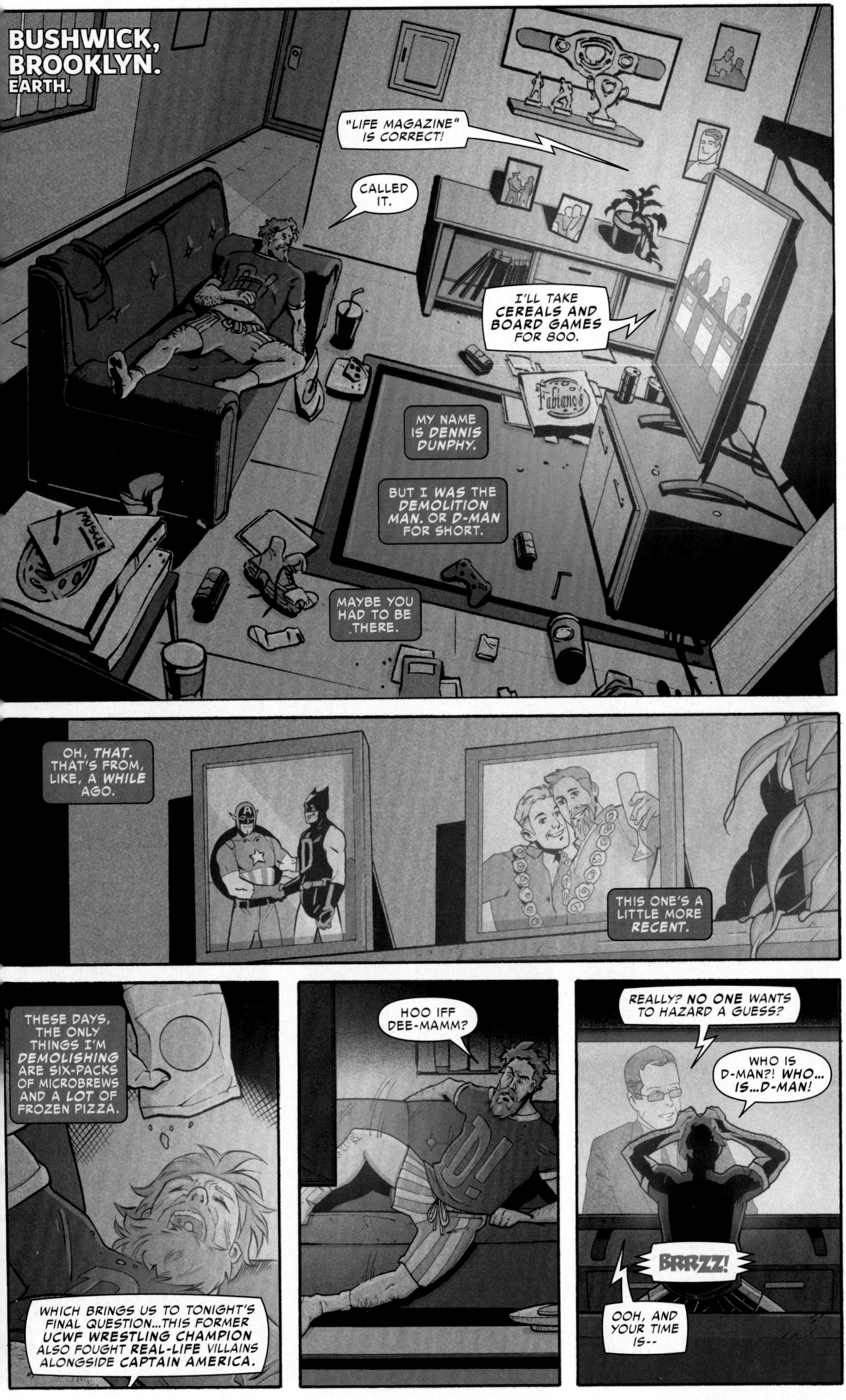

BUSHWICK, BROOKLYN.
EARTH.
"LIFE MAGAZINE" IS CORRECT!
CALLED IT.
I'LL TAKE CEREALS AND BOARD GAMES FOR 800.
Fabiano's
MY NAME IS DENNIS DUNPHY.
BUT I WAS THE DEMOLITION MAN. OR D-MAN FOR SHORT.
MUSCLE
MAYBE YOU HAD TO BE THERE.
OH, THAT. THAT'S FROM, LIKE, A WHILE AGO.
THIS ONE'S A LITTLE MORE RECENT.
THESE DAYS, THE ONLY THINGS I'M DEMOLISHING ARE SIX-PACKS OF MICROBREWS AND A LOT OF FROZEN PIZZA.
WHICH BRINGS US TO TONIGHT'S FINAL QUESTION...THIS FORMER UCWF WRESTLING CHAMPION ALSO FOUGHT REAL-LIFE VILLAINS ALONGSIDE CAPTAIN AMERICA.
HOO IFF DEE-MAMM?
REALLY? NO ONE WANTS TO HAZARD A GUESS?
WHO IS D-MAN?! WHO... IS...D-MAN!
BRRZZ!
OOH, AND YOUR TIME IS--

WHO...IS... D-MAN?!

KRASH

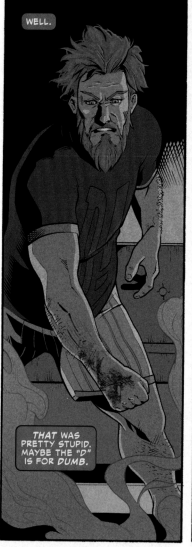

WELL.

THAT WAS PRETTY STUPID. MAYBE THE "D" IS FOR DUMB.

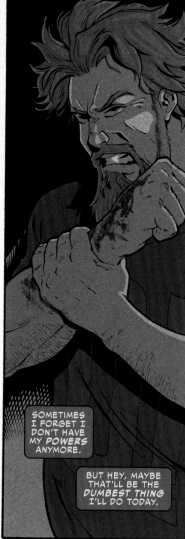

SOMETIMES I FORGET I DON'T HAVE MY POWERS ANYMORE.

BUT HEY, MAYBE THAT'LL BE THE DUMBEST THING I'LL DO TODAY.

BARK

BARK

BARK

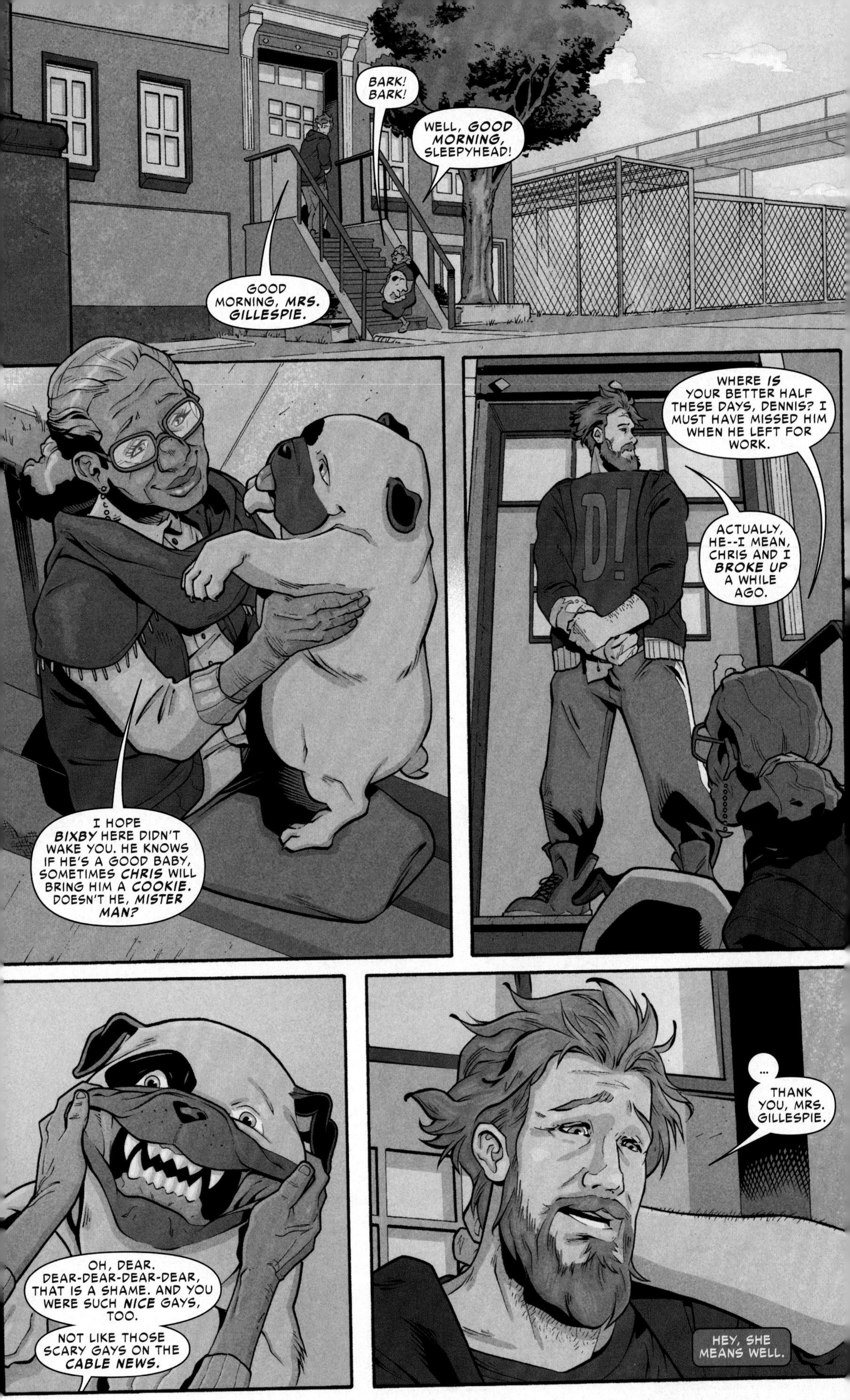

BARK! BARK!
WELL, GOOD MORNING, SLEEPYHEAD!
GOOD MORNING, MRS. GILLESPIE.
I HOPE BIXBY HERE DIDN'T WAKE YOU. HE KNOWS IF HE'S A GOOD BABY, SOMETIMES CHRIS WILL BRING HIM A COOKIE. DOESN'T HE, MISTER MAN?
WHERE IS YOUR BETTER HALF THESE DAYS, DENNIS? I MUST HAVE MISSED HIM WHEN HE LEFT FOR WORK.
ACTUALLY, HE--I MEAN, CHRIS AND I BROKE UP A WHILE AGO.
OH, DEAR. DEAR-DEAR-DEAR-DEAR, THAT IS A SHAME. AND YOU WERE SUCH NICE GAYS, TOO.
NOT LIKE THOSE SCARY GAYS ON THE CABLE NEWS.
...
THANK YOU, MRS. GILLESPIE.
HEY, SHE MEANS WELL.

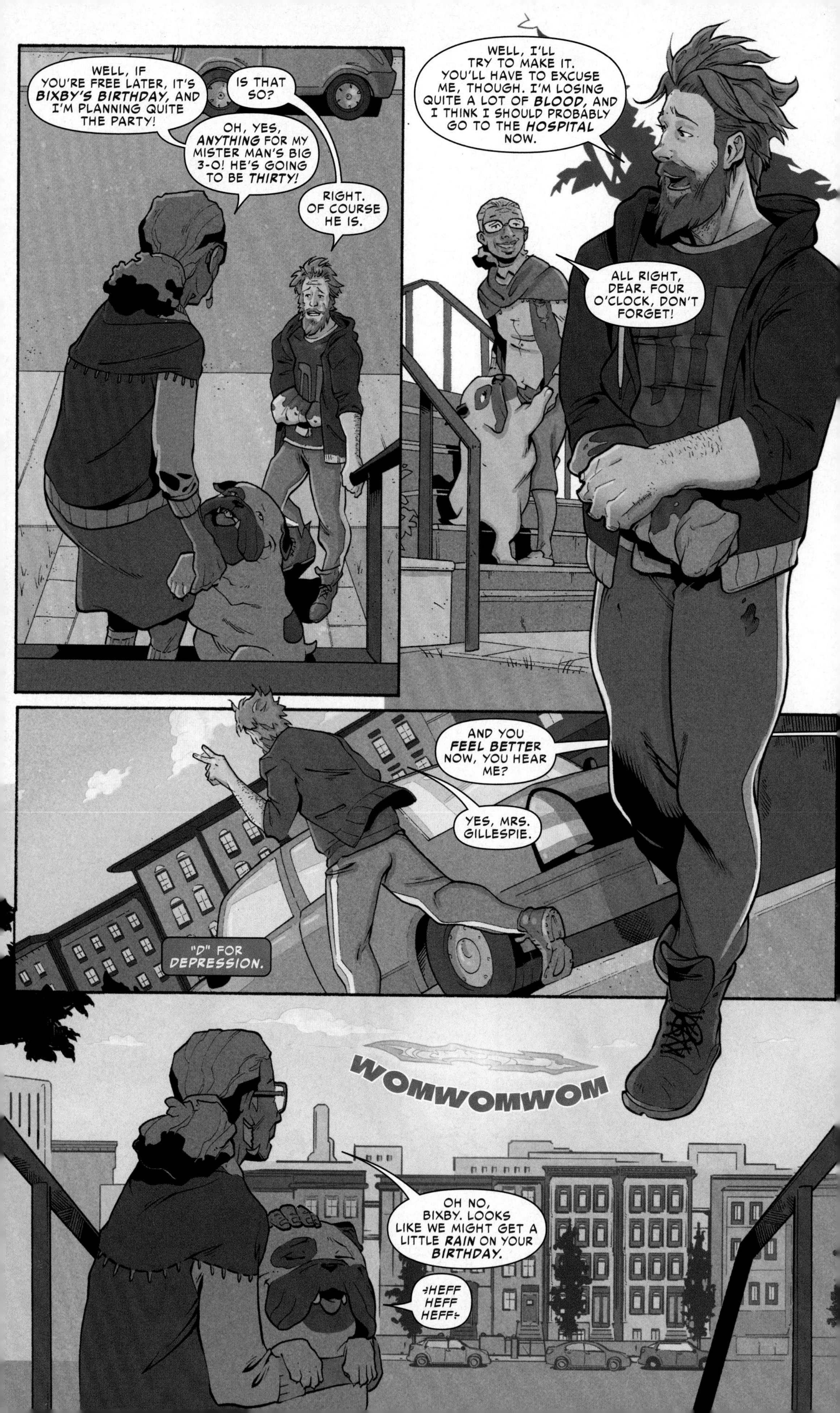
WELL, IF YOU'RE FREE LATER, IT'S BIXBY'S BIRTHDAY, AND I'M PLANNING QUITE THE PARTY!
IS THAT SO?
OH, YES, ANYTHING FOR MY MISTER MAN'S BIG 3-0! HE'S GOING TO BE THIRTY!
RIGHT. OF COURSE HE IS.
WELL, I'LL TRY TO MAKE IT. YOU'LL HAVE TO EXCUSE ME, THOUGH. I'M LOSING QUITE A LOT OF BLOOD, AND I THINK I SHOULD PROBABLY GO TO THE HOSPITAL NOW.
ALL RIGHT, DEAR. FOUR O'CLOCK, DON'T FORGET!
AND YOU FEEL BETTER NOW, YOU HEAR ME?
YES, MRS. GILLESPIE.
"D" FOR DEPRESSION.
WOMWOMWOM
OH NO, BIXBY. LOOKS LIKE WE MIGHT GET A LITTLE RAIN ON YOUR BIRTHDAY.
HEFF HEFF HEFF

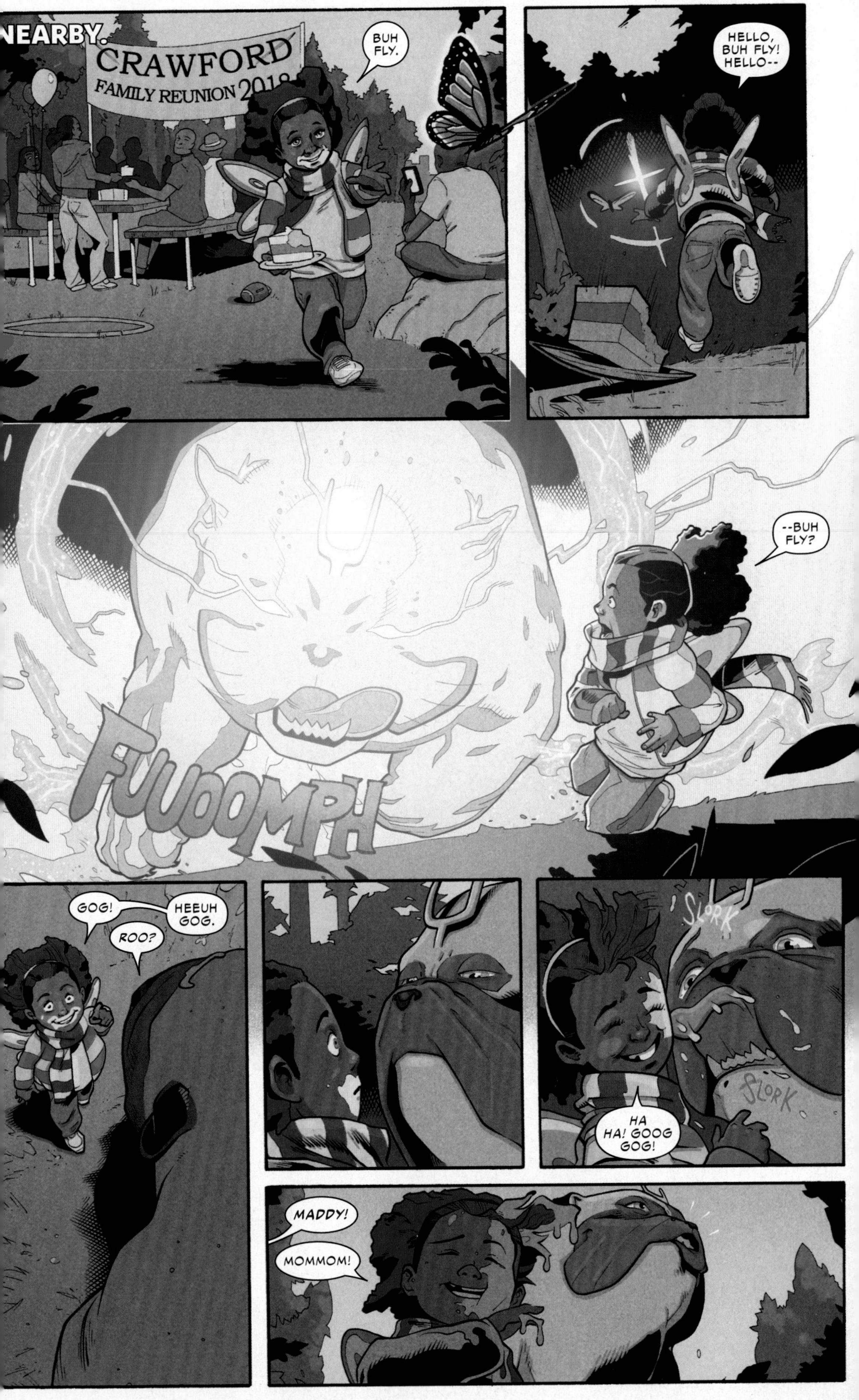
NEARBY.
CRAWFORD
FAMILY REUNION 2018
BUH FLY.
HELLO, BUH FLY! HELLO--
--BUH FLY?
FUUOOMPH
GOG!
HEEUH GOG.
ROO?
SLORK
SLORK
HA HA! GOOG GOG!
MADDY!
MOMMOM!

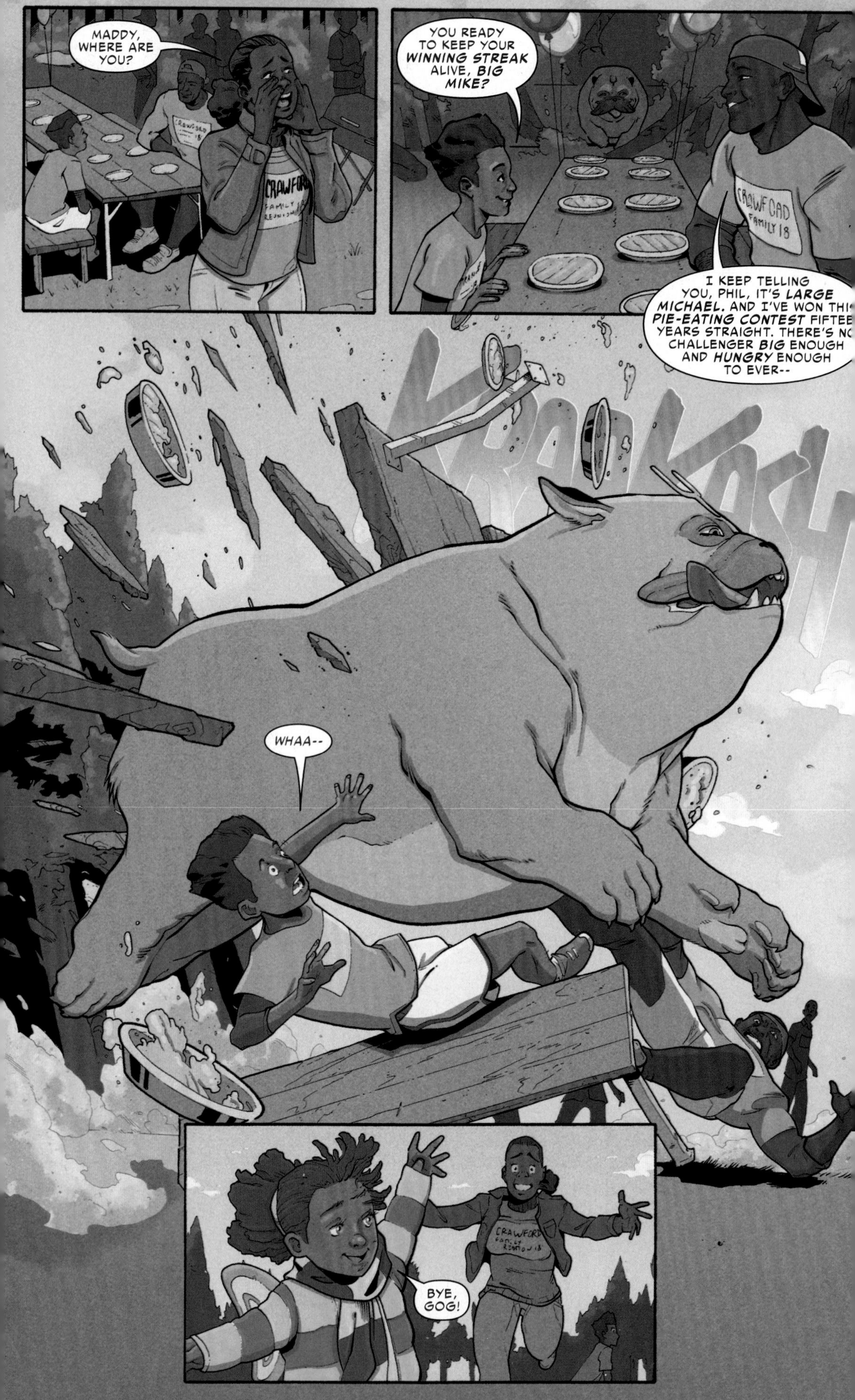

MADDY, WHERE ARE YOU?
YOU READY TO KEEP YOUR WINNING STREAK ALIVE, BIG MIKE?
I KEEP TELLING YOU, PHIL, IT'S LARGE MICHAEL. AND I'VE WON THI PIE-EATING CONTEST FIFTEE YEARS STRAIGHT. THERE'S NO CHALLENGER BIG ENOUGH AND HUNGRY ENOUGH TO EVER--
WHAA--
BYE, GOG!

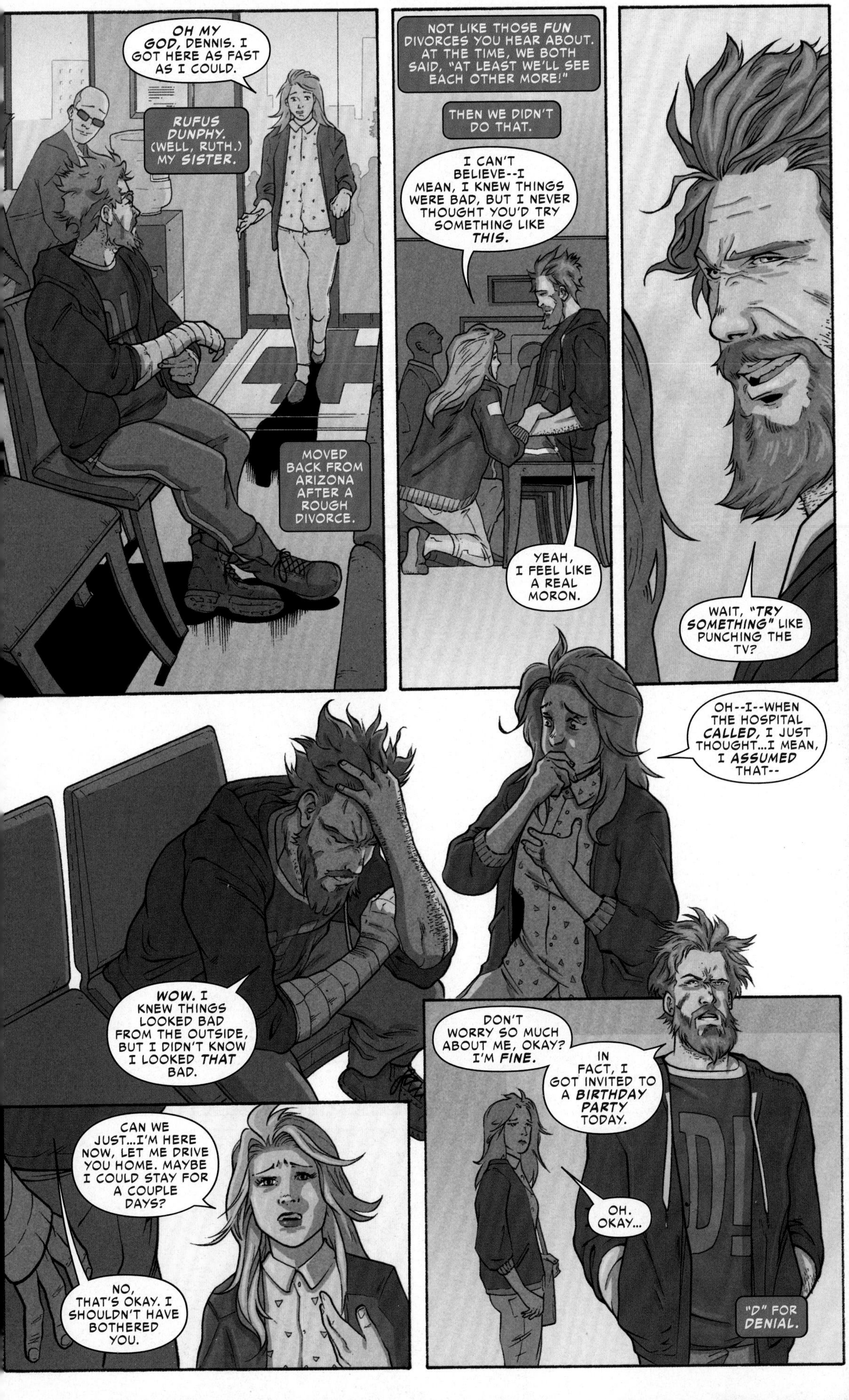

OH MY GOD, DENNIS. I GOT HERE AS FAST AS I COULD.
RUFUS DUNPHY. (WELL, RUTH.) MY SISTER.
MOVED BACK FROM ARIZONA AFTER A ROUGH DIVORCE.
NOT LIKE THOSE FUN DIVORCES YOU HEAR ABOUT. AT THE TIME, WE BOTH SAID, "AT LEAST WE'LL SEE EACH OTHER MORE!"
THEN WE DIDN'T DO THAT.
I CAN'T BELIEVE--I MEAN, I KNEW THINGS WERE BAD, BUT I NEVER THOUGHT YOU'D TRY SOMETHING LIKE THIS.
YEAH, I FEEL LIKE A REAL MORON.
WAIT, "TRY SOMETHING" LIKE PUNCHING THE TV?
OH--I--WHEN THE HOSPITAL CALLED, I JUST THOUGHT...I MEAN, I ASSUMED THAT--
WOW. I KNEW THINGS LOOKED BAD FROM THE OUTSIDE, BUT I DIDN'T KNOW I LOOKED THAT BAD.
CAN WE JUST...I'M HERE NOW, LET ME DRIVE YOU HOME. MAYBE I COULD STAY FOR A COUPLE DAYS?
NO, THAT'S OKAY. I SHOULDN'T HAVE BOTHERED YOU.
DON'T WORRY SO MUCH ABOUT ME, OKAY? I'M FINE.
IN FACT, I GOT INVITED TO A BIRTHDAY PARTY TODAY.
OH. OKAY...
"D" FOR DENIAL.

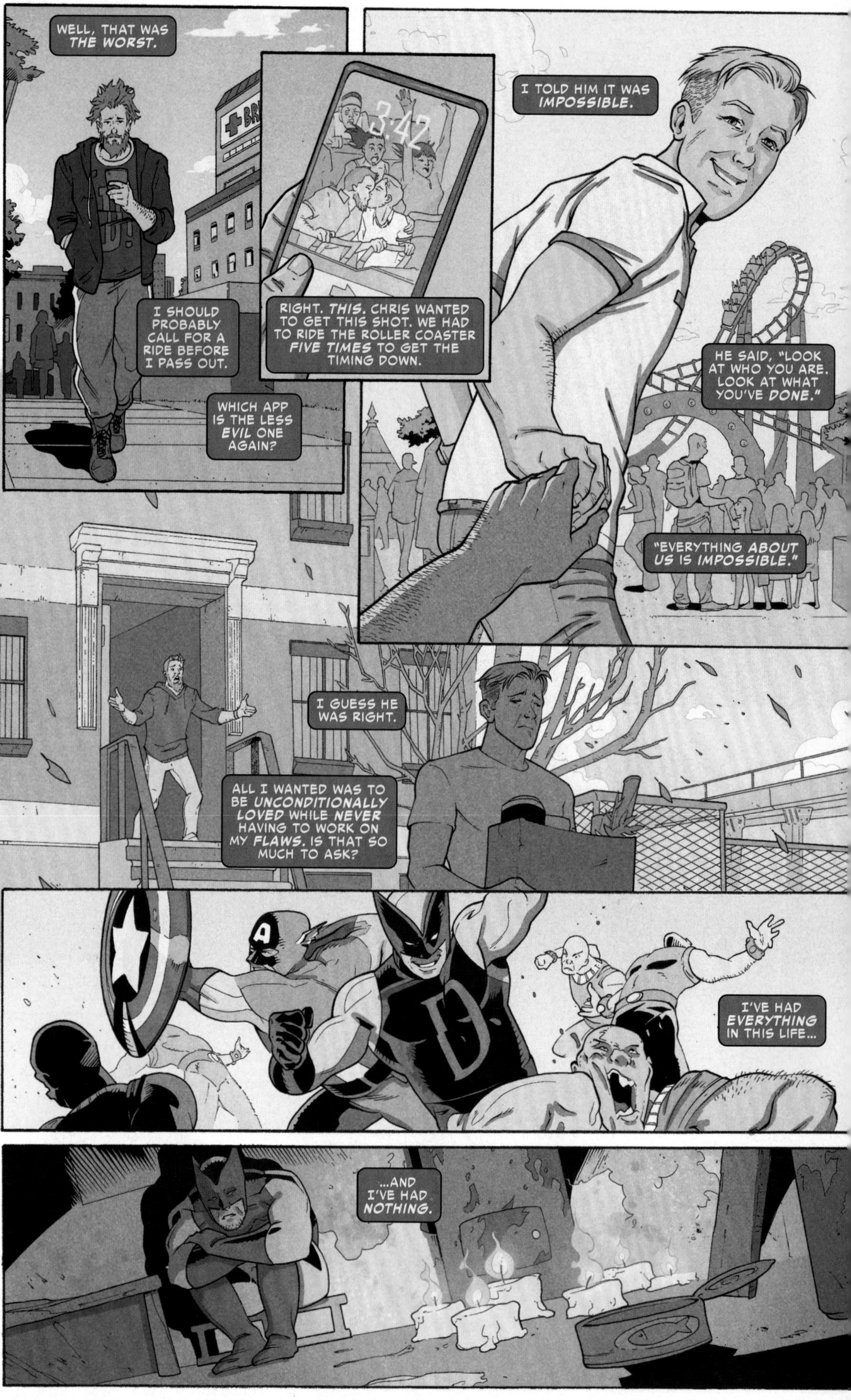
WELL, THAT WAS THE WORST.
I SHOULD PROBABLY CALL FOR A RIDE BEFORE I PASS OUT.
WHICH APP IS THE LESS EVIL ONE AGAIN?
3:42
RIGHT. THIS. CHRIS WANTED TO GET THIS SHOT. WE HAD TO RIDE THE ROLLER COASTER FIVE TIMES TO GET THE TIMING DOWN.
I TOLD HIM IT WAS IMPOSSIBLE.
HE SAID, "LOOK AT WHO YOU ARE. LOOK AT WHAT YOU'VE DONE."
"EVERYTHING ABOUT US IS IMPOSSIBLE."
I GUESS HE WAS RIGHT.
ALL I WANTED WAS TO BE UNCONDITIONALLY LOVED WHILE NEVER HAVING TO WORK ON MY FLAWS. IS THAT SO MUCH TO ASK?
I'VE HAD EVERYTHING IN THIS LIFE...
...AND I'VE HAD NOTHING.

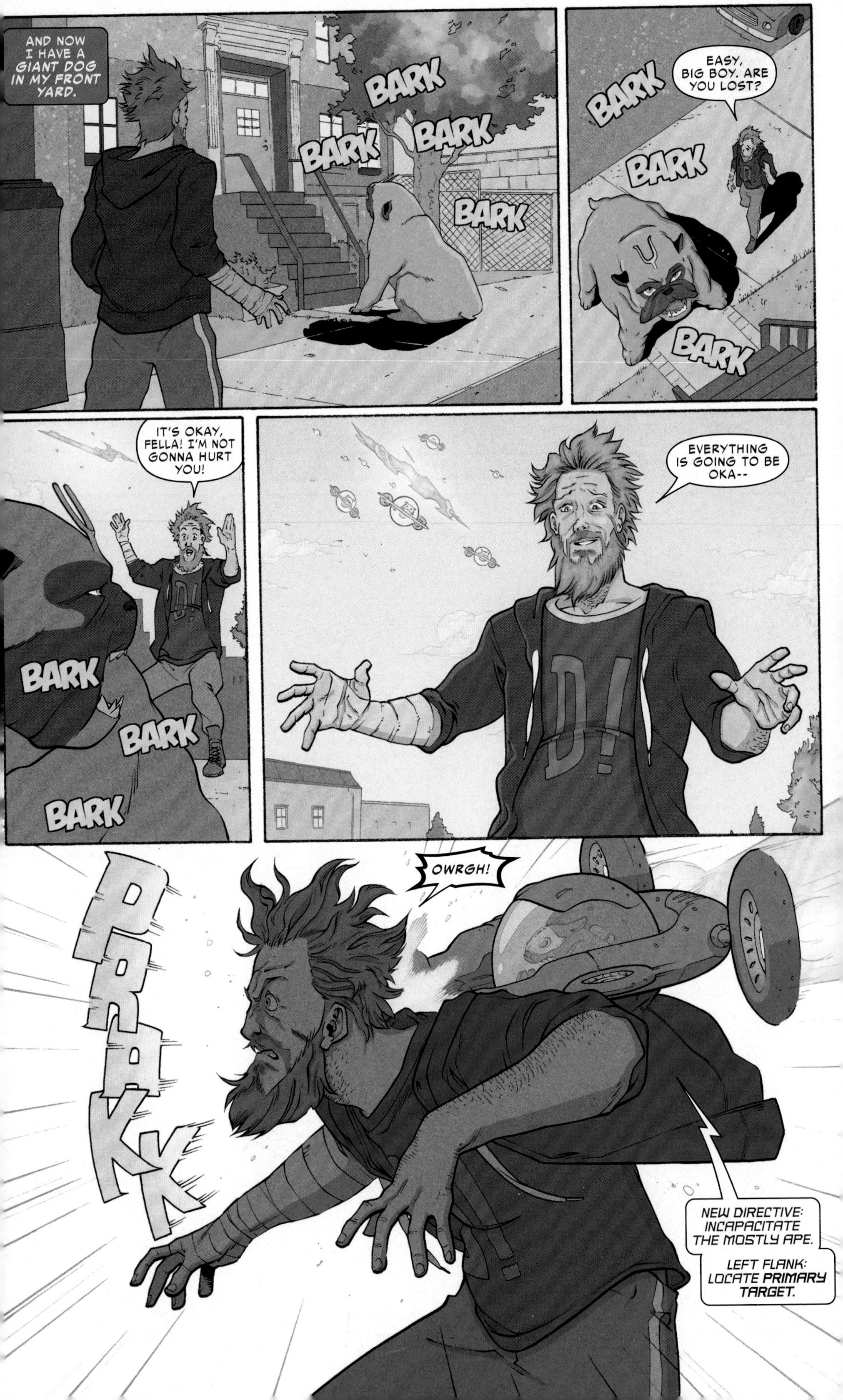
AND NOW I HAVE A GIANT DOG IN MY FRONT YARD.
BARK
BARK
BARK
BARK
BARK
EASY, BIG BOY. ARE YOU LOST?
BARK
BARK
IT'S OKAY, FELLA! I'M NOT GONNA HURT YOU!
BARK
BARK
BARK
EVERYTHING IS GOING TO BE OKA--
PRRAKK
OWRGH!
NEW DIRECTIVE: INCAPACITATE THE MOSTLY APE.
LEFT FLANK: LOCATE PRIMARY TARGET.

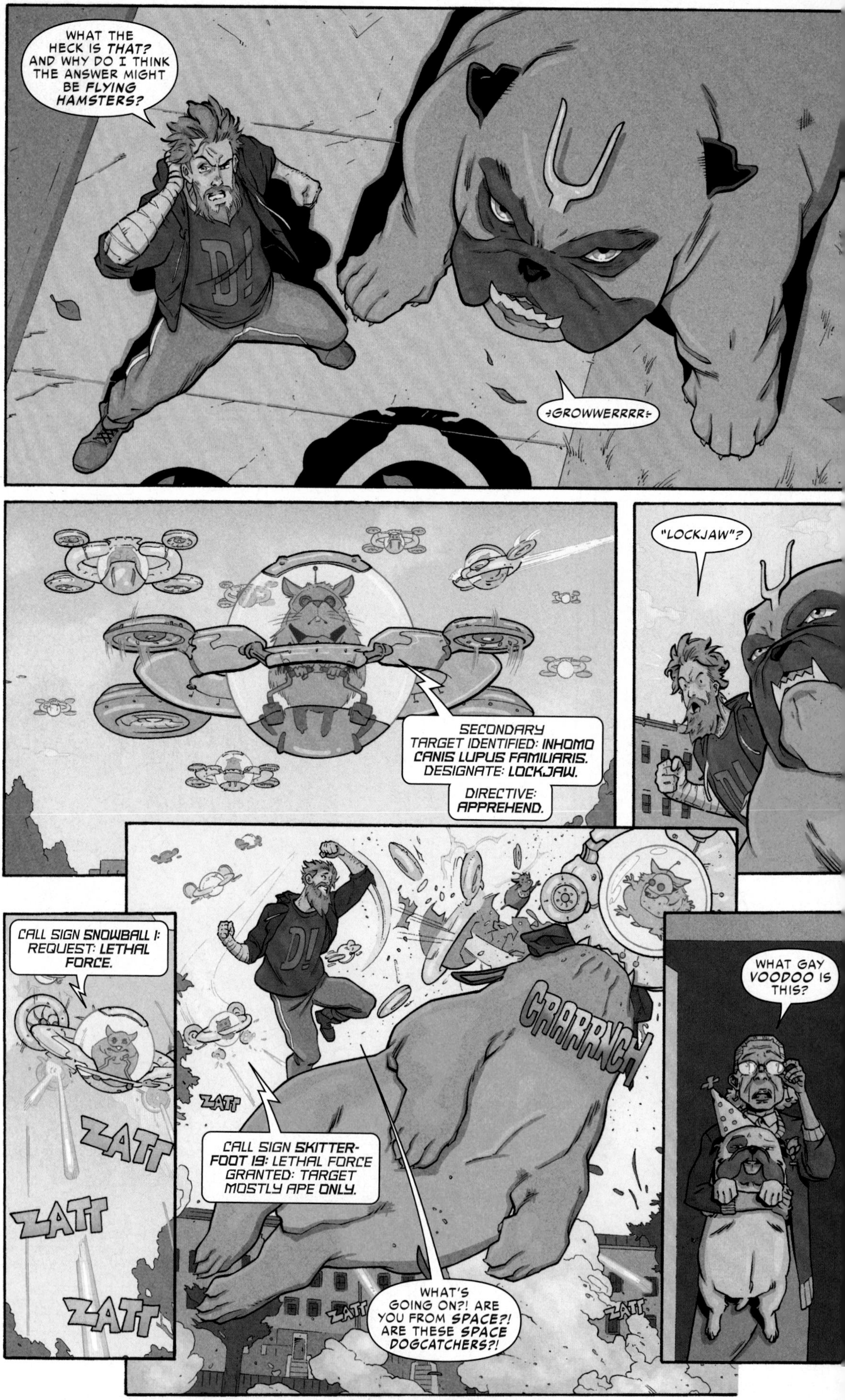
WHAT THE HECK IS THAT? AND WHY DO I THINK THE ANSWER MIGHT BE FLYING HAMSTERS?
GROWWERRRR
SECONDARY TARGET IDENTIFIED: INHOMO CANIS LUPUS FAMILIARIS. DESIGNATE: LOCKJAW.
DIRECTIVE: APPREHEND.
"LOCKJAW"?
CALL SIGN SNOWBALL 1: REQUEST: LETHAL FORCE.
ZATT
ZATT
ZATT
CRARRNCH
ZATT
CALL SIGN SKITTER-FOOT 19: LETHAL FORCE GRANTED: TARGET MOSTLY APE ONLY.
ZATT
ZATT
WHAT'S GOING ON?! ARE YOU FROM SPACE?! ARE THESE SPACE DOGCATCHERS?!
WHAT GAY VOODOO IS THIS?

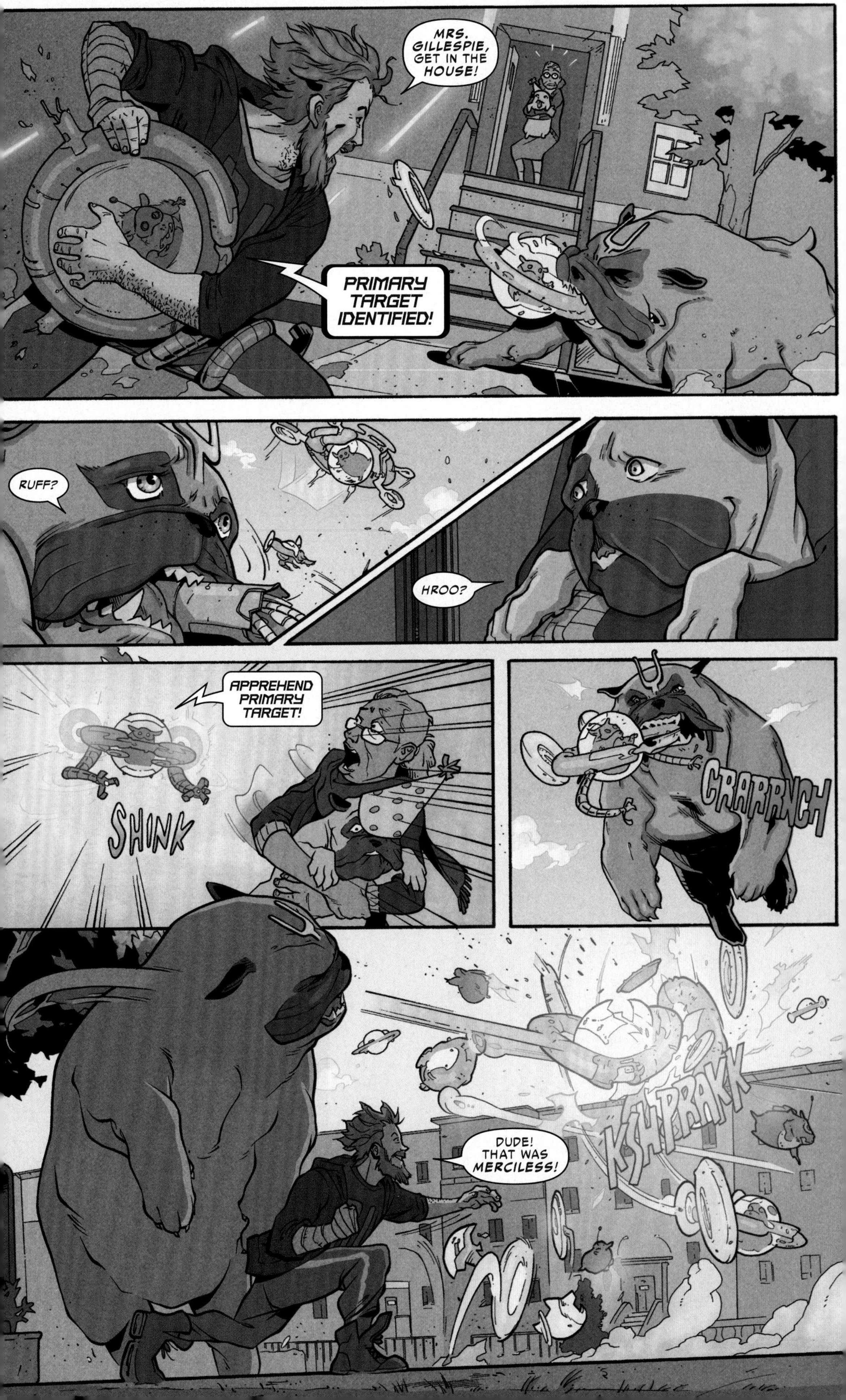
MRS. GILLESPIE, GET IN THE HOUSE!
PRIMARY TARGET IDENTIFIED!
RUFF?
HROO?
APPREHEND PRIMARY TARGET!
SHINK
CRARRNCH
DUDE! THAT WAS MERCILESS!
KSHPRAKK

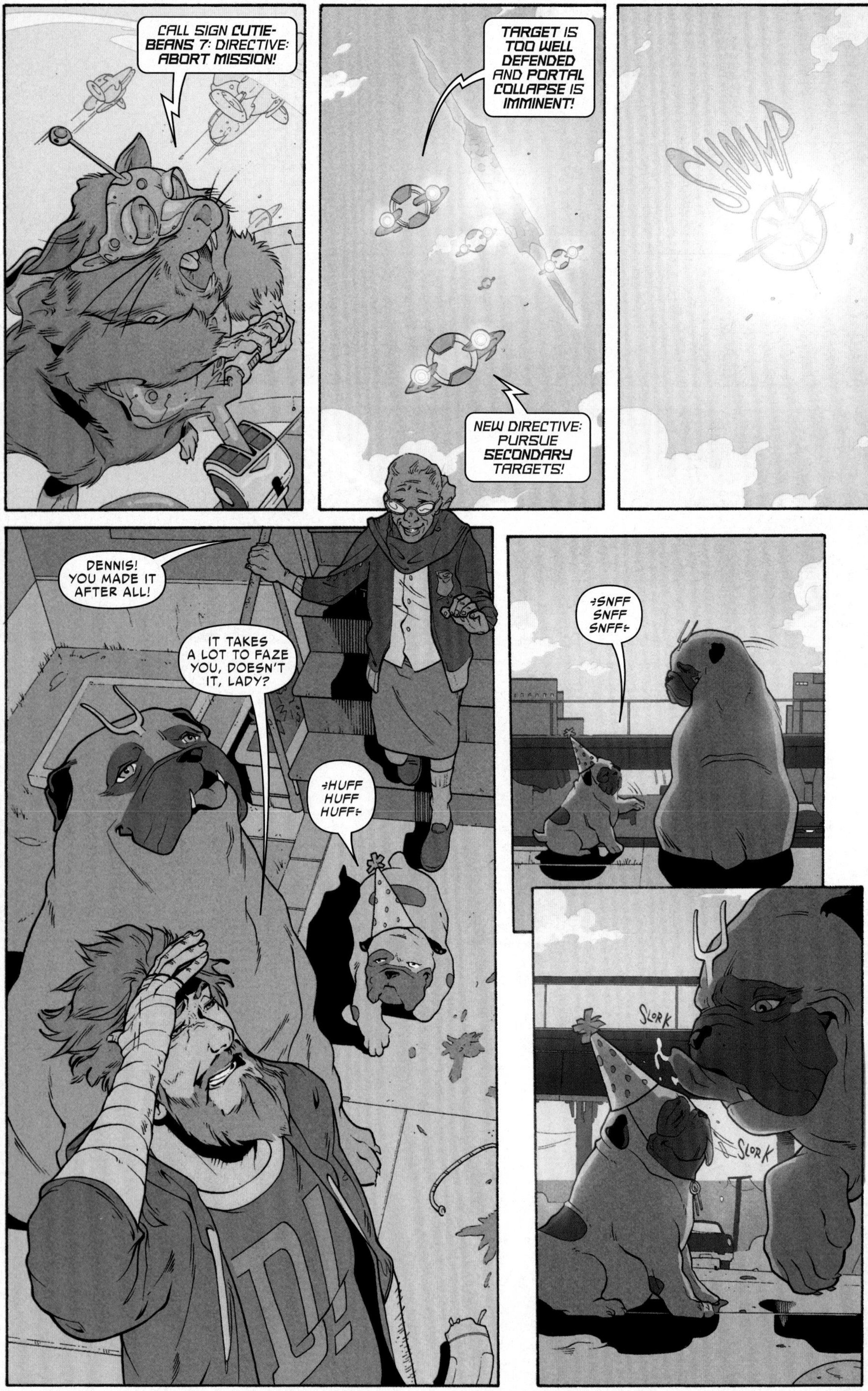
CALL SIGN CUTIE-BEANS 7: DIRECTIVE: ABORT MISSION!
TARGET IS TOO WELL DEFENDED AND PORTAL COLLAPSE IS IMMINENT!
NEW DIRECTIVE: PURSUE SECONDARY TARGETS!
SHOOMP
DENNIS! YOU MADE IT AFTER ALL!
IT TAKES A LOT TO FAZE YOU, DOESN'T IT, LADY?
HUFF HUFF HUFF
SNFF SNFF SNFF
SLORK
SLORK

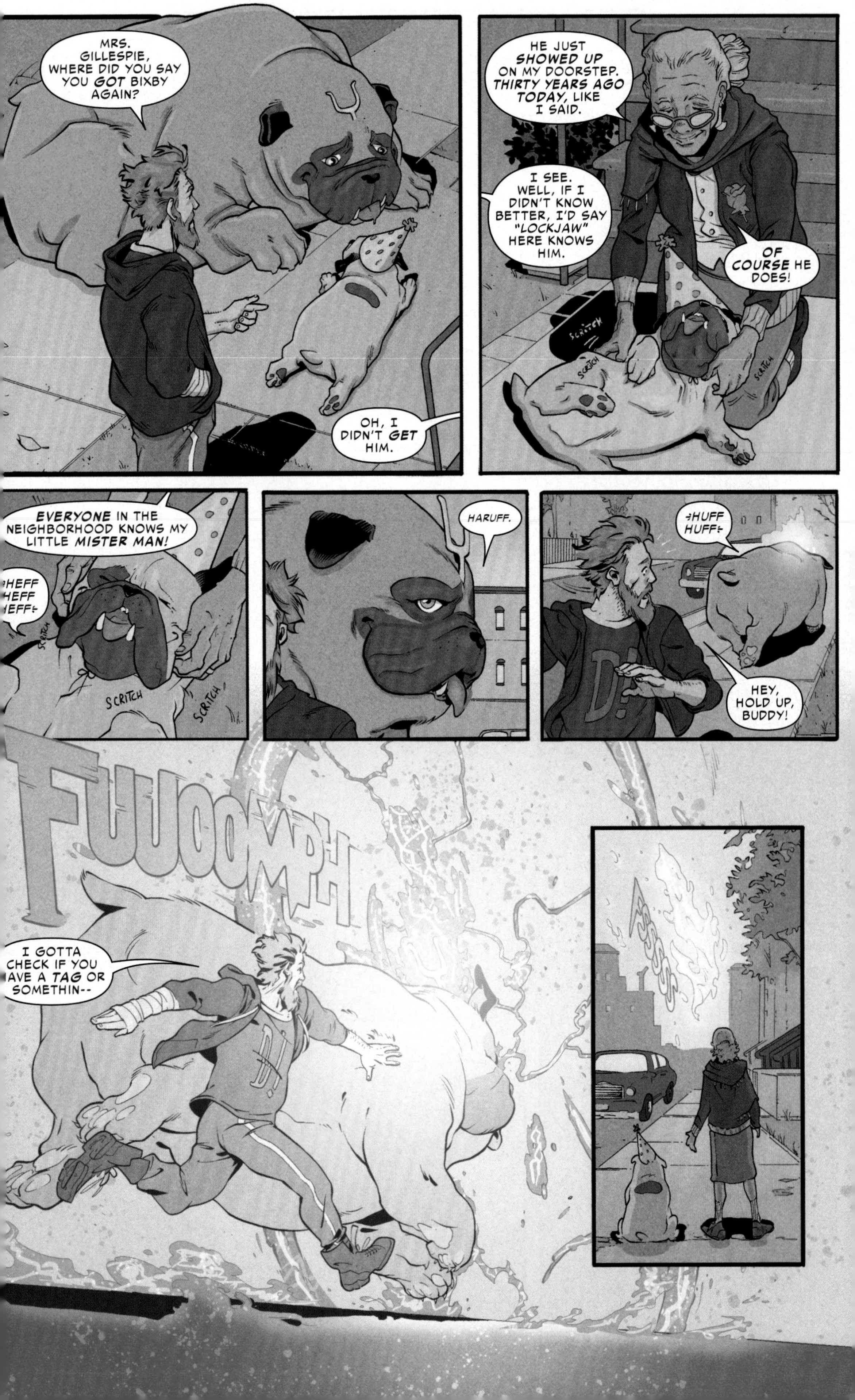

MRS. GILLESPIE, WHERE DID YOU SAY YOU GOT BIXBY AGAIN?
OH, I DIDN'T GET HIM.
HE JUST SHOWED UP ON MY DOORSTEP. THIRTY YEARS AGO TODAY, LIKE I SAID.
I SEE. WELL, IF I DIDN'T KNOW BETTER, I'D SAY "LOCKJAW" HERE KNOWS HIM.
OF COURSE HE DOES!
SCRITCH
SCRITCH
SCRITCH
EVERYONE IN THE NEIGHBORHOOD KNOWS MY LITTLE MISTER MAN!
HEFF HEFF HEFF
SCRITCH
SCRITCH
SCRITCH
HARUFF.
HUFF HUFF
HEY, HOLD UP, BUDDY!
FUUOOMPH
I GOTTA CHECK IF YOU AVE A TAG OR SOMETHIN--
SSSSS

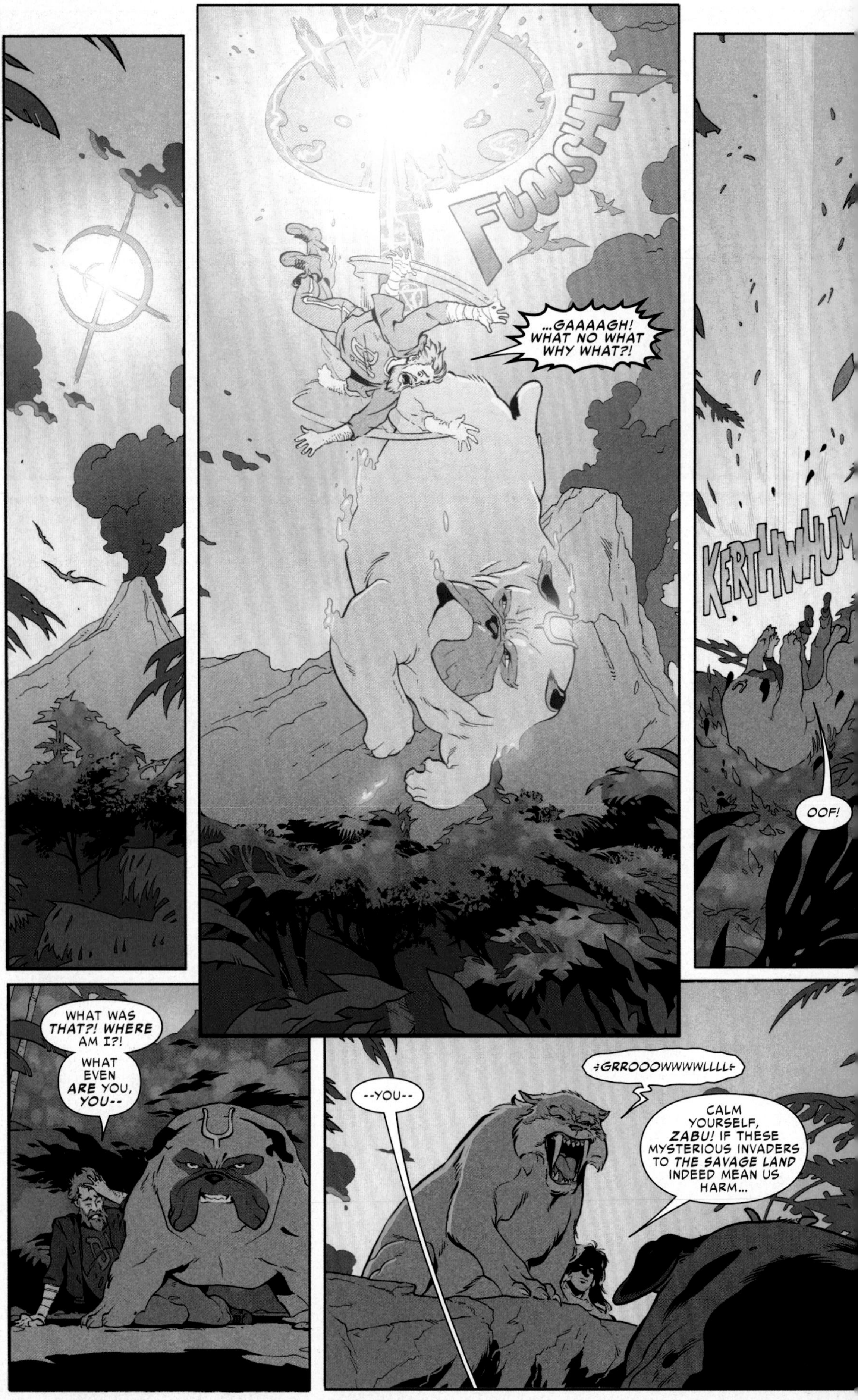
FWOOSH
...GAAAAGH! WHAT NO WHAT WHY WHAT?!
KERTHWHUM
OOF!
WHAT WAS THAT?! WHERE AM I?!
WHAT EVEN ARE YOU, YOU--
--YOU--
GRROOOWWWWLLLL
CALM YOURSELF, ZABU! IF THESE MYSTERIOUS INVADERS TO THE SAVAGE LAND INDEED MEAN US HARM...

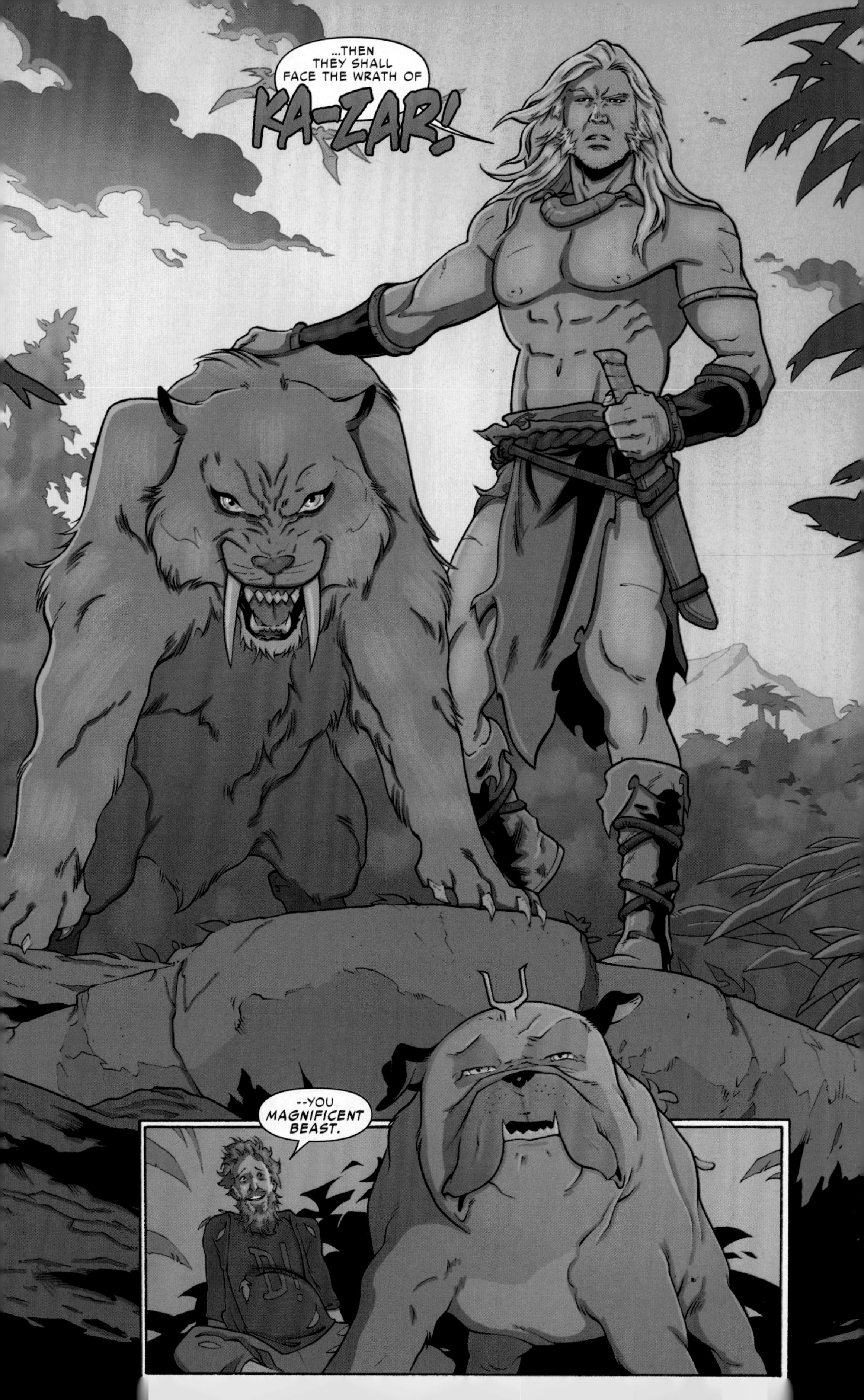

...THEN THEY SHALL FACE THE WRATH OF
KA-ZAR!
--YOU MAGNIFICENT BEAST.

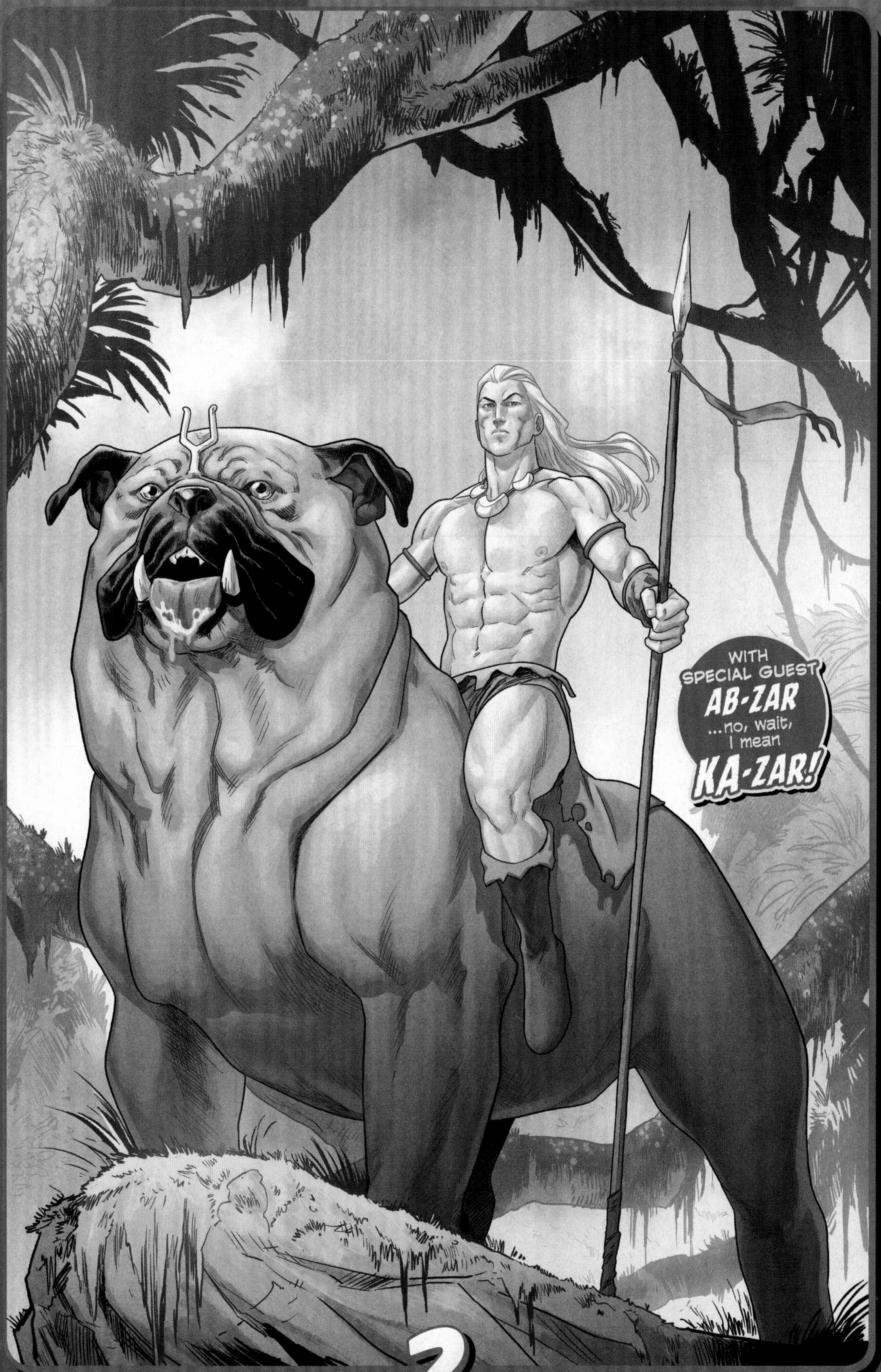
WITH SPECIAL GUEST
AB-ZAR
...no, wait, I mean
KA-ZAR!
2

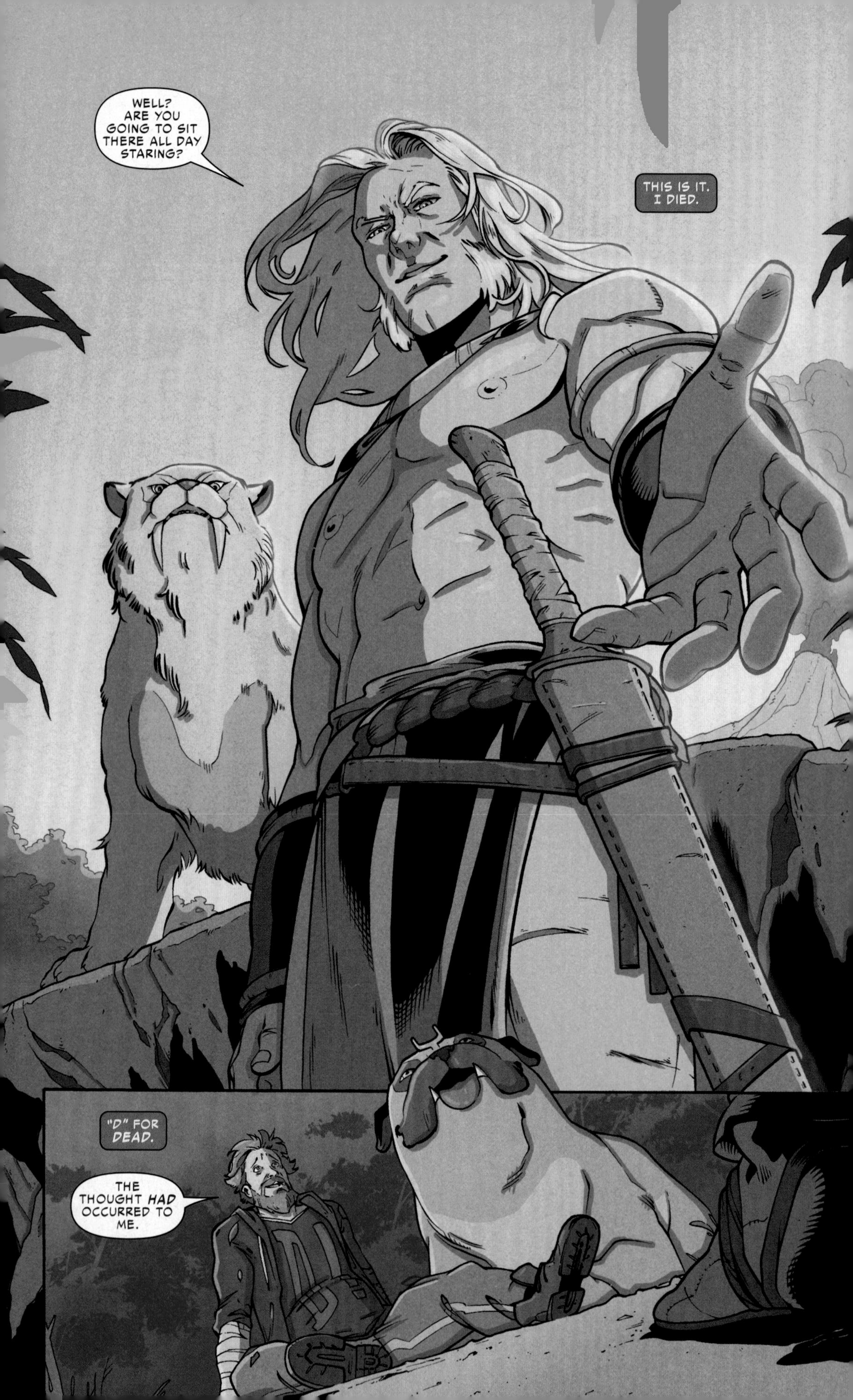
WELL? ARE YOU GOING TO SIT THERE ALL DAY STARING?
THIS IS IT. I DIED.
"D" FOR DEAD.
THE THOUGHT HAD OCCURRED TO ME.

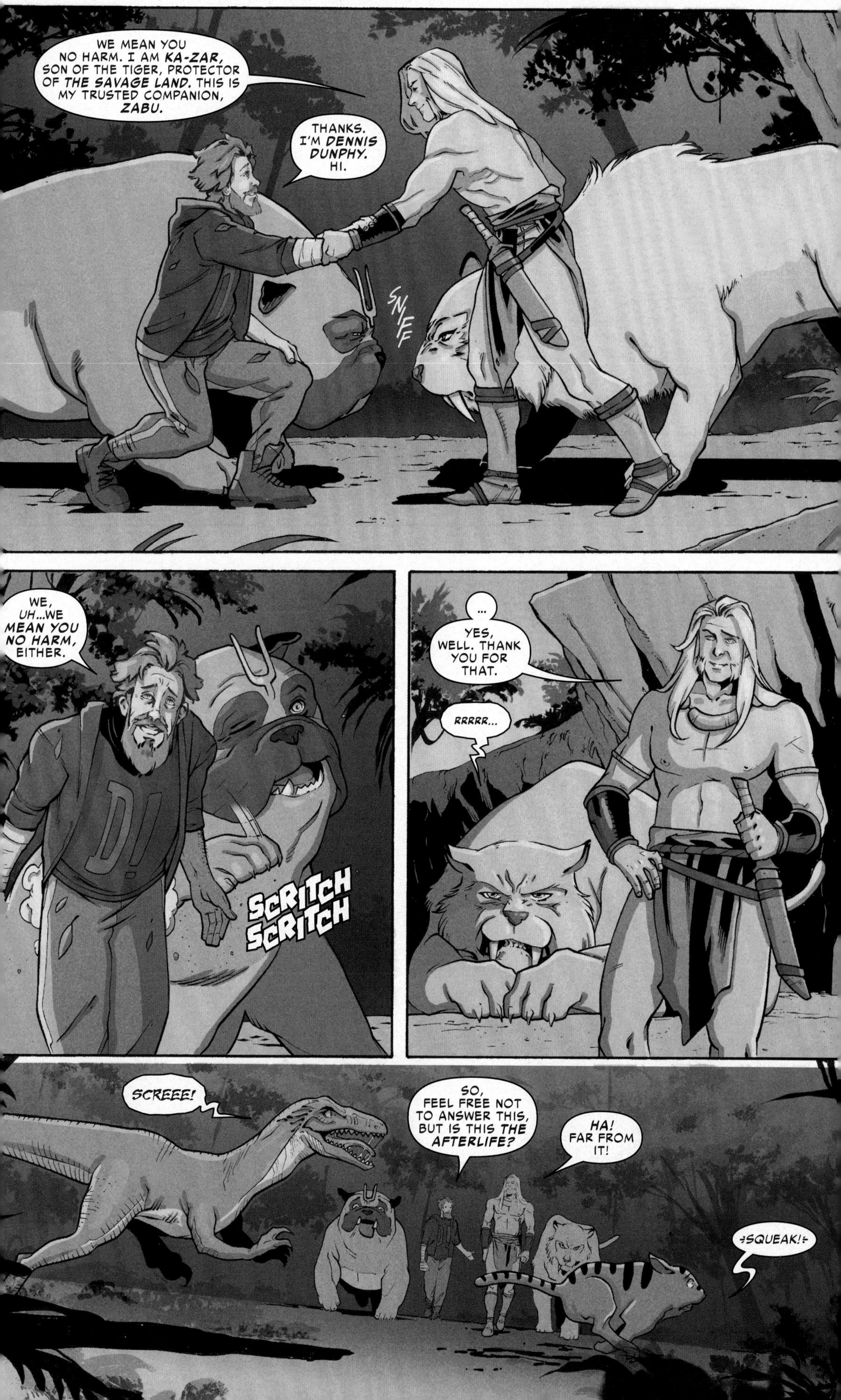
WE MEAN YOU NO HARM. I AM KA-ZAR, SON OF THE TIGER, PROTECTOR OF THE SAVAGE LAND. THIS IS MY TRUSTED COMPANION, ZABU.
THANKS. I'M DENNIS DUNPHY. HI.
SNIFF
WE, UH...WE MEAN YOU NO HARM, EITHER.
SCRITCH SCRITCH
...
YES, WELL. THANK YOU FOR THAT.
RRRRR...
SCREEE!
SO, FEEL FREE NOT TO ANSWER THIS, BUT IS THIS THE AFTERLIFE?
HA! FAR FROM IT!
SQUEAK!

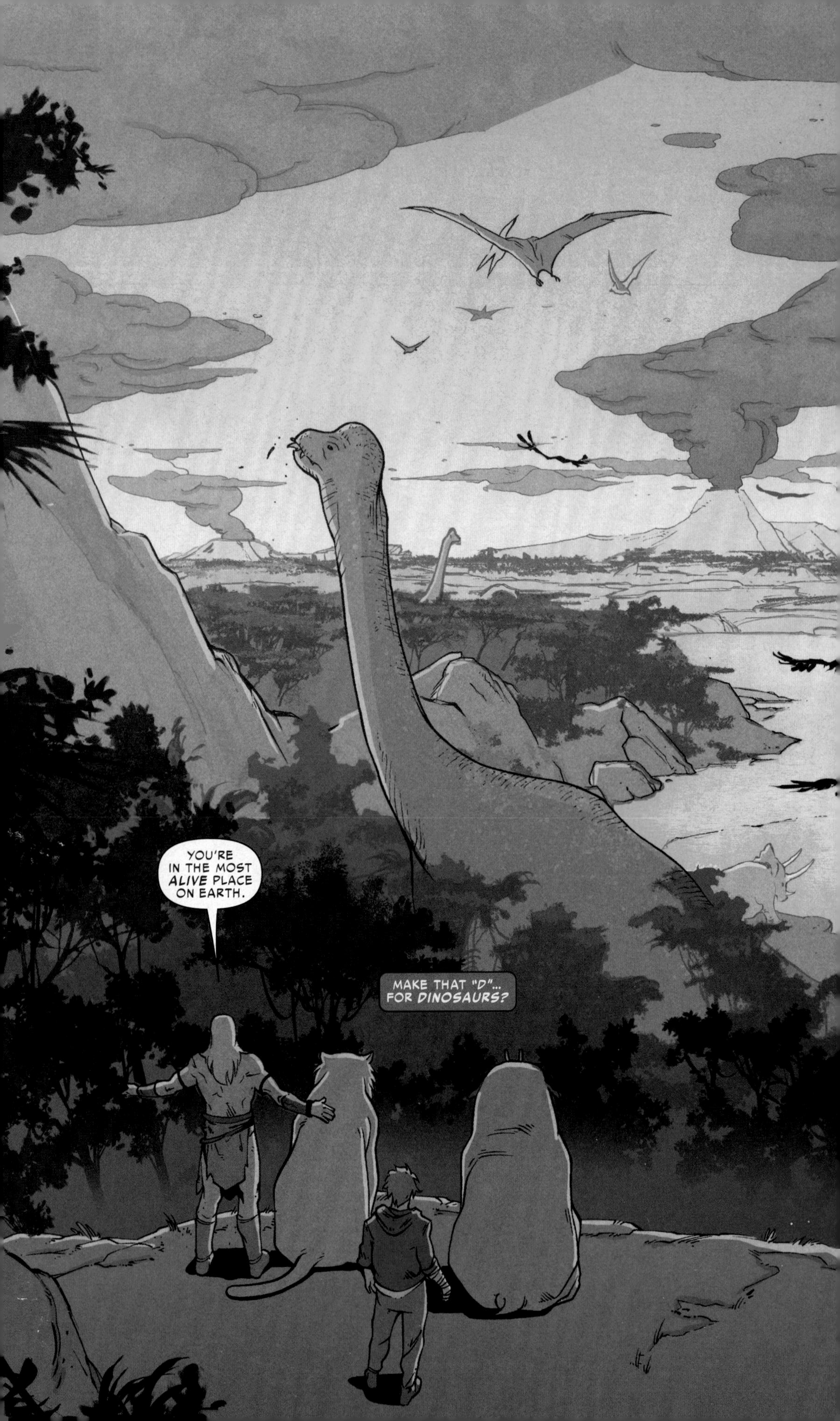
YOU'RE IN THE MOST *ALIVE* PLACE ON EARTH.
MAKE THAT "D"... FOR *DINOSAURS?*

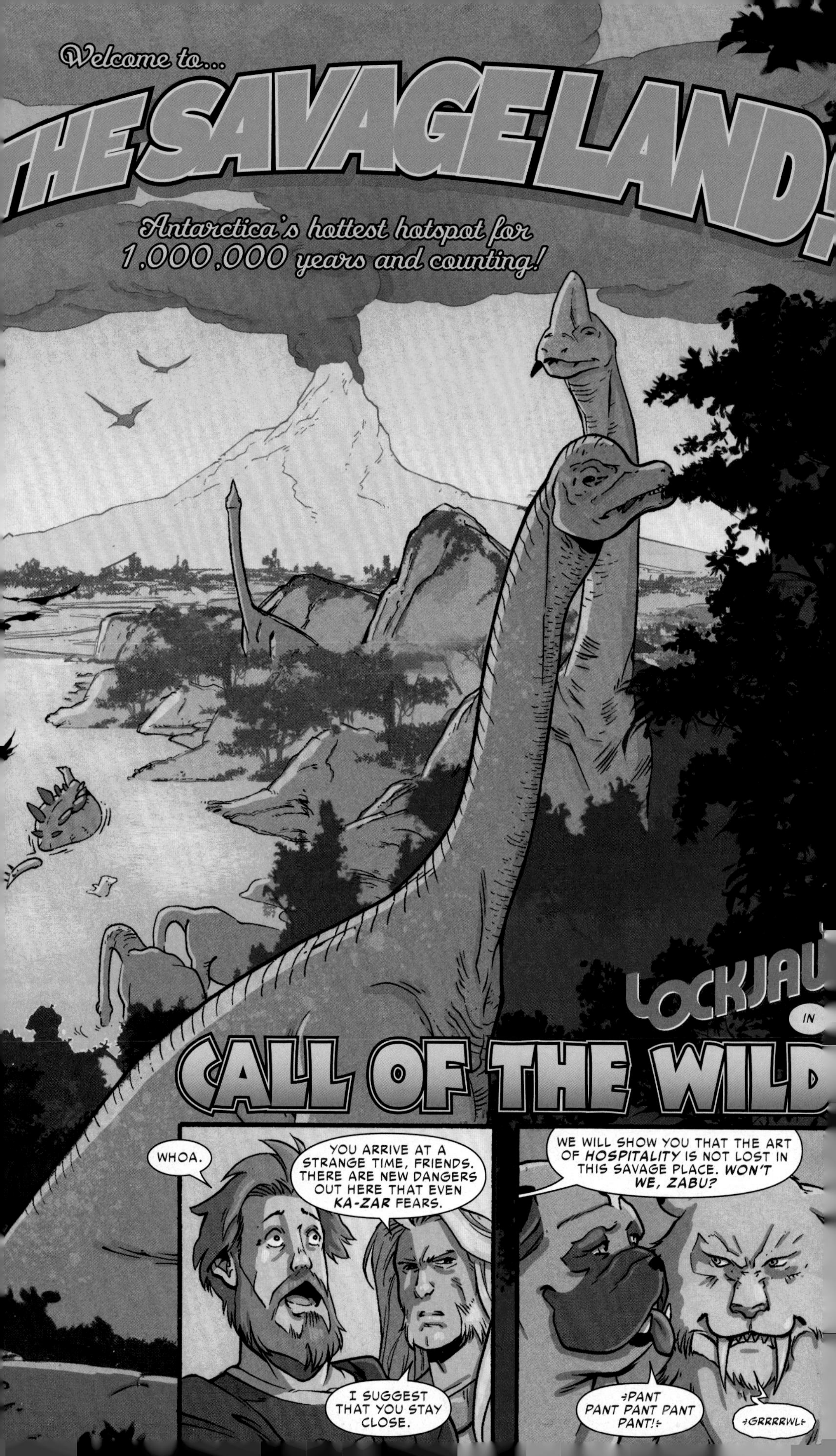

Welcome to...
THE SAVAGE LAND!
Antarctica's hottest hotspot for 1,000,000 years and counting!
LOCKJAW
IN
CALL OF THE WILD
WHOA.
YOU ARRIVE AT A STRANGE TIME, FRIENDS. THERE ARE NEW DANGERS OUT HERE THAT EVEN KA-ZAR FEARS.
I SUGGEST THAT YOU STAY CLOSE.
WE WILL SHOW YOU THAT THE ART OF HOSPITALITY IS NOT LOST IN THIS SAVAGE PLACE. WON'T WE, ZABU?
PANT PANT PANT PANT PANT!
GRRRRWL

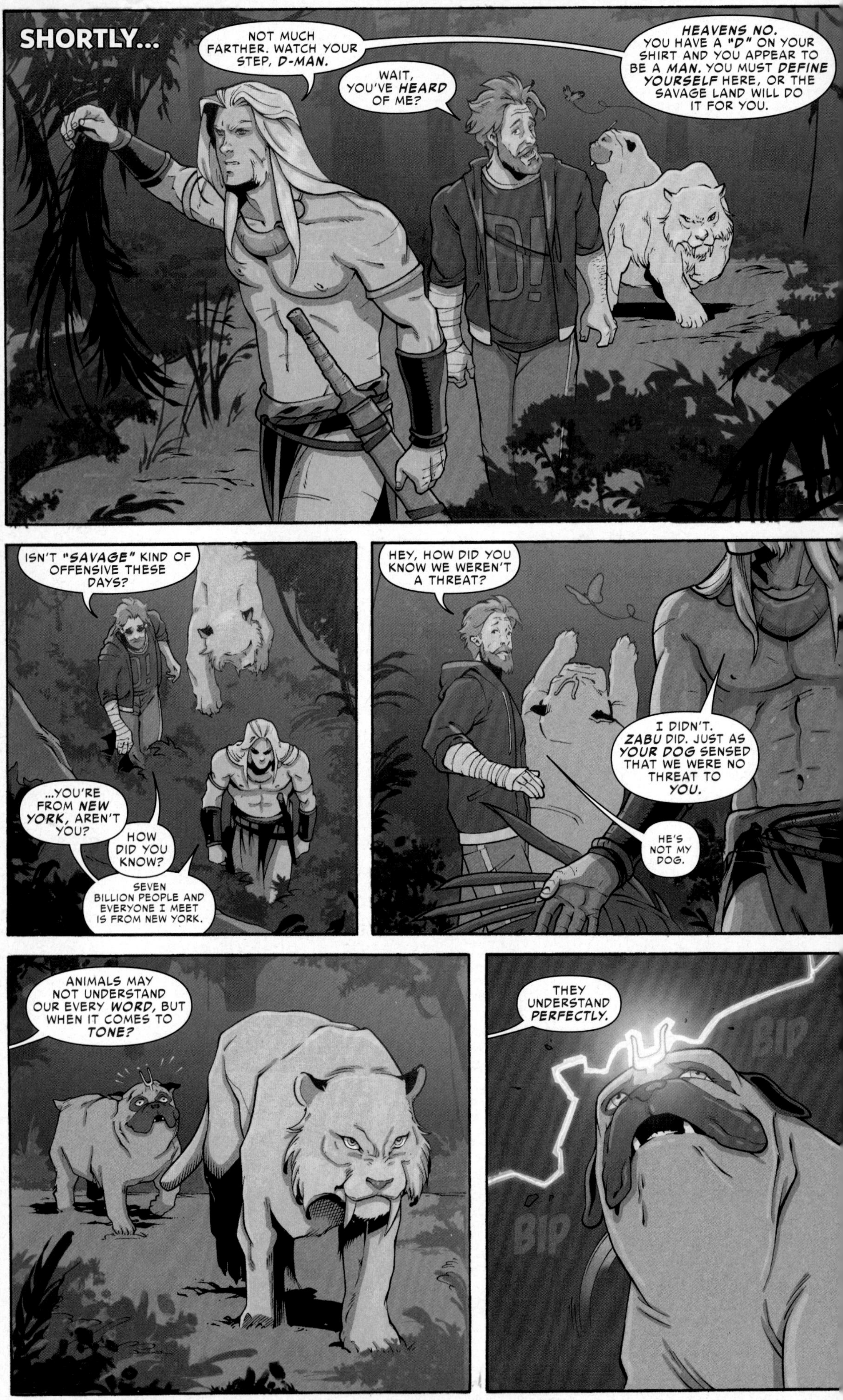
SHORTLY...
NOT MUCH FARTHER. WATCH YOUR STEP, D-MAN.
WAIT, YOU'VE HEARD OF ME?
HEAVENS NO. YOU HAVE A "D" ON YOUR SHIRT AND YOU APPEAR TO BE A MAN. YOU MUST DEFINE YOURSELF HERE, OR THE SAVAGE LAND WILL DO IT FOR YOU.
ISN'T "SAVAGE" KIND OF OFFENSIVE THESE DAYS?
...YOU'RE FROM NEW YORK, AREN'T YOU?
HOW DID YOU KNOW?
SEVEN BILLION PEOPLE AND EVERYONE I MEET IS FROM NEW YORK.
HEY, HOW DID YOU KNOW WE WEREN'T A THREAT?
I DIDN'T. ZABU DID. JUST AS YOUR DOG SENSED THAT WE WERE NO THREAT TO YOU.
HE'S NOT MY DOG.
ANIMALS MAY NOT UNDERSTAND OUR EVERY WORD, BUT WHEN IT COMES TO TONE?
THEY UNDERSTAND PERFECTLY.
BIP
BIP

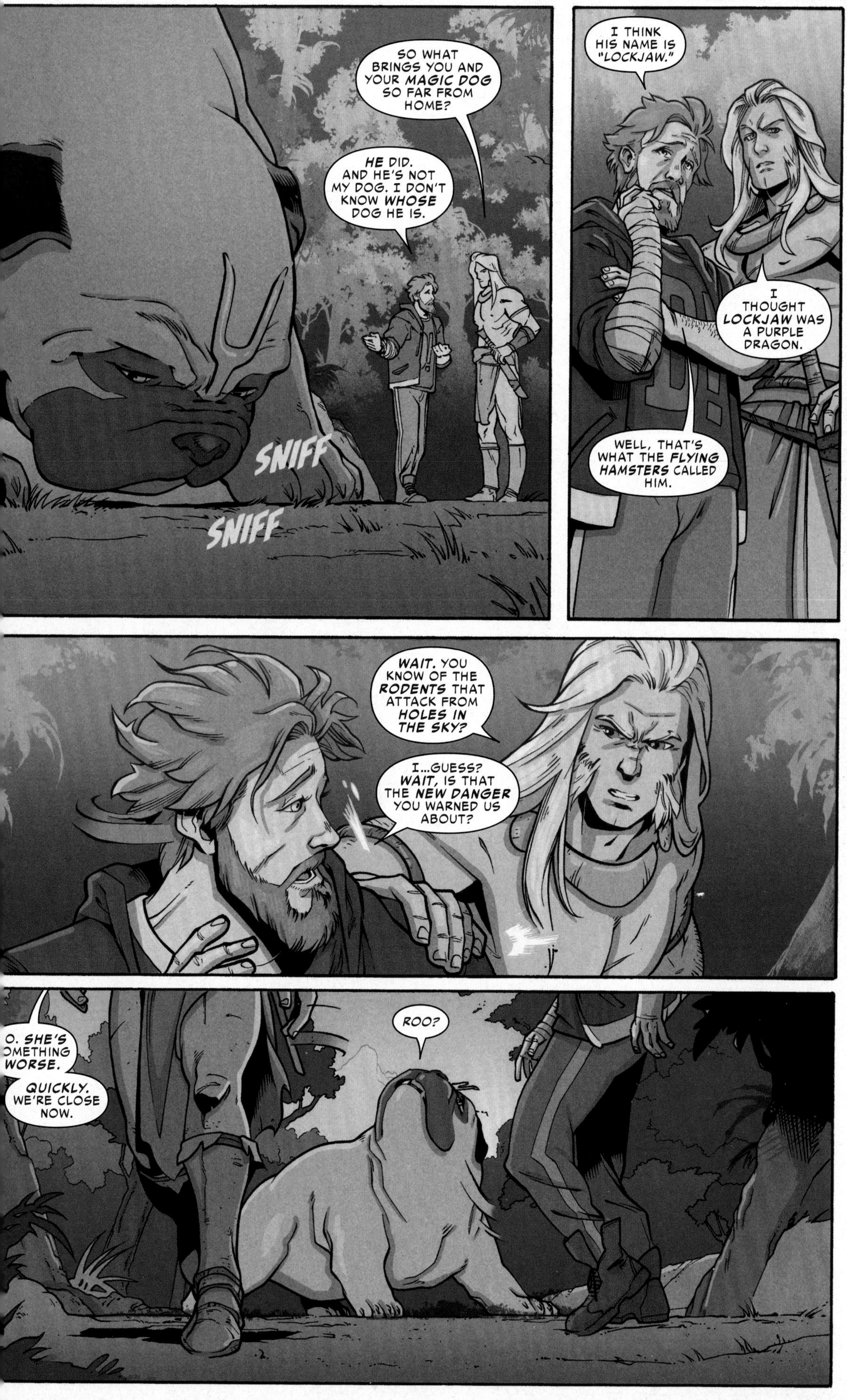
SO WHAT BRINGS YOU AND YOUR MAGIC DOG SO FAR FROM HOME?
HE DID. AND HE'S NOT MY DOG. I DON'T KNOW WHOSE DOG HE IS.
SNIFF
SNIFF
I THINK HIS NAME IS "LOCKJAW."
I THOUGHT LOCKJAW WAS A PURPLE DRAGON.
WELL, THAT'S WHAT THE FLYING HAMSTERS CALLED HIM.
WAIT. YOU KNOW OF THE RODENTS THAT ATTACK FROM HOLES IN THE SKY?
I...GUESS? WAIT, IS THAT THE NEW DANGER YOU WARNED US ABOUT?
O. SHE'S OMETHING WORSE.
QUICKLY. WE'RE CLOSE NOW.
ROO?

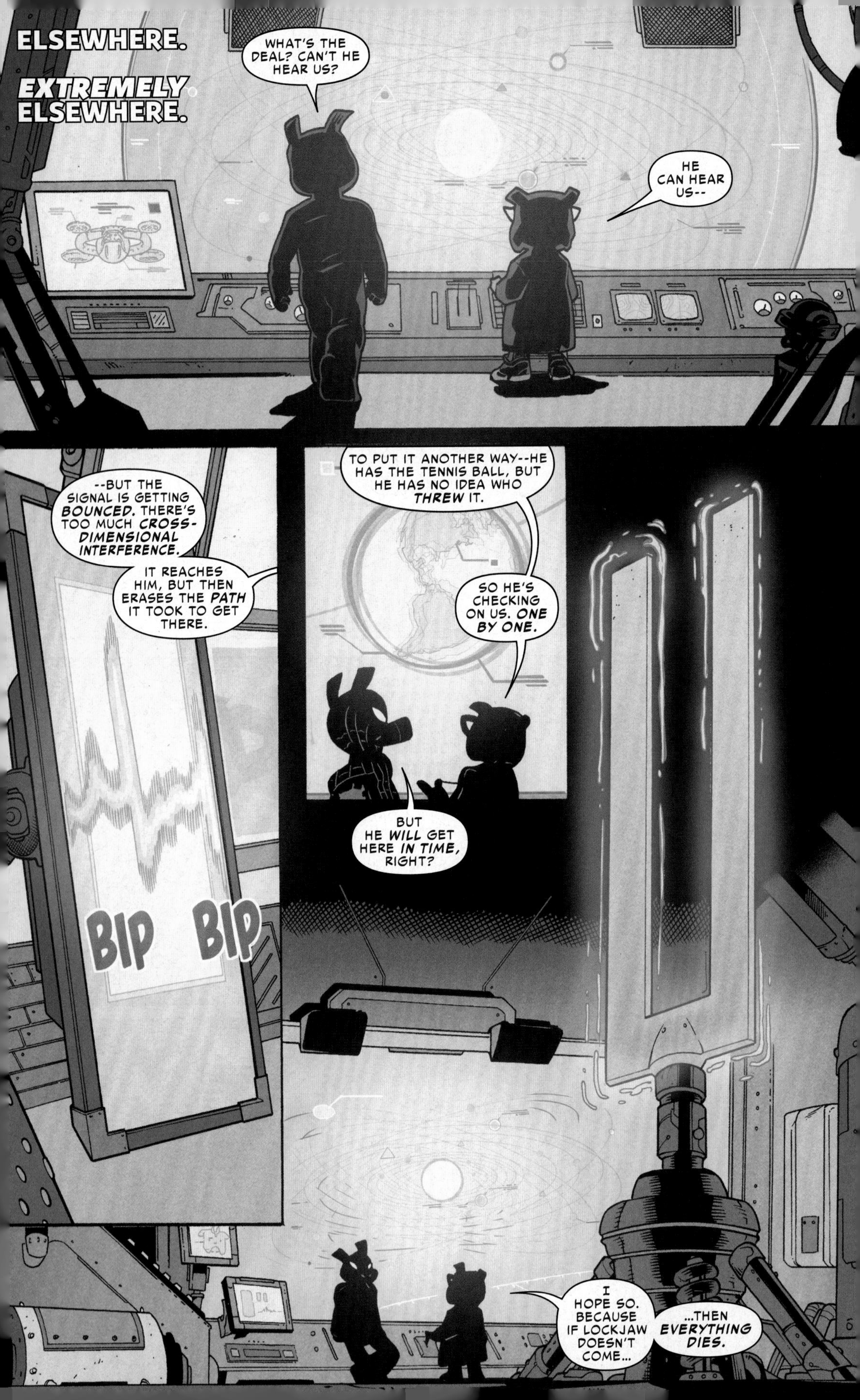

ELSEWHERE.
EXTREMELY ELSEWHERE.
WHAT'S THE DEAL? CAN'T HE HEAR US?
HE CAN HEAR US--
--BUT THE SIGNAL IS GETTING BOUNCED. THERE'S TOO MUCH CROSS-DIMENSIONAL INTERFERENCE.
IT REACHES HIM, BUT THEN ERASES THE PATH IT TOOK TO GET THERE.
TO PUT IT ANOTHER WAY--HE HAS THE TENNIS BALL, BUT HE HAS NO IDEA WHO THREW IT.
SO HE'S CHECKING ON US. ONE BY ONE.
BUT HE WILL GET HERE IN TIME, RIGHT?
BIP BIP
I HOPE SO. BECAUSE IF LOCKJAW DOESN'T COME...
...THEN EVERYTHING DIES.

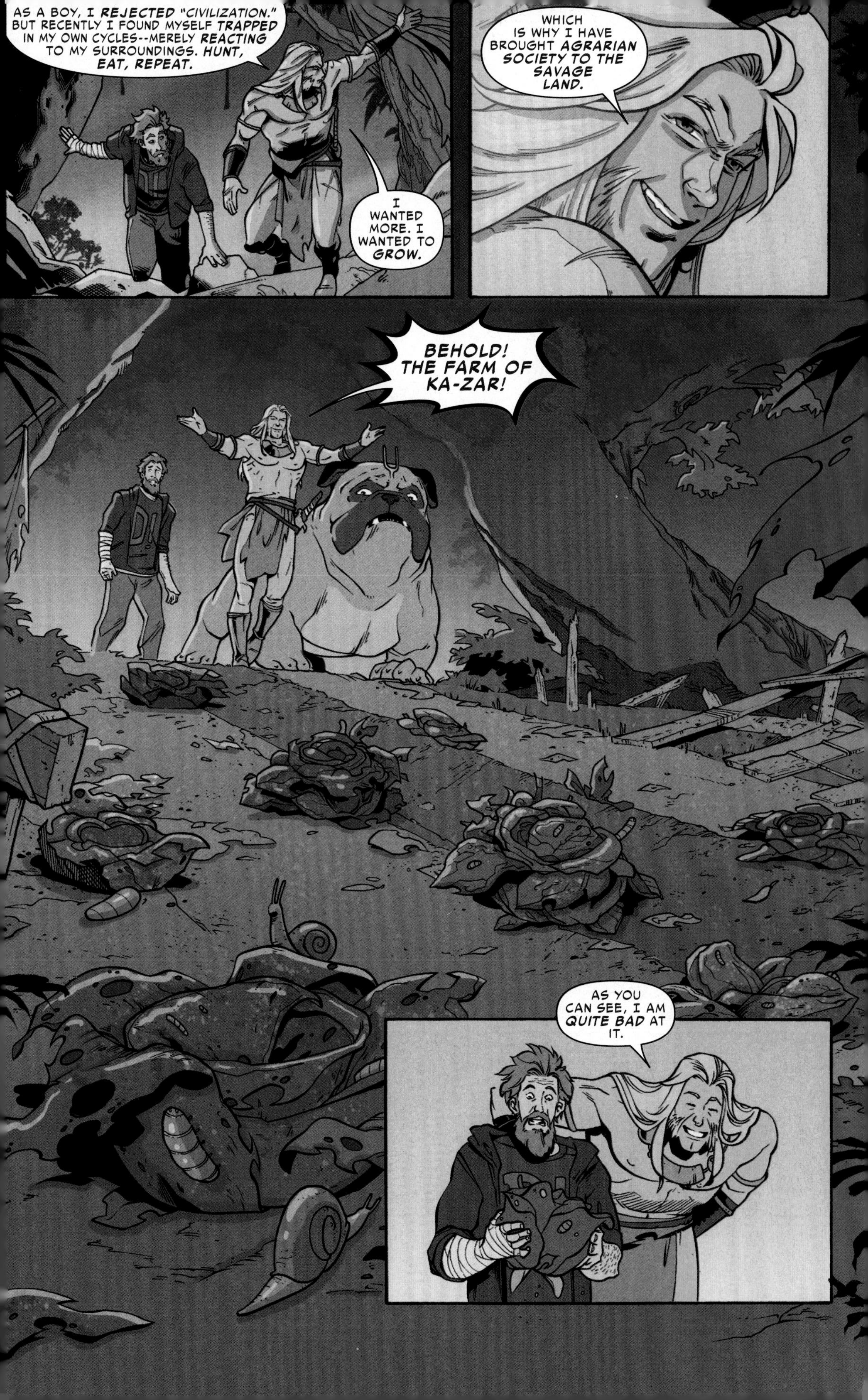
AS A BOY, I REJECTED "CIVILIZATION." BUT RECENTLY I FOUND MYSELF TRAPPED IN MY OWN CYCLES--MERELY REACTING TO MY SURROUNDINGS. HUNT, EAT, REPEAT.
I WANTED MORE. I WANTED TO GROW.
WHICH IS WHY I HAVE BROUGHT AGRARIAN SOCIETY TO THE SAVAGE LAND.
BEHOLD! THE FARM OF KA-ZAR!
AS YOU CAN SEE, I AM QUITE BAD AT IT.

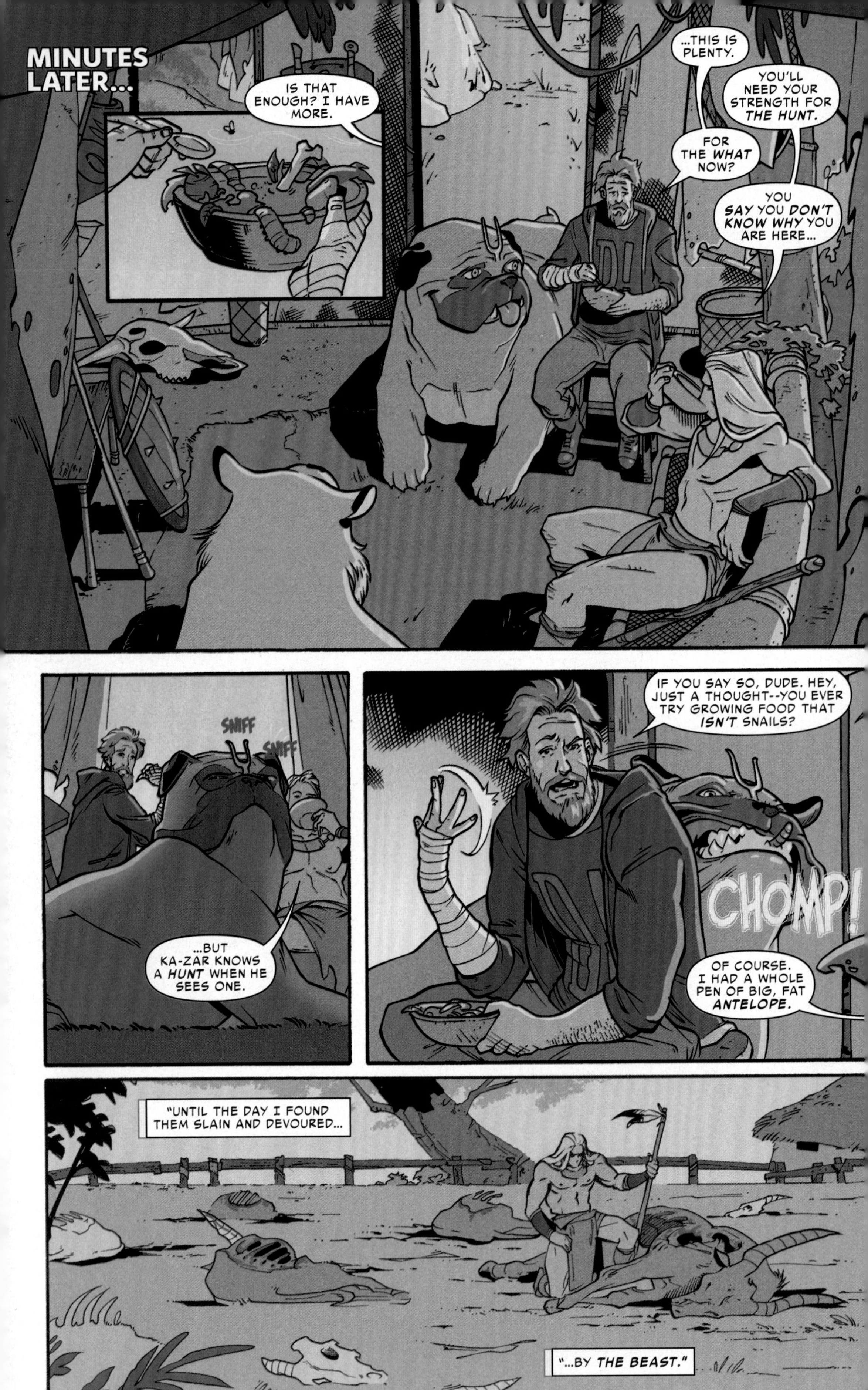
MINUTES LATER...
IS THAT ENOUGH? I HAVE MORE.
...THIS IS PLENTY.
YOU'LL NEED YOUR STRENGTH FOR THE HUNT.
FOR THE WHAT NOW?
YOU SAY YOU DON'T KNOW WHY YOU ARE HERE...
SNIFF
SNIFF
...BUT KA-ZAR KNOWS A HUNT WHEN HE SEES ONE.
IF YOU SAY SO, DUDE. HEY, JUST A THOUGHT--YOU EVER TRY GROWING FOOD THAT ISN'T SNAILS?
CHOMP!
OF COURSE. I HAD A WHOLE PEN OF BIG, FAT ANTELOPE.
"UNTIL THE DAY I FOUND THEM SLAIN AND DEVOURED...
"...BY THE BEAST."

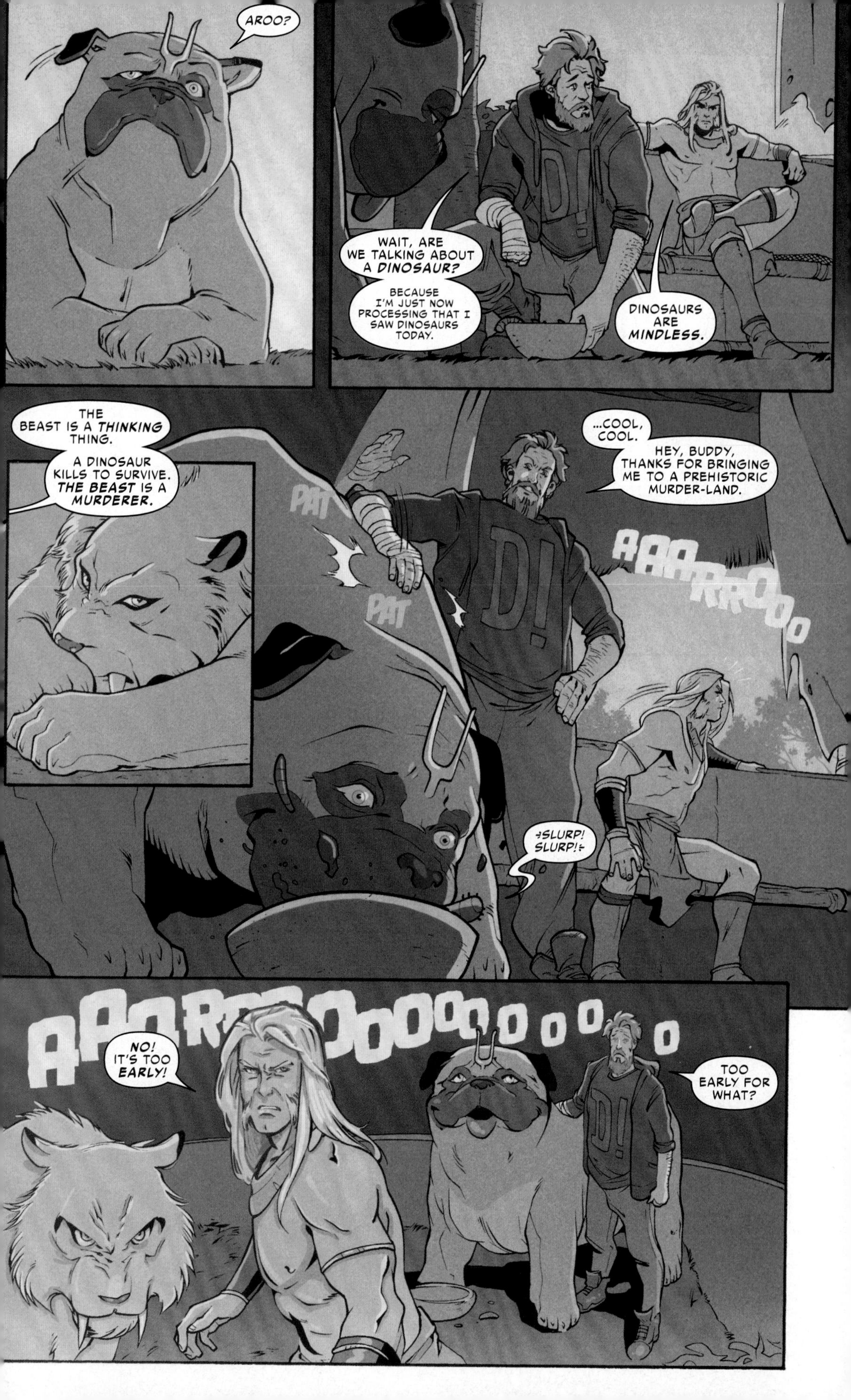

AROO?
WAIT, ARE WE TALKING ABOUT A *DINOSAUR?*
BECAUSE I'M JUST NOW PROCESSING THAT I SAW DINOSAURS TODAY.
DINOSAURS ARE *MINDLESS.*
THE BEAST IS A *THINKING* THING.
A DINOSAUR KILLS TO SURVIVE. *THE BEAST* IS A *MURDERER.*
...COOL, COOL.
HEY, BUDDY, THANKS FOR BRINGING ME TO A PREHISTORIC MURDER-LAND.
PAT
PAT
AAARROOO
SLURP! SLURP!
AAARRROOOOOOOOO
NO! IT'S TOO *EARLY!*
TOO EARLY FOR WHAT?

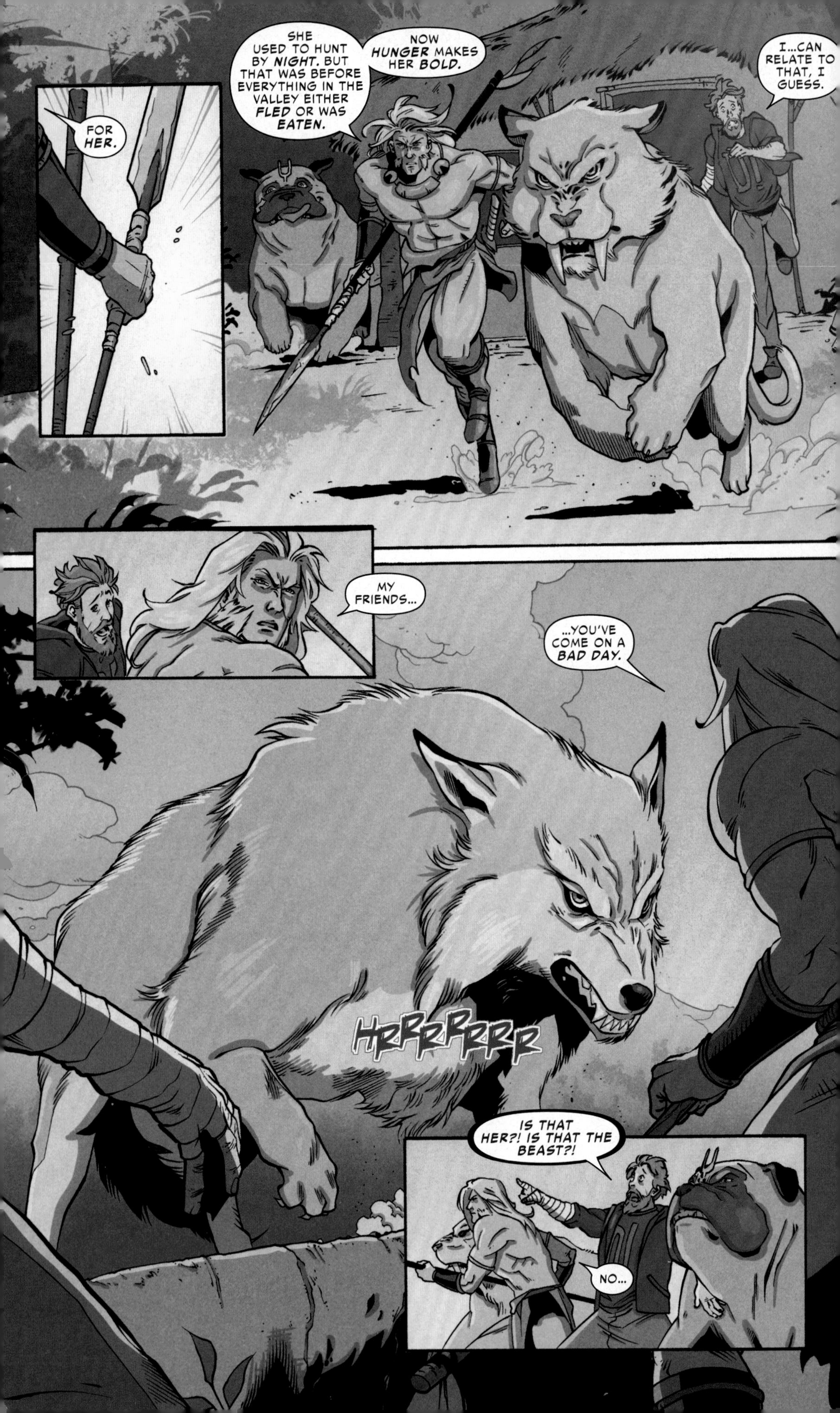
FOR HER.
SHE USED TO HUNT BY NIGHT. BUT THAT WAS BEFORE EVERYTHING IN THE VALLEY EITHER FLED OR WAS EATEN.
NOW HUNGER MAKES HER BOLD.
I...CAN RELATE TO THAT, I GUESS.
MY FRIENDS...
...YOU'VE COME ON A BAD DAY.
HRRRRRRR
IS THAT HER?! IS THAT THE BEAST?!
NO...

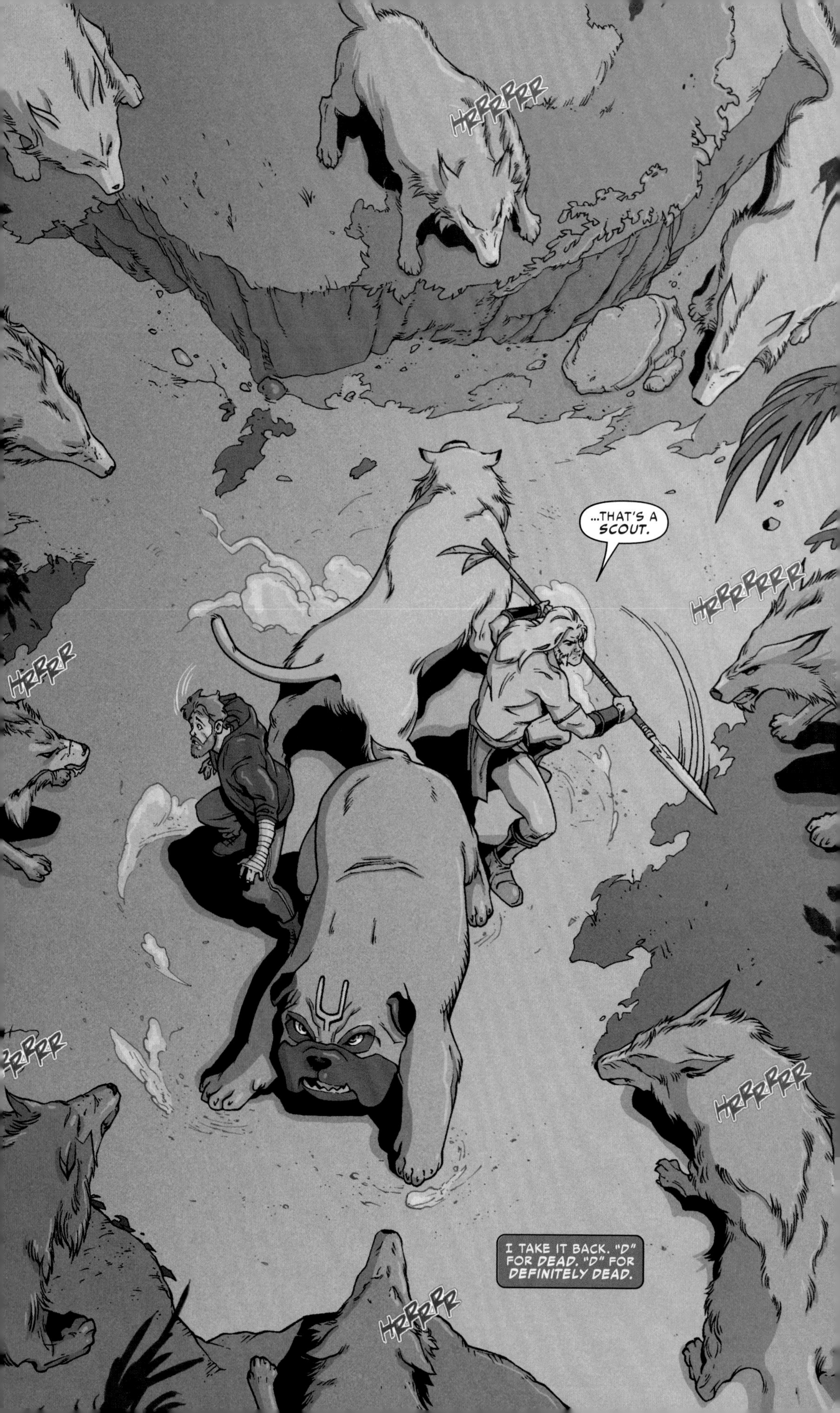
HRRRRR
...THAT'S A SCOUT.
HRRRRRR
HRRRR
HRRRR
HRRRRRR
I TAKE IT BACK. "D" FOR DEAD. "D" FOR DEFINITELY DEAD.
HRRRR

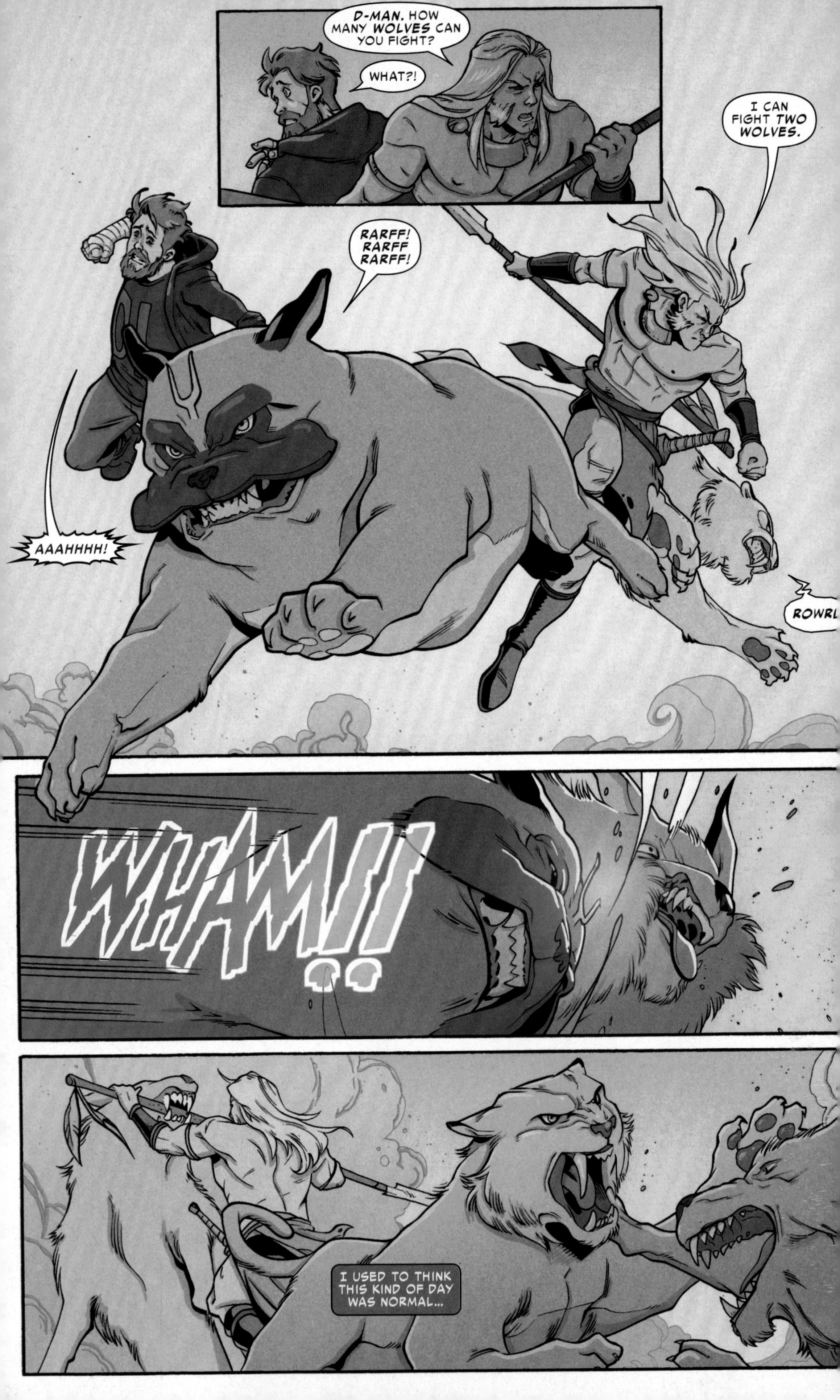
D-MAN. HOW MANY WOLVES CAN YOU FIGHT?
WHAT?!
I CAN FIGHT TWO WOLVES.
RARFF! RARFF RARFF!
AAAHHHH!
ROWRL
WHAM!!
I USED TO THINK THIS KIND OF DAY WAS NORMAL...

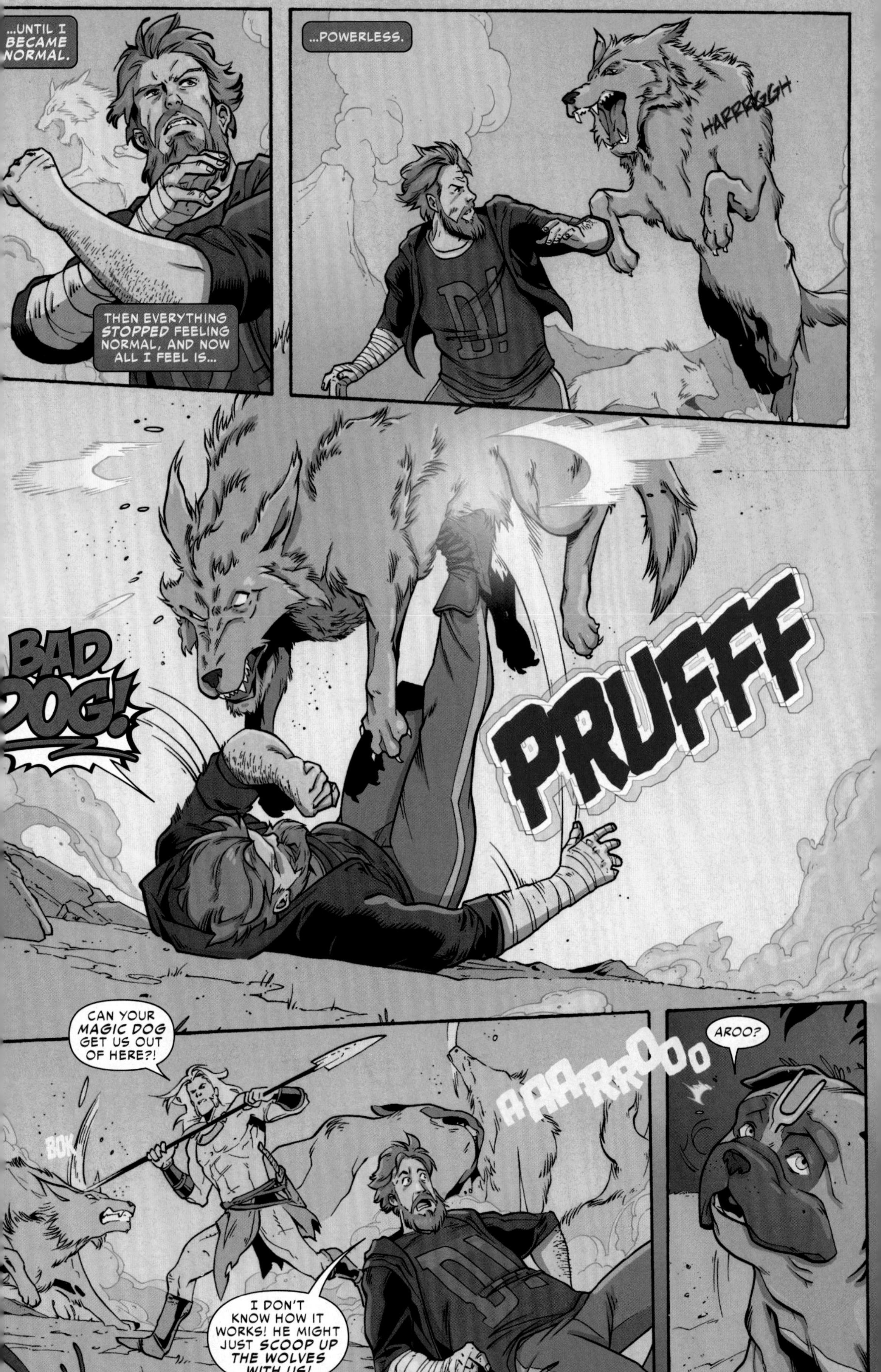

...UNTIL I BECAME NORMAL.
THEN EVERYTHING STOPPED FEELING NORMAL, AND NOW ALL I FEEL IS...
...POWERLESS.
HARRRGGH
BAD DOG!
PRUFFF
CAN YOUR MAGIC DOG GET US OUT OF HERE?!
BOK
AAARRROOo
I DON'T KNOW HOW IT WORKS! HE MIGHT JUST SCOOP UP THE WOLVES WITH US!
AROO?

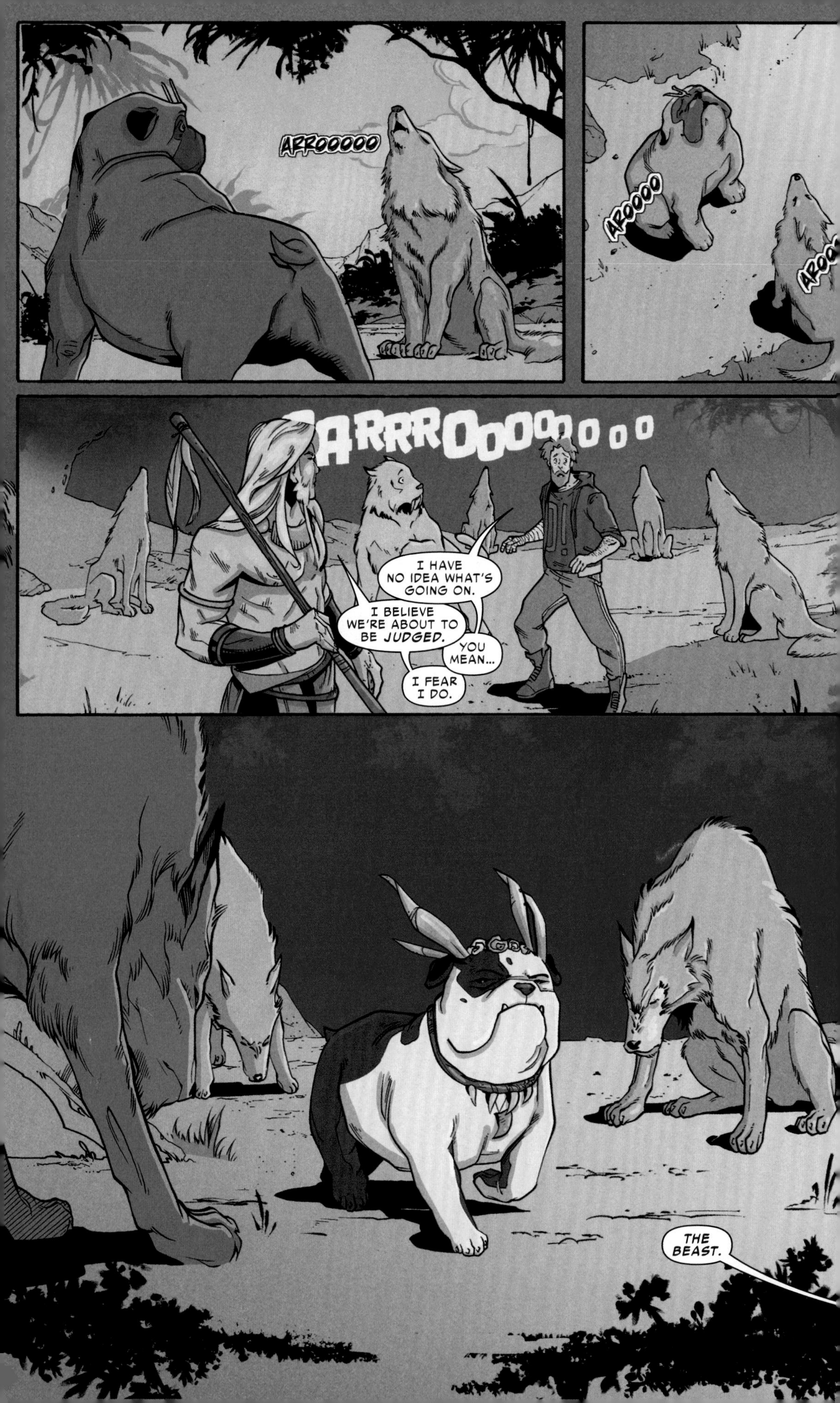
ARROOOOO
AROOOO
AROO
ARRRROOOooooo
I HAVE NO IDEA WHAT'S GOING ON.
I BELIEVE WE'RE ABOUT TO BE *JUDGED.*
YOU MEAN...
I FEAR I DO.
THE BEAST.

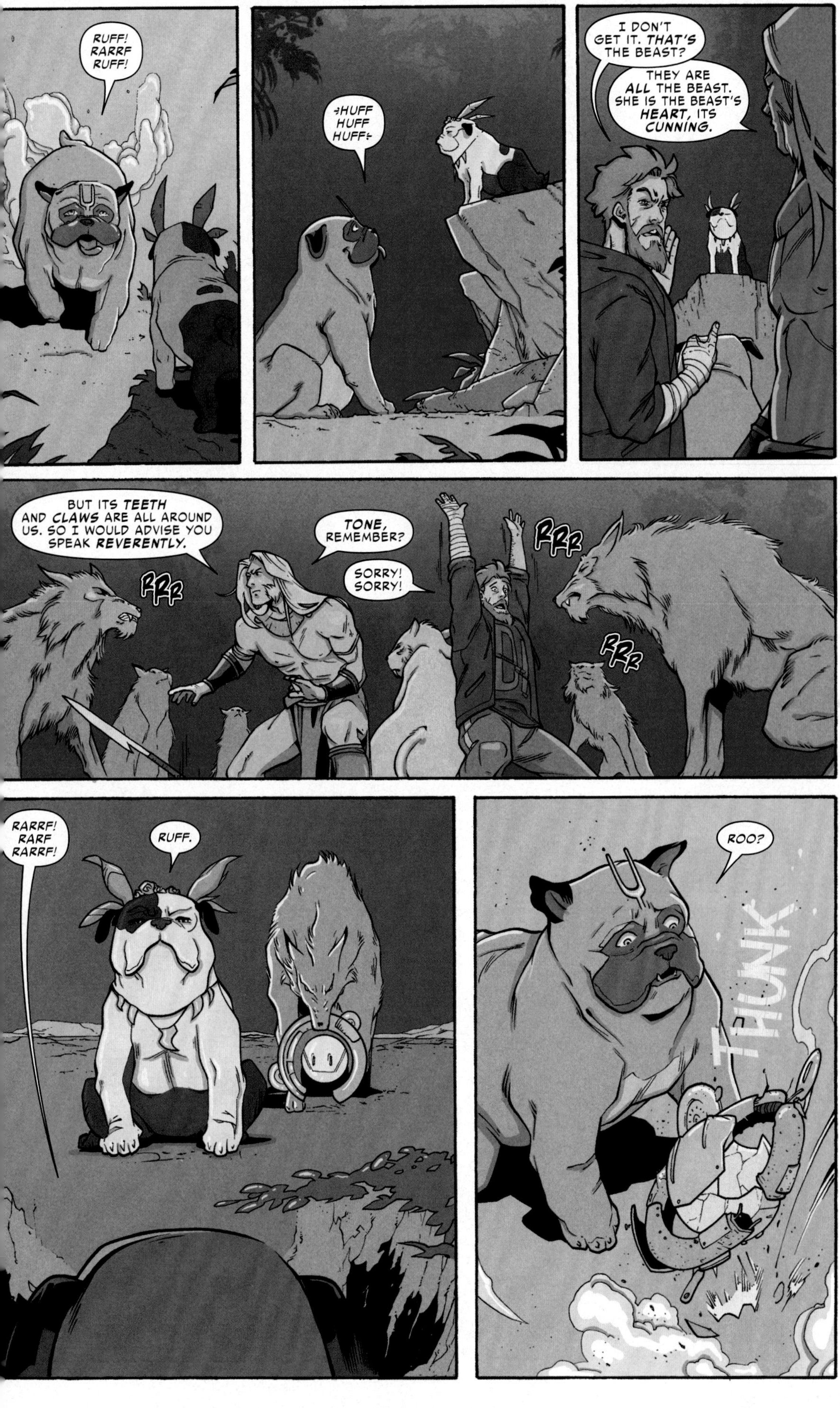
RUFF! RARRF RUFF!
HUFF HUFF HUFF
I DON'T GET IT. THAT'S THE BEAST?
THEY ARE ALL THE BEAST. SHE IS THE BEAST'S HEART, ITS CUNNING.
BUT ITS TEETH AND CLAWS ARE ALL AROUND US. SO I WOULD ADVISE YOU SPEAK REVERENTLY.
TONE, REMEMBER?
SORRY! SORRY!
RRR
RRR
RRR
RARRF! RARF RARRF!
RUFF.
ROO?
THUNK

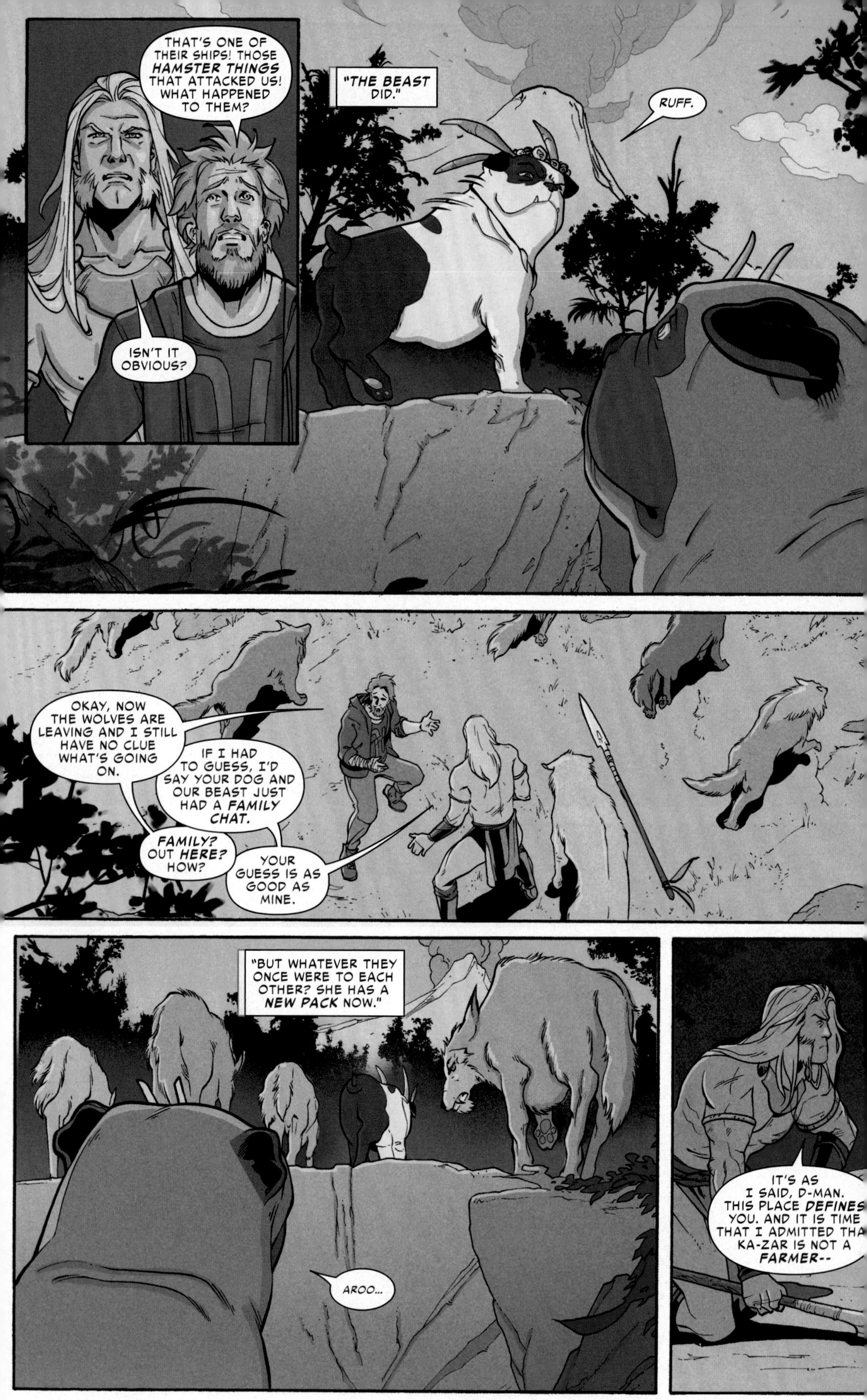
THAT'S ONE OF THEIR SHIPS! THOSE HAMSTER THINGS THAT ATTACKED US! WHAT HAPPENED TO THEM?
ISN'T IT OBVIOUS?
"THE BEAST DID."
RUFF.
OKAY, NOW THE WOLVES ARE LEAVING AND I STILL HAVE NO CLUE WHAT'S GOING ON.
IF I HAD TO GUESS, I'D SAY YOUR DOG AND OUR BEAST JUST HAD A FAMILY CHAT.
FAMILY? OUT HERE? HOW?
YOUR GUESS IS AS GOOD AS MINE.
"BUT WHATEVER THEY ONCE WERE TO EACH OTHER? SHE HAS A NEW PACK NOW."
AROO...
IT'S AS I SAID, D-MAN. THIS PLACE DEFINES YOU. AND IT IS TIME THAT I ADMITTED THA KA-ZAR IS NOT A FARMER--

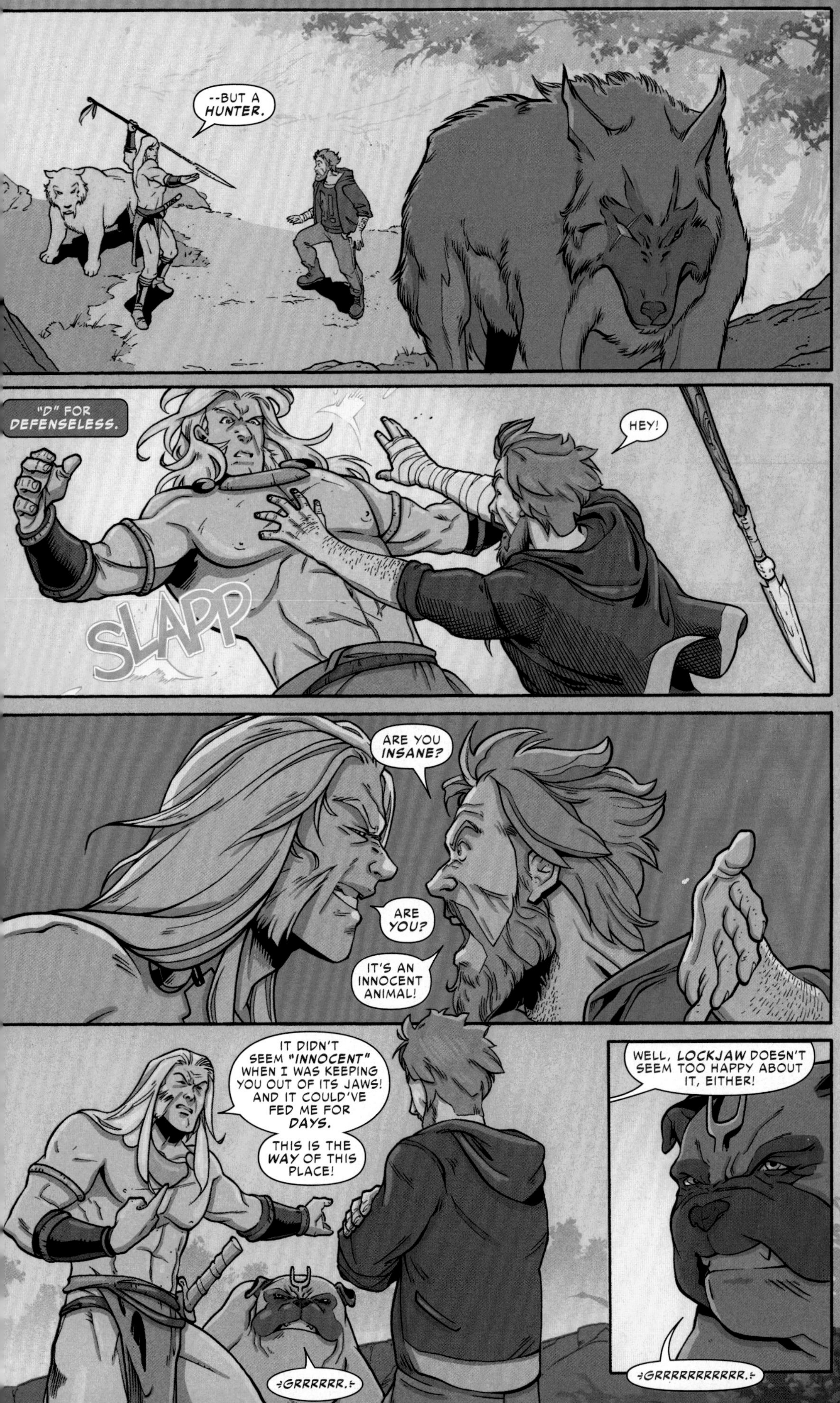
--BUT A HUNTER.
"D" FOR DEFENSELESS.
SLAPP
HEY!
ARE YOU INSANE?
ARE YOU?
IT'S AN INNOCENT ANIMAL!
IT DIDN'T SEEM "INNOCENT" WHEN I WAS KEEPING YOU OUT OF ITS JAWS! AND IT COULD'VE FED ME FOR DAYS.
THIS IS THE WAY OF THIS PLACE!
GRRRRRR.
WELL, LOCKJAW DOESN'T SEEM TOO HAPPY ABOUT IT, EITHER!
GRRRRRRRRRRR.

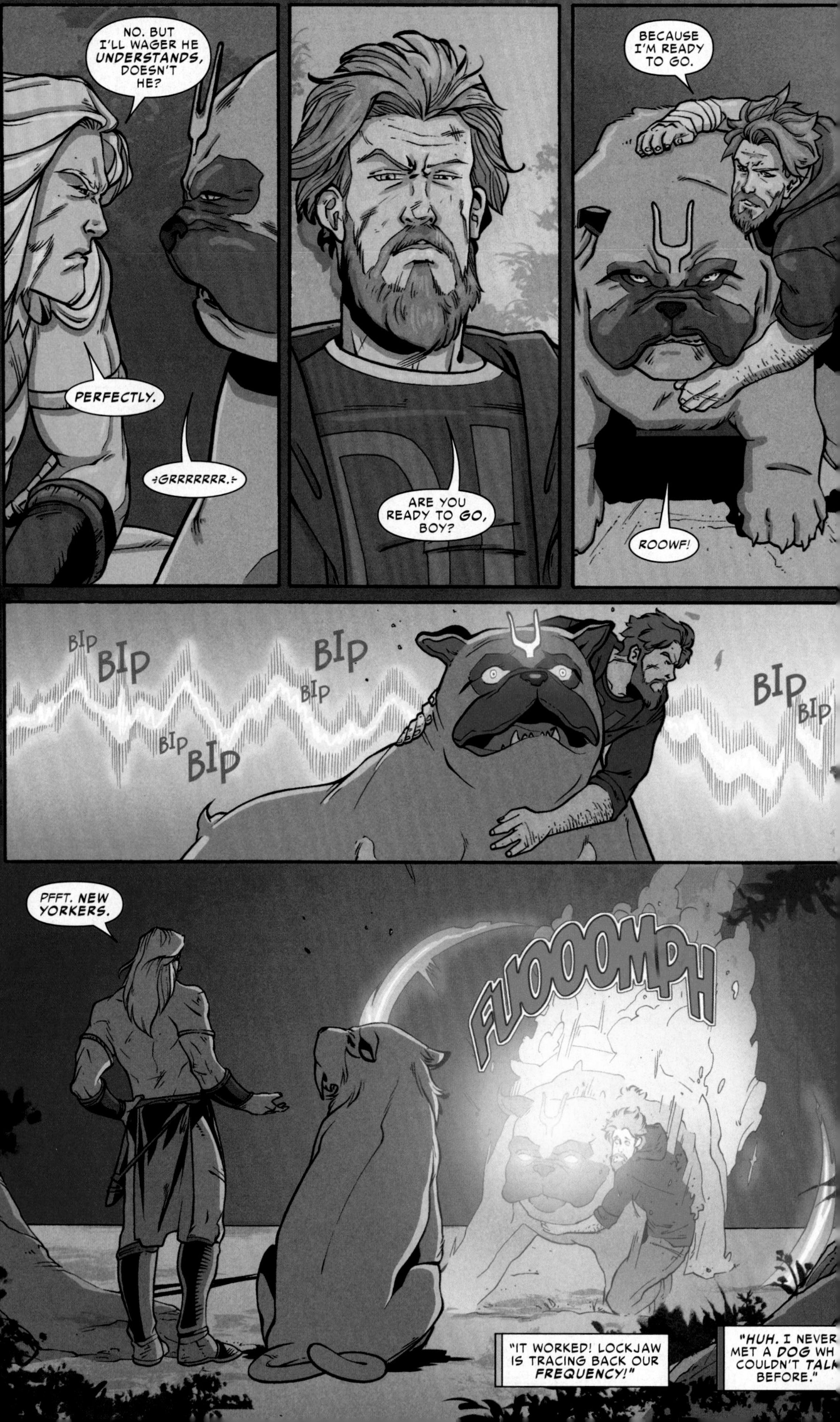
NO. BUT I'LL WAGER HE UNDERSTANDS, DOESN'T HE?
PERFECTLY.
GRRRRRRR.
ARE YOU READY TO GO, BOY?
BECAUSE I'M READY TO GO.
ROOWF!
BIP BIP
BIP BIP
BIP BIP
BIP BIP
PFFT. NEW YORKERS.
FLOOOMPH
"IT WORKED! LOCKJAW IS TRACING BACK OUR FREQUENCY!"
"HUH. I NEVER MET A DOG WH COULDN'T TAL BEFORE."

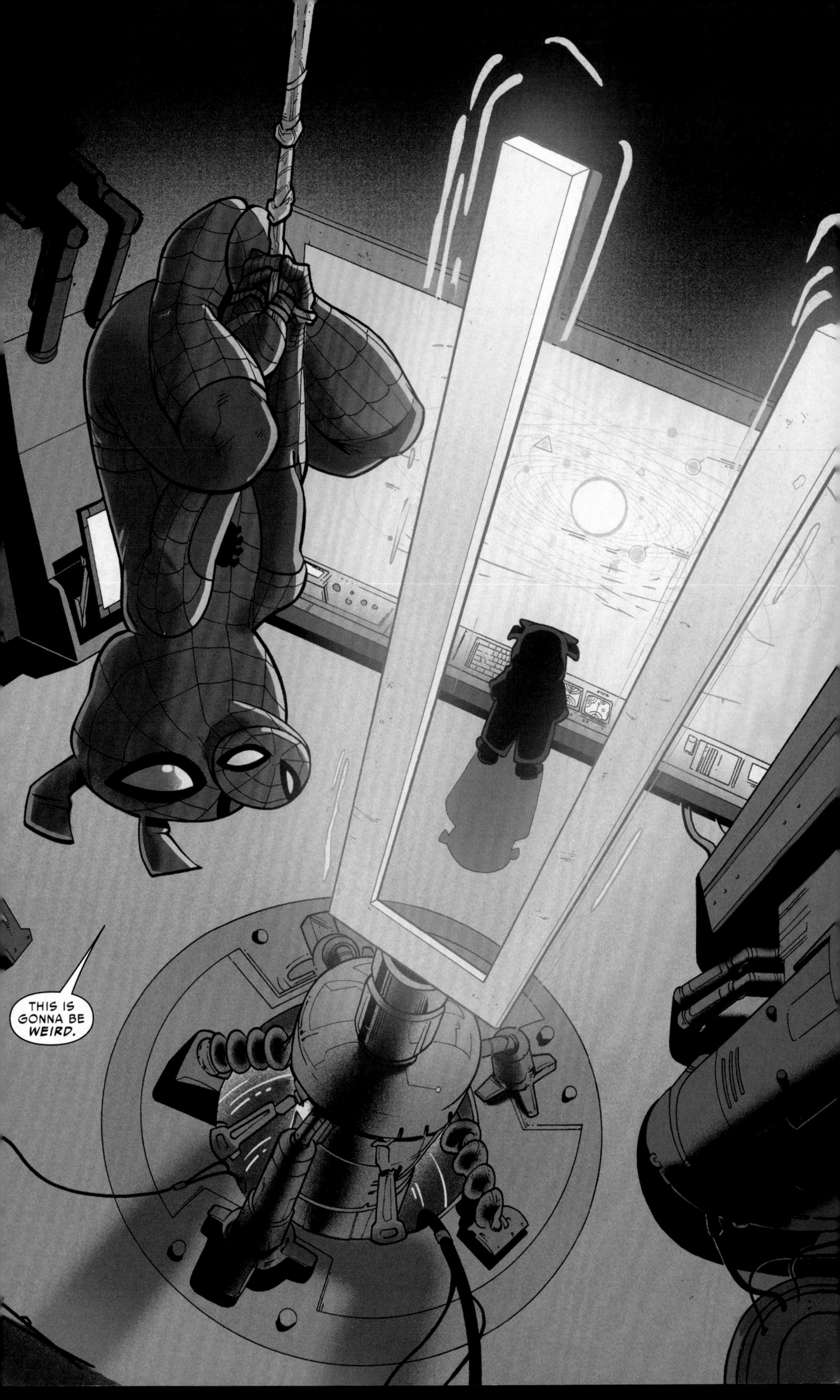
THIS IS GONNA BE WEIRD.

LOCKJAW
IMPERILING: SPIDER-HAM
THE WORLD WILL MARVEL AT THE AWESOME MIGHT OF SPIDER-HAM AND LOCKJAW...
...AND LOCKJAW'S MIGHTY WEIGHT! GEEZ, DOG, LAY OFF THE BACON!
WOOF!
ALSO IN THIS ISSUE:
AN IMPORTANT MESSAGE TO YOU, FROM D-MAN -- ABOUT THE NEW LEASH LAWS!
3

HEY, IT'S ME! LOCKJAW!

THIS SURE HAS BEEN ONE CRAZY ADVENTURE! FIRST *FLYING HAMSTERS* IN BROOKLYN AND THEN *THE SAVAGE LAND!*

TALK ABOUT *TRUTH* IN ADVERTISING.

YOU SURE TOOK A NASTY *BUMP* WHEN WE LANDED.

SORRY ABOUT THAT--MY *TELEPORTS* HAVE BEEN A LITTLE *OFF* LATELY. KINDA GOIN' THROUGH SOME STUFF.

ARE YOU OKAY?

DENNIS?

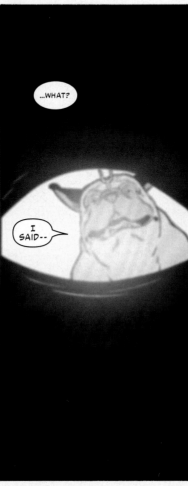

...WHAT?

I SAID--

BARK

BARK

BARK

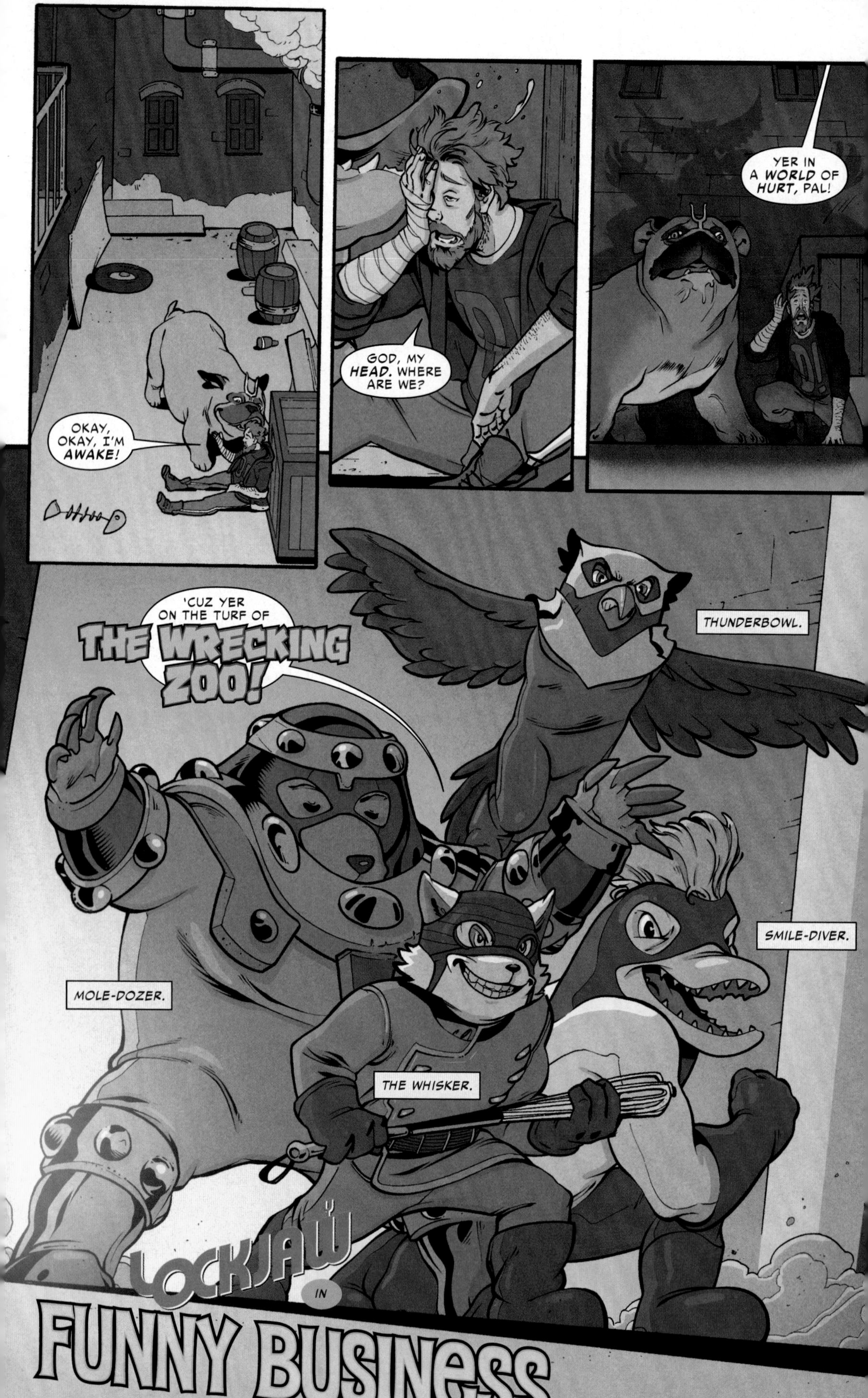

OKAY, OKAY, I'M AWAKE!
GOD, MY HEAD. WHERE ARE WE?
YER IN A WORLD OF HURT, PAL!
'CUZ YER ON THE TURF OF THE WRECKING ZOO!
THUNDERBOWL.
SMILE-DIVER.
MOLE-DOZER.
THE WHISKER.
LOCKJAW IN
FUNNY BUSINESS

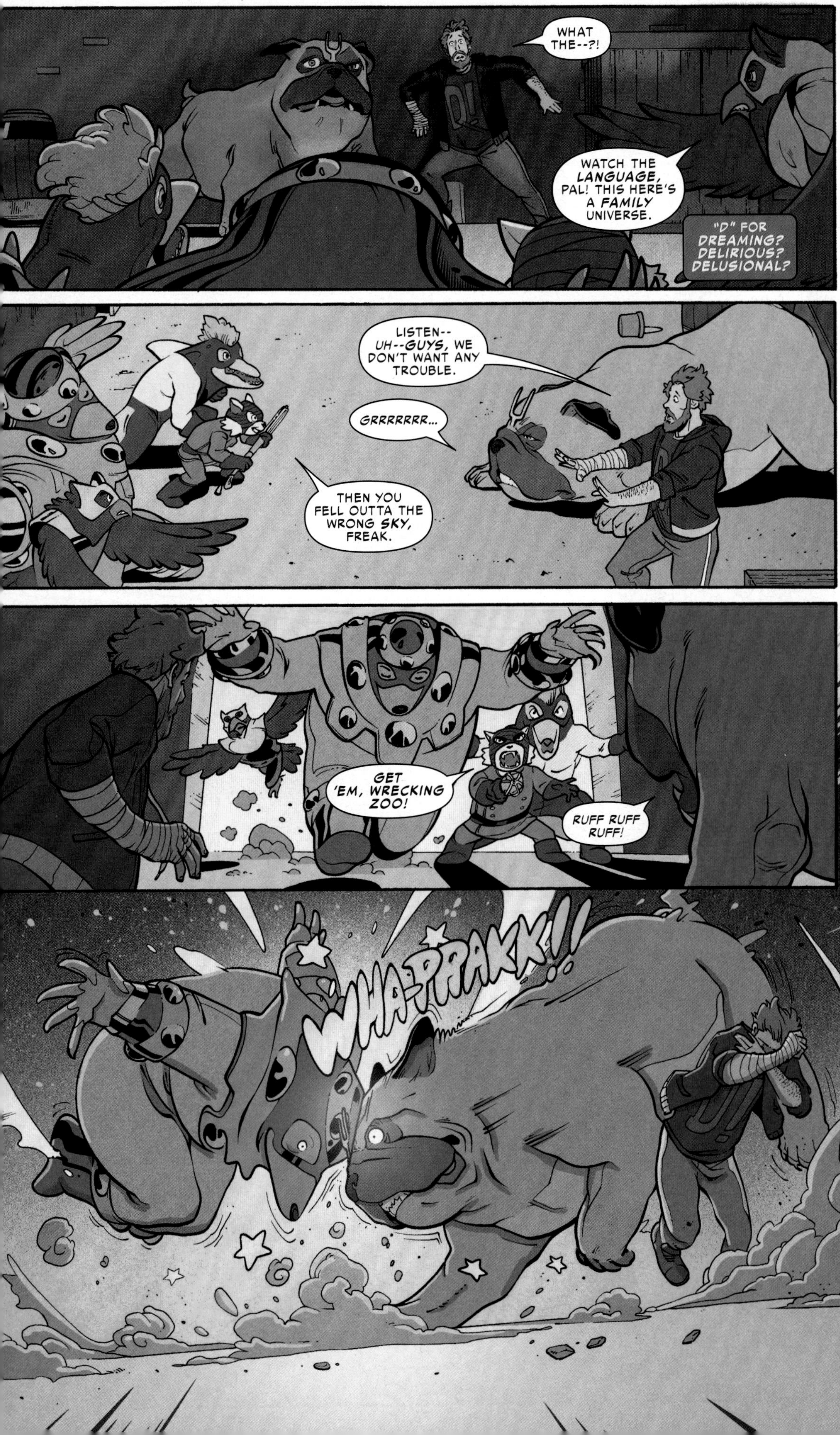
WHAT THE--?!
WATCH THE *LANGUAGE*, PAL! THIS HERE'S A *FAMILY* UNIVERSE.
"D" FOR *DREAMING? DELIRIOUS? DELUSIONAL?*
LISTEN-- *UH--GUYS*, WE DON'T WANT ANY TROUBLE.
GRRRRRRR...
THEN YOU FELL OUTTA THE WRONG *SKY*, FREAK.
GET 'EM, WRECKING ZOO!
RUFF RUFF RUFF!
WHA-PAKK!!

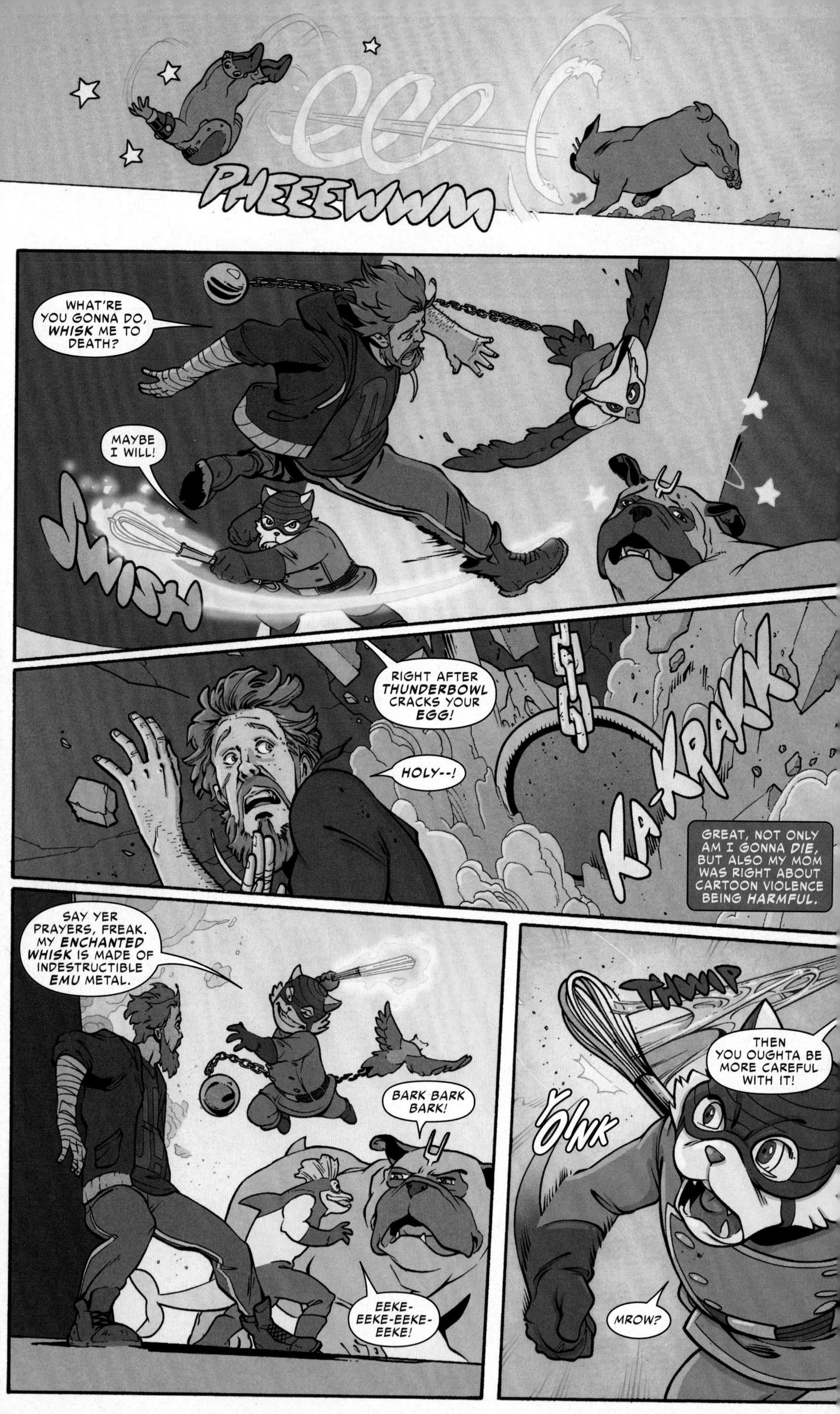
PHEEEWWM
WHAT'RE YOU GONNA DO, WHISK ME TO DEATH?
MAYBE I WILL!
SWISH
RIGHT AFTER THUNDERBOWL CRACKS YOUR EGG!
HOLY--!
KA-KRAKK
GREAT, NOT ONLY AM I GONNA DIE, BUT ALSO MY MOM WAS RIGHT ABOUT CARTOON VIOLENCE BEING HARMFUL.
SAY YER PRAYERS, FREAK. MY ENCHANTED WHISK IS MADE OF INDESTRUCTIBLE EMU METAL.
BARK BARK BARK!
EEKE-EEKE-EEKE-EEKE!
THWIP
THEN YOU OUGHTA BE MORE CAREFUL WITH IT!
YOINK
MROW?

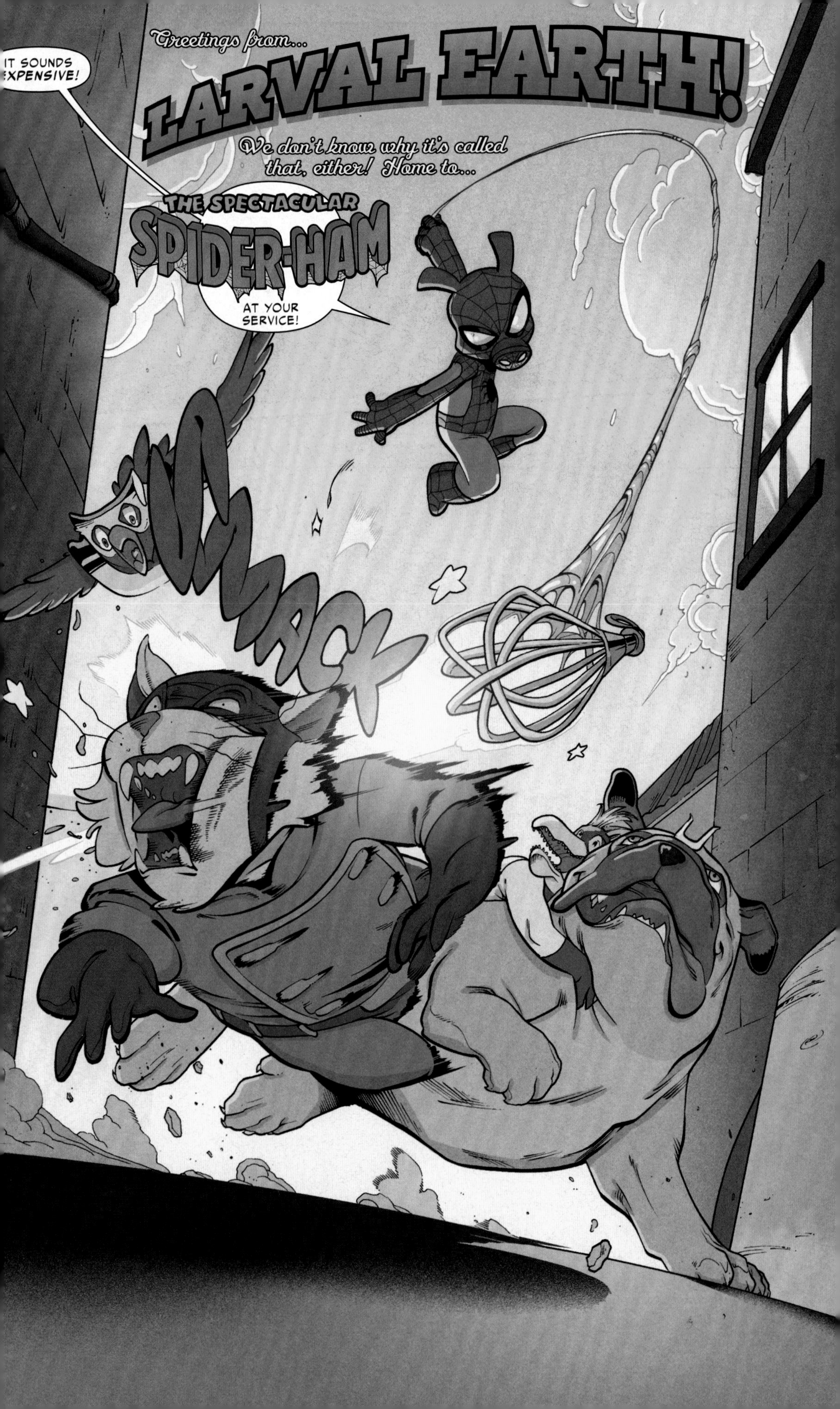
IT SOUNDS EXPENSIVE!
Greetings from...
LARVAL EARTH!
We don't know why it's called that, either! Home to...
THE SPECTACULAR SPIDER-HAM
AT YOUR SERVICE!
WHACK

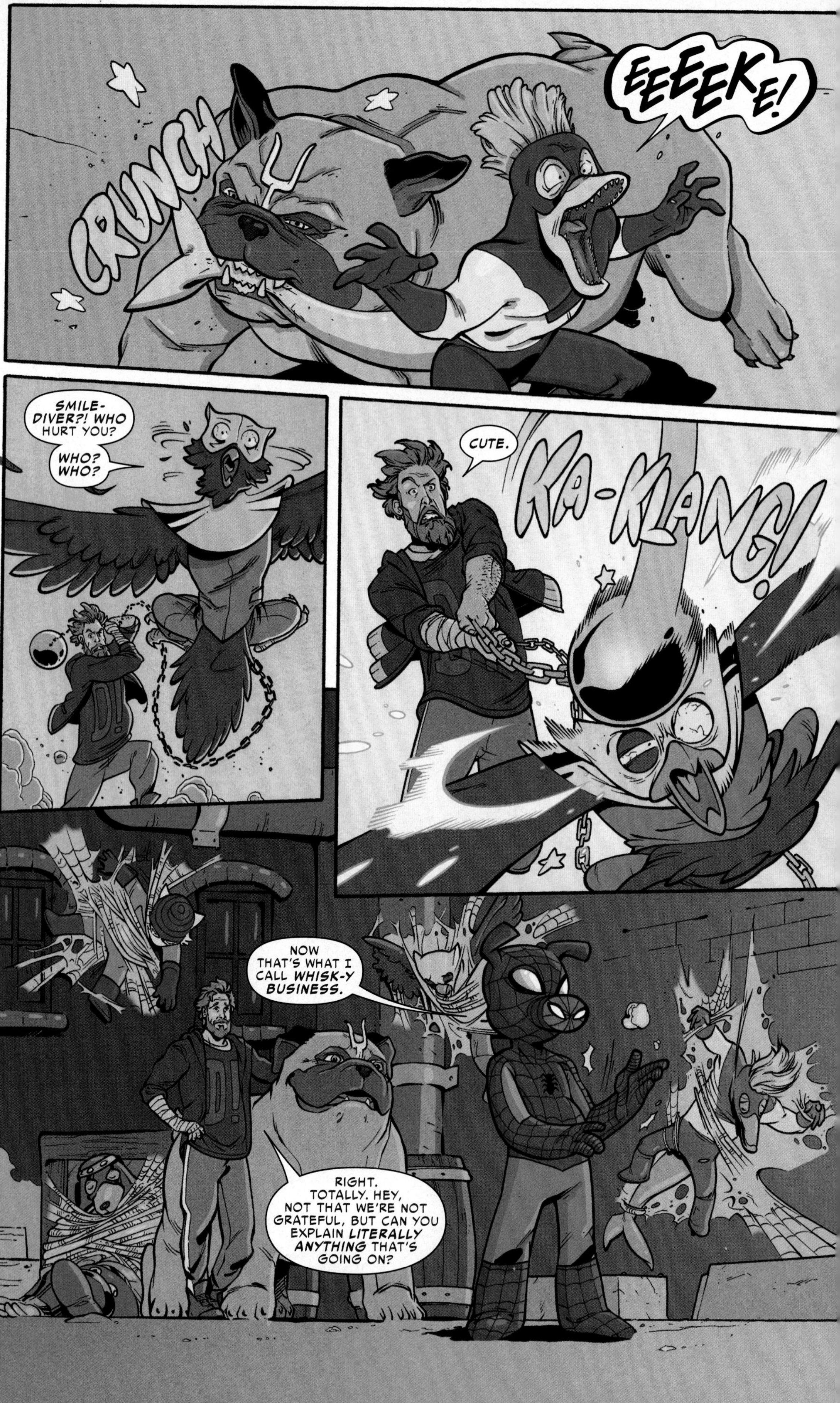

CRUNCH
EEEEKE!
SMILE-DIVER?! WHO HURT YOU?
WHO? WHO?
CUTE.
KA-KLANG!
NOW THAT'S WHAT I CALL WHISK-Y BUSINESS.
RIGHT. TOTALLY. HEY, NOT THAT WE'RE NOT GRATEFUL, BUT CAN YOU EXPLAIN LITERALLY ANYTHING THAT'S GOING ON?

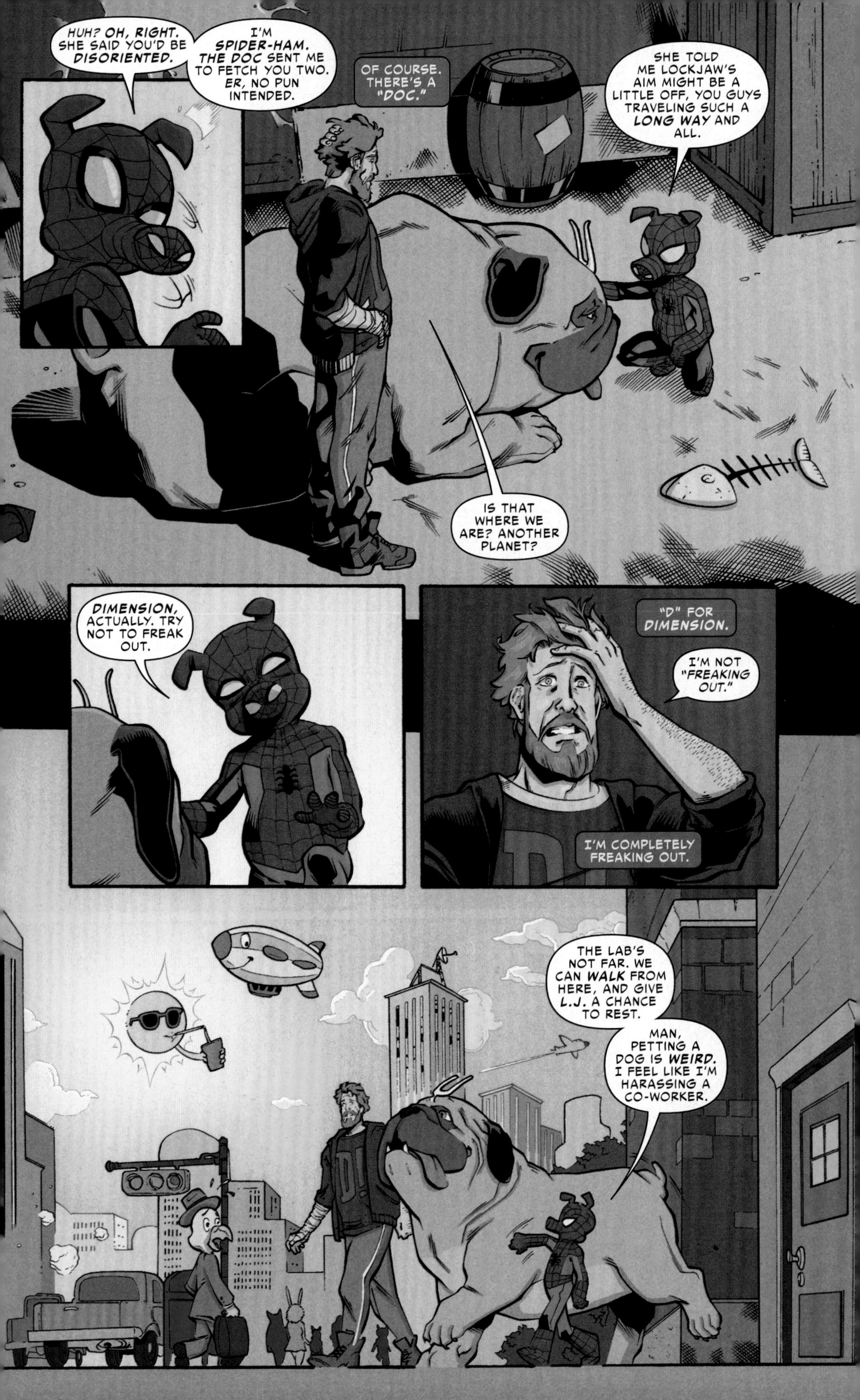
HUH? OH, RIGHT. SHE SAID YOU'D BE DISORIENTED.
I'M SPIDER-HAM. THE DOC SENT ME TO FETCH YOU TWO. ER, NO PUN INTENDED.
OF COURSE. THERE'S A "DOC."
SHE TOLD ME LOCKJAW'S AIM MIGHT BE A LITTLE OFF, YOU GUYS TRAVELING SUCH A LONG WAY AND ALL.
IS THAT WHERE WE ARE? ANOTHER PLANET?
DIMENSION, ACTUALLY. TRY NOT TO FREAK OUT.
"D" FOR DIMENSION.
I'M NOT "FREAKING OUT."
I'M COMPLETELY FREAKING OUT.
THE LAB'S NOT FAR. WE CAN WALK FROM HERE, AND GIVE L.J. A CHANCE TO REST.
MAN, PETTING A DOG IS WEIRD. I FEEL LIKE I'M HARASSING A CO-WORKER.

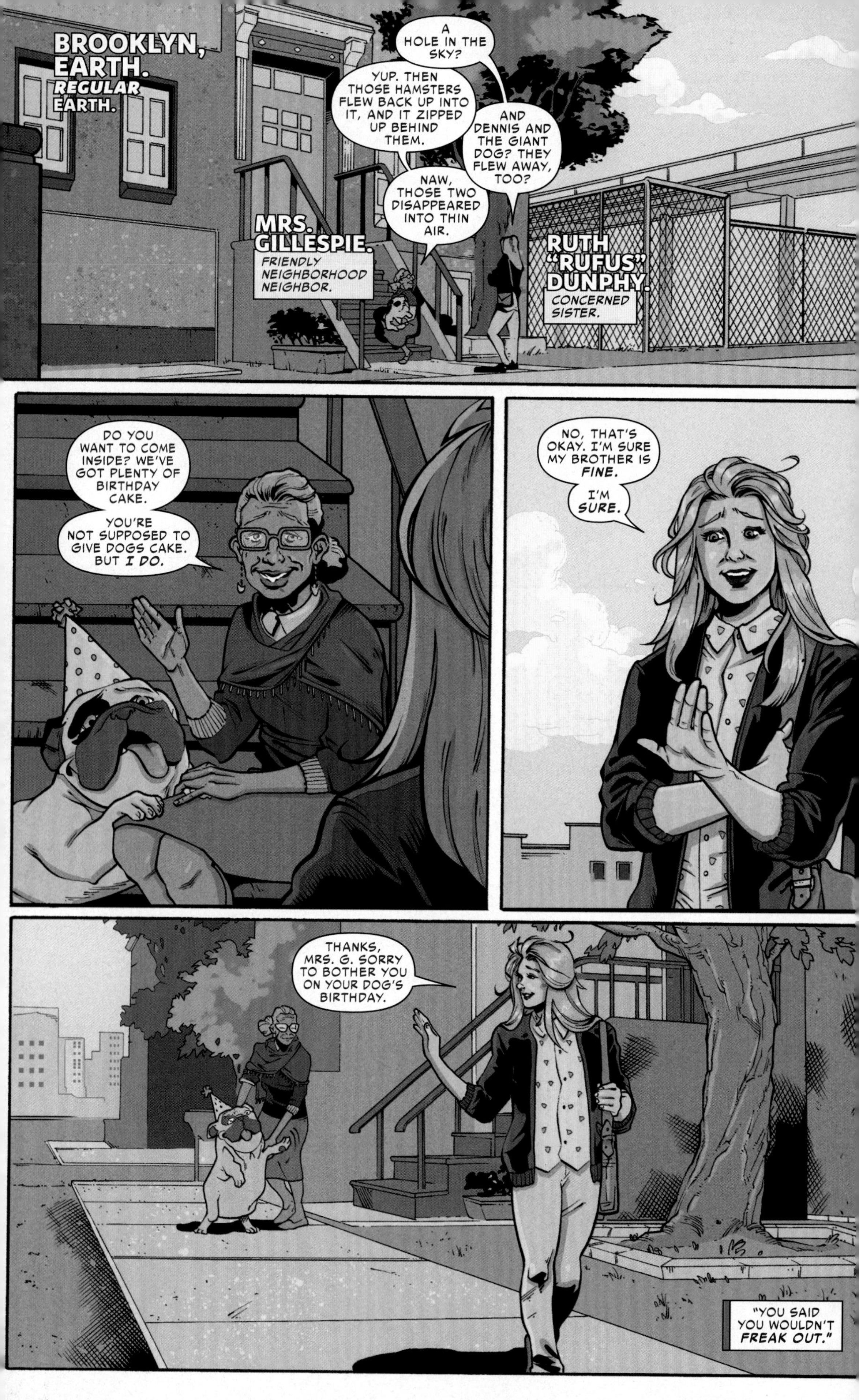
BROOKLYN, EARTH. REGULAR EARTH.
A HOLE IN THE SKY?
YUP. THEN THOSE HAMSTERS FLEW BACK UP INTO IT, AND IT ZIPPED UP BEHIND THEM.
AND DENNIS AND THE GIANT DOG? THEY FLEW AWAY, TOO?
NAW, THOSE TWO DISAPPEARED INTO THIN AIR.
MRS. GILLESPIE. FRIENDLY NEIGHBORHOOD NEIGHBOR.
RUTH "RUFUS" DUNPHY. CONCERNED SISTER.
DO YOU WANT TO COME INSIDE? WE'VE GOT PLENTY OF BIRTHDAY CAKE.
YOU'RE NOT SUPPOSED TO GIVE DOGS CAKE. BUT I DO.
NO, THAT'S OKAY. I'M SURE MY BROTHER IS FINE.
I'M SURE.
THANKS, MRS. G. SORRY TO BOTHER YOU ON YOUR DOG'S BIRTHDAY.
"YOU SAID YOU WOULDN'T FREAK OUT."

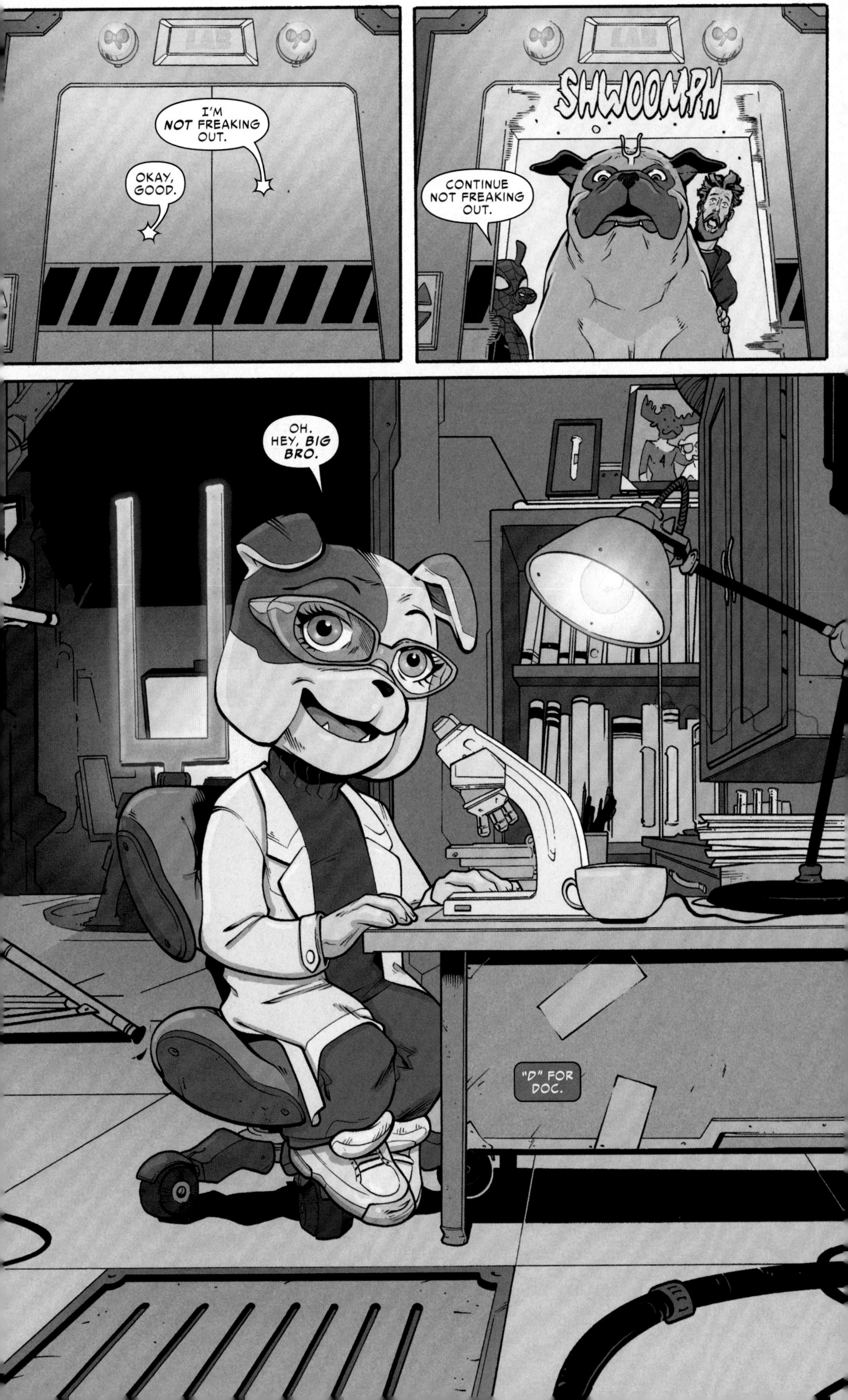
LAB
I'M NOT FREAKING OUT.
OKAY, GOOD.
LAB
SHWOOMPH
CONTINUE NOT FREAKING OUT.
OH. HEY, BIG BRO.
"D" FOR DOC.

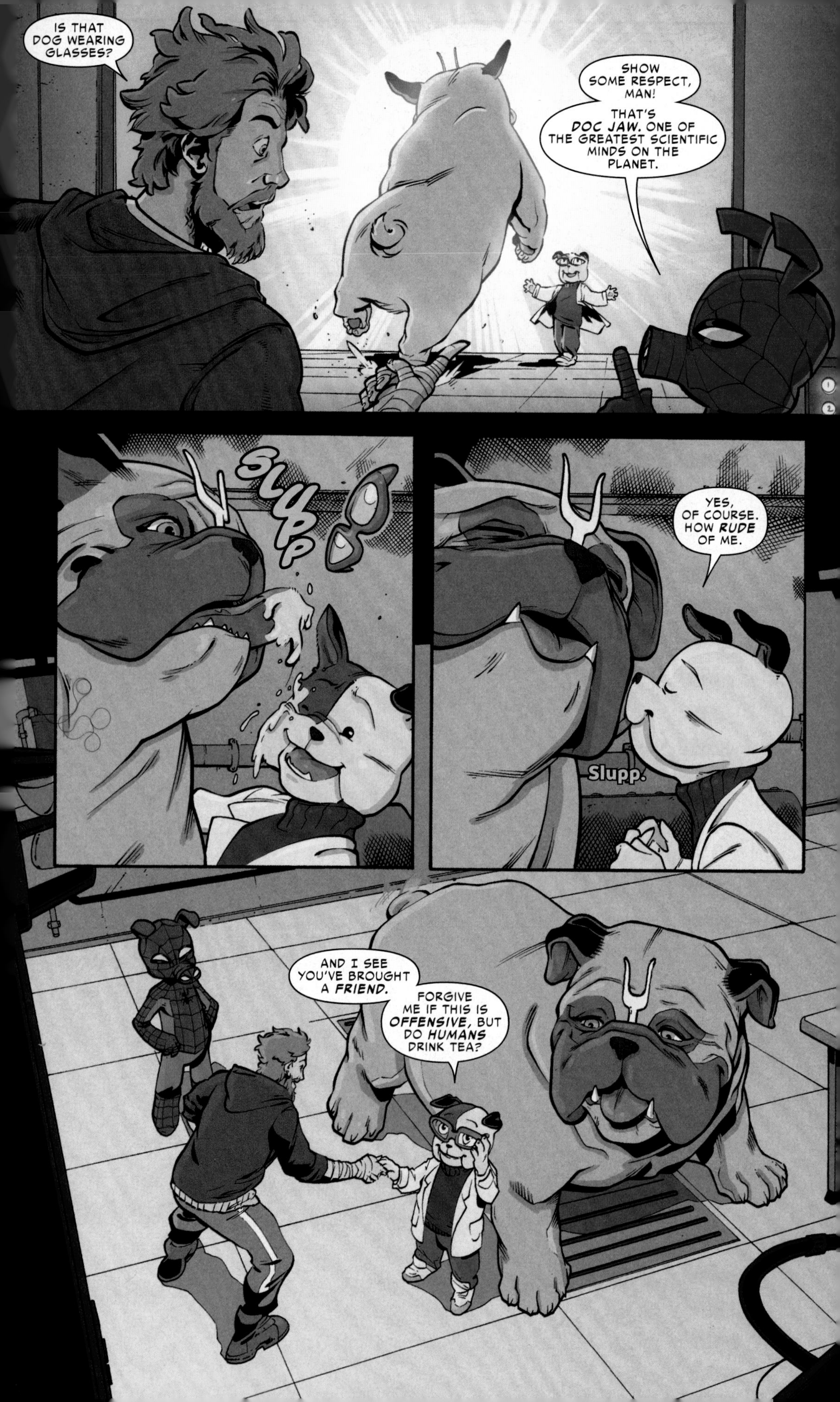
IS THAT DOG WEARING GLASSES?
SHOW SOME RESPECT, MAN!
THAT'S DOC JAW. ONE OF THE GREATEST SCIENTIFIC MINDS ON THE PLANET.
SLUPP
YES, OF COURSE. HOW RUDE OF ME.
Slupp.
AND I SEE YOU'VE BROUGHT A FRIEND.
FORGIVE ME IF THIS IS OFFENSIVE, BUT DO HUMANS DRINK TEA?

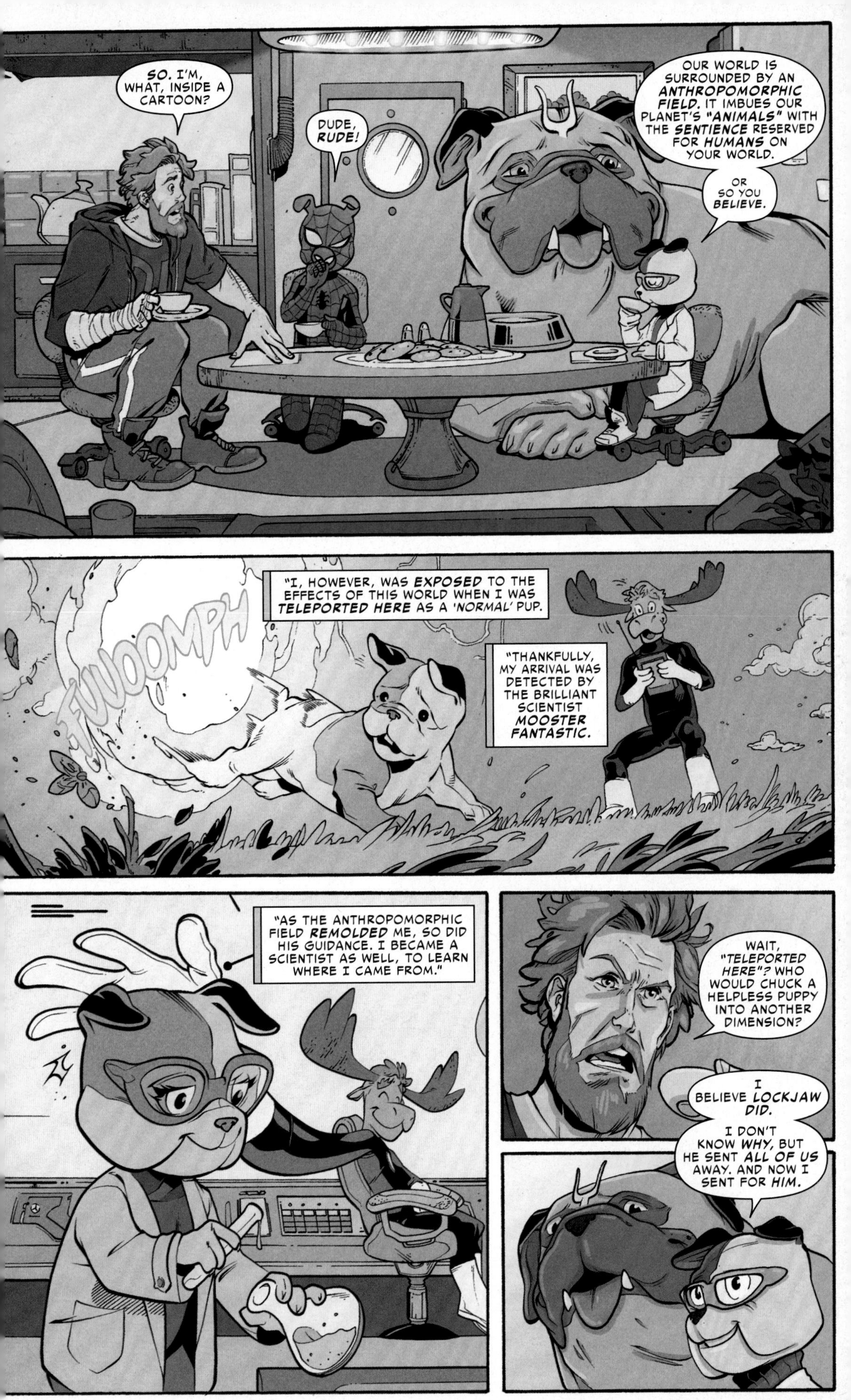

SO. I'M, WHAT, INSIDE A CARTOON?
DUDE, RUDE!
OUR WORLD IS SURROUNDED BY AN ANTHROPOMORPHIC FIELD. IT IMBUES OUR PLANET'S "ANIMALS" WITH THE SENTIENCE RESERVED FOR HUMANS ON YOUR WORLD.
OR SO YOU BELIEVE.
"I, HOWEVER, WAS EXPOSED TO THE EFFECTS OF THIS WORLD WHEN I WAS TELEPORTED HERE AS A 'NORMAL' PUP.
FUUOOMPH
"THANKFULLY, MY ARRIVAL WAS DETECTED BY THE BRILLIANT SCIENTIST MOOSTER FANTASTIC.
"AS THE ANTHROPOMORPHIC FIELD REMOLDED ME, SO DID HIS GUIDANCE. I BECAME A SCIENTIST AS WELL, TO LEARN WHERE I CAME FROM."
WAIT, "TELEPORTED HERE"? WHO WOULD CHUCK A HELPLESS PUPPY INTO ANOTHER DIMENSION?
I BELIEVE LOCKJAW DID.
I DON'T KNOW WHY, BUT HE SENT ALL OF US AWAY. AND NOW I SENT FOR HIM.

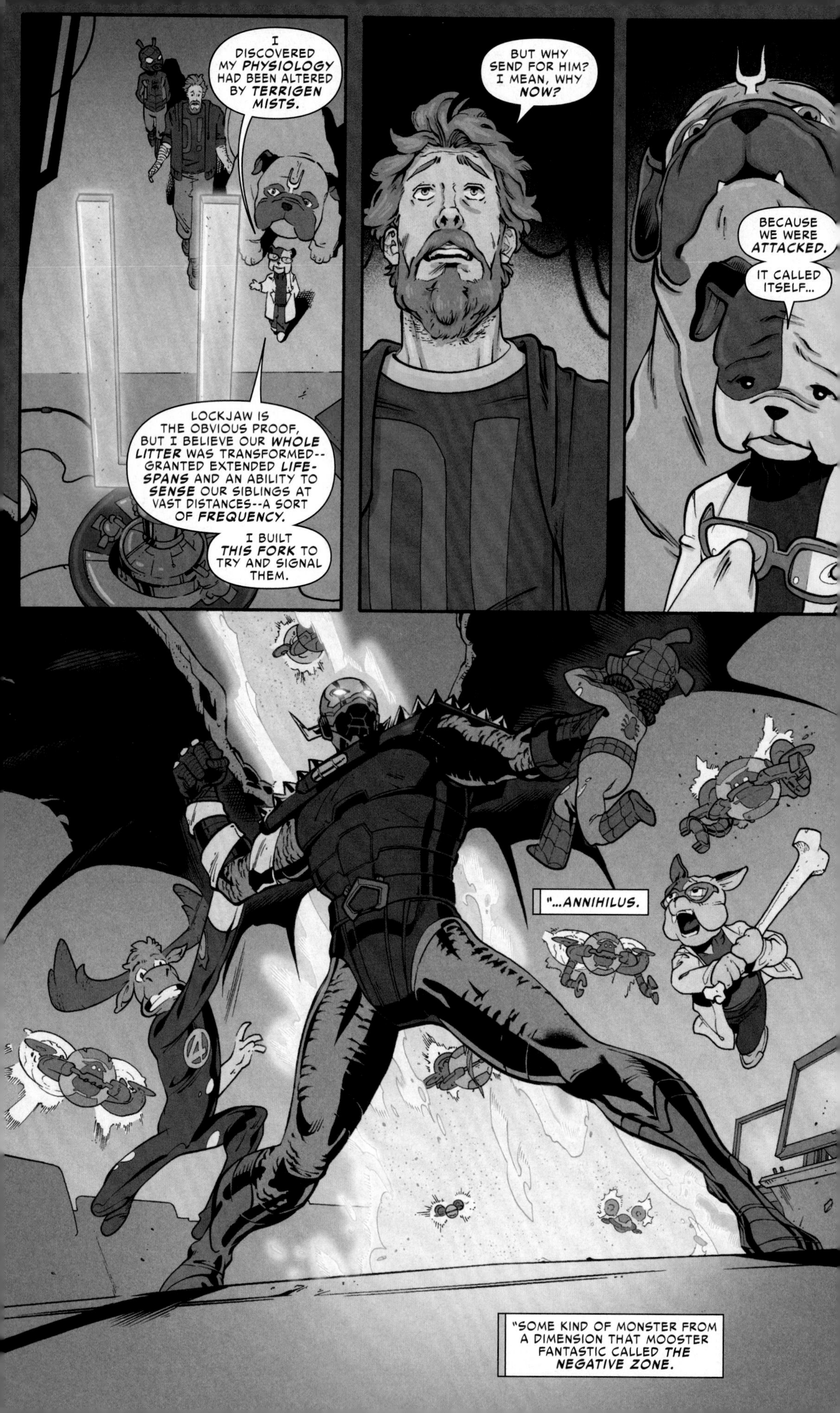

I DISCOVERED MY PHYSIOLOGY HAD BEEN ALTERED BY TERRIGEN MISTS.
LOCKJAW IS THE OBVIOUS PROOF, BUT I BELIEVE OUR WHOLE LITTER WAS TRANSFORMED--GRANTED EXTENDED LIFE-SPANS AND AN ABILITY TO SENSE OUR SIBLINGS AT VAST DISTANCES--A SORT OF FREQUENCY.
I BUILT THIS FORK TO TRY AND SIGNAL THEM.
BUT WHY SEND FOR HIM? I MEAN, WHY NOW?
BECAUSE WE WERE ATTACKED.
IT CALLED ITSELF...
"...ANNIHILUS.
"SOME KIND OF MONSTER FROM A DIMENSION THAT MOOSTER FANTASTIC CALLED THE NEGATIVE ZONE.

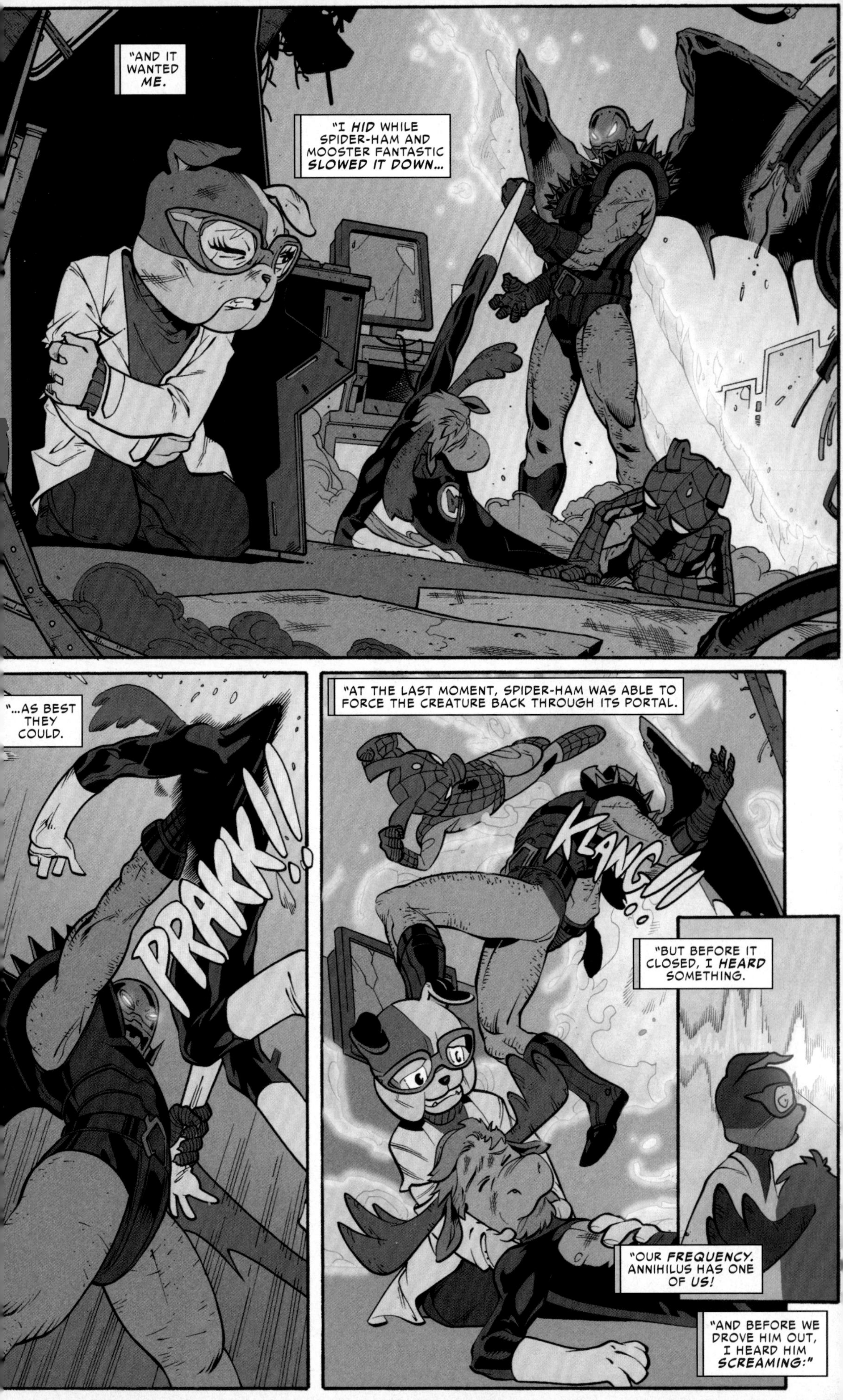
"AND IT WANTED *ME.*
"I *HID* WHILE SPIDER-HAM AND MOOSTER FANTASTIC *SLOWED IT DOWN...*
"...AS BEST THEY COULD.
PRAKK!!
"AT THE LAST MOMENT, SPIDER-HAM WAS ABLE TO FORCE THE CREATURE BACK THROUGH ITS PORTAL.
KLANG!!
"BUT BEFORE IT CLOSED, I *HEARD* SOMETHING.
"OUR *FREQUENCY.* ANNIHILUS HAS ONE OF *US!*
"AND BEFORE WE DROVE HIM OUT, I HEARD HIM *SCREAMING:"*

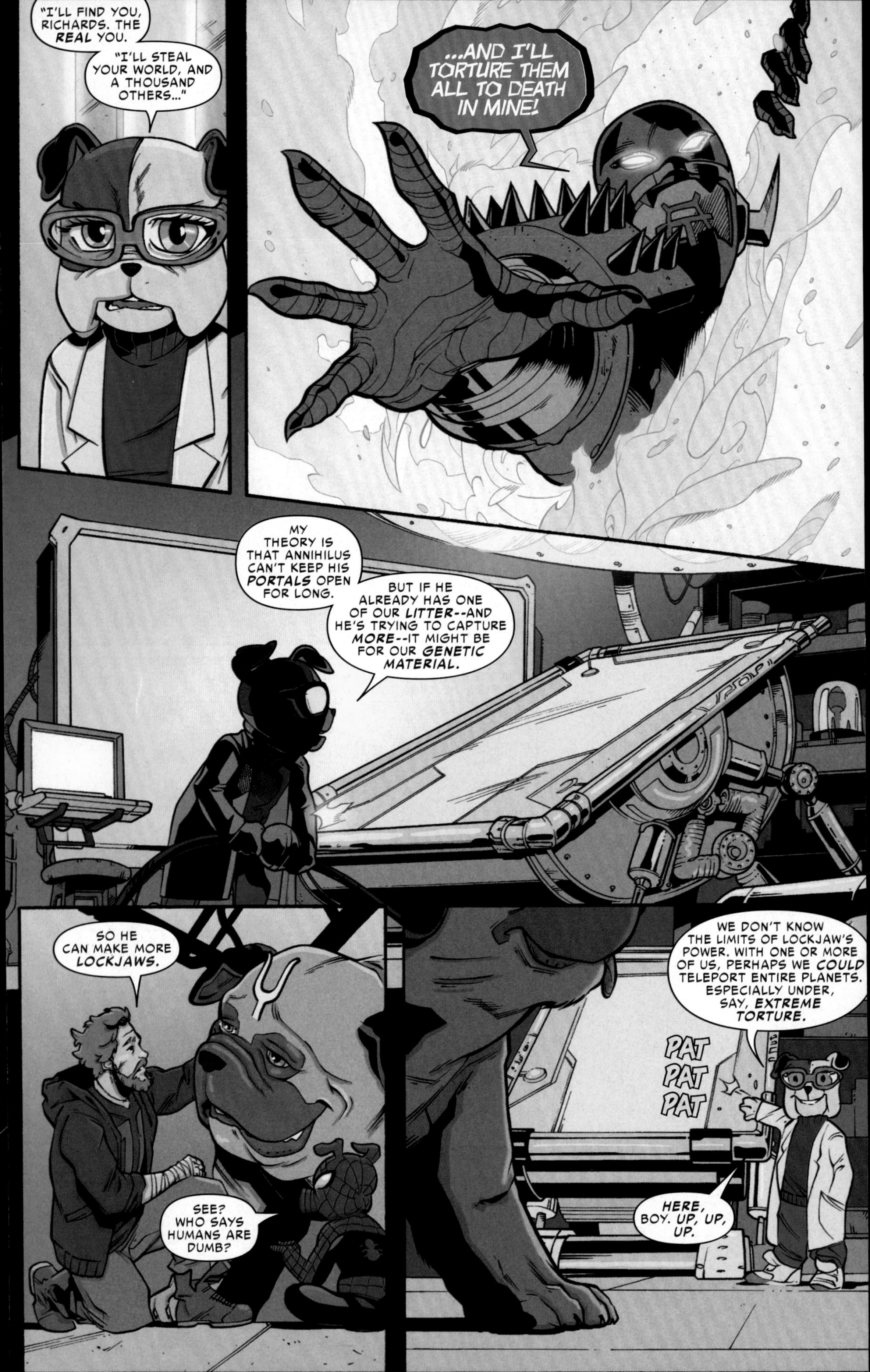
"I'LL FIND YOU, RICHARDS. THE REAL YOU.
"I'LL STEAL YOUR WORLD, AND A THOUSAND OTHERS..."
...AND I'LL TORTURE THEM ALL TO DEATH IN MINE!
MY THEORY IS THAT ANNIHILUS CAN'T KEEP HIS PORTALS OPEN FOR LONG.
BUT IF HE ALREADY HAS ONE OF OUR LITTER--AND HE'S TRYING TO CAPTURE MORE--IT MIGHT BE FOR OUR GENETIC MATERIAL.
SO HE CAN MAKE MORE LOCKJAWS.
SEE? WHO SAYS HUMANS ARE DUMB?
WE DON'T KNOW THE LIMITS OF LOCKJAW'S POWER. WITH ONE OR MORE OF US, PERHAPS WE COULD TELEPORT ENTIRE PLANETS. ESPECIALLY UNDER, SAY, EXTREME TORTURE.
PAT PAT PAT
HERE, BOY. UP, UP, UP.

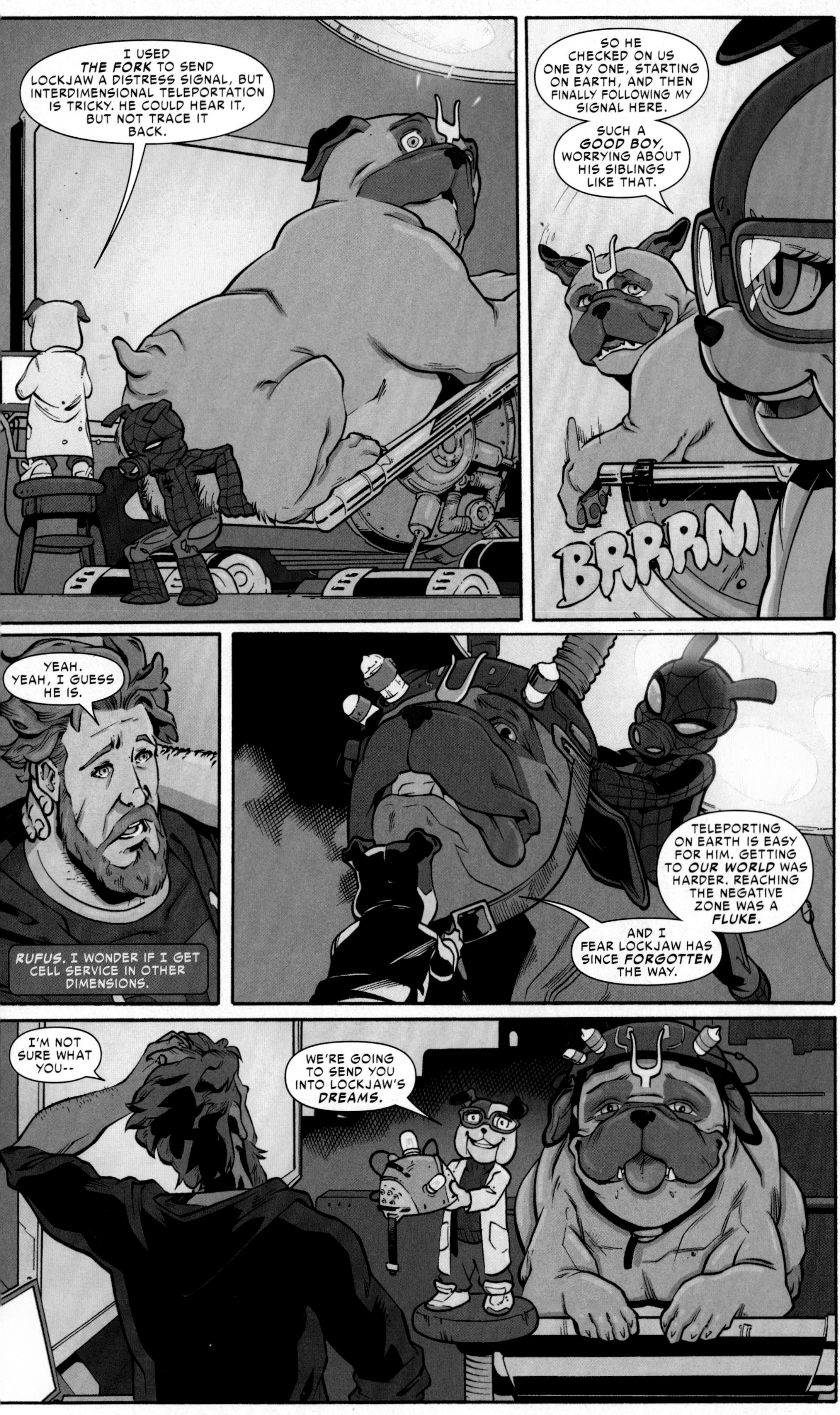

I USED THE FORK TO SEND LOCKJAW A DISTRESS SIGNAL, BUT INTERDIMENSIONAL TELEPORTATION IS TRICKY. HE COULD HEAR IT, BUT NOT TRACE IT BACK.
SO HE CHECKED ON US ONE BY ONE, STARTING ON EARTH, AND THEN FINALLY FOLLOWING MY SIGNAL HERE.
SUCH A GOOD BOY, WORRYING ABOUT HIS SIBLINGS LIKE THAT.
BRRRM
YEAH. YEAH, I GUESS HE IS.
RUFUS. I WONDER IF I GET CELL SERVICE IN OTHER DIMENSIONS.
TELEPORTING ON EARTH IS EASY FOR HIM. GETTING TO OUR WORLD WAS HARDER. REACHING THE NEGATIVE ZONE WAS A FLUKE.
AND I FEAR LOCKJAW HAS SINCE FORGOTTEN THE WAY.
I'M NOT SURE WHAT YOU--
WE'RE GOING TO SEND YOU INTO LOCKJAW'S DREAMS.

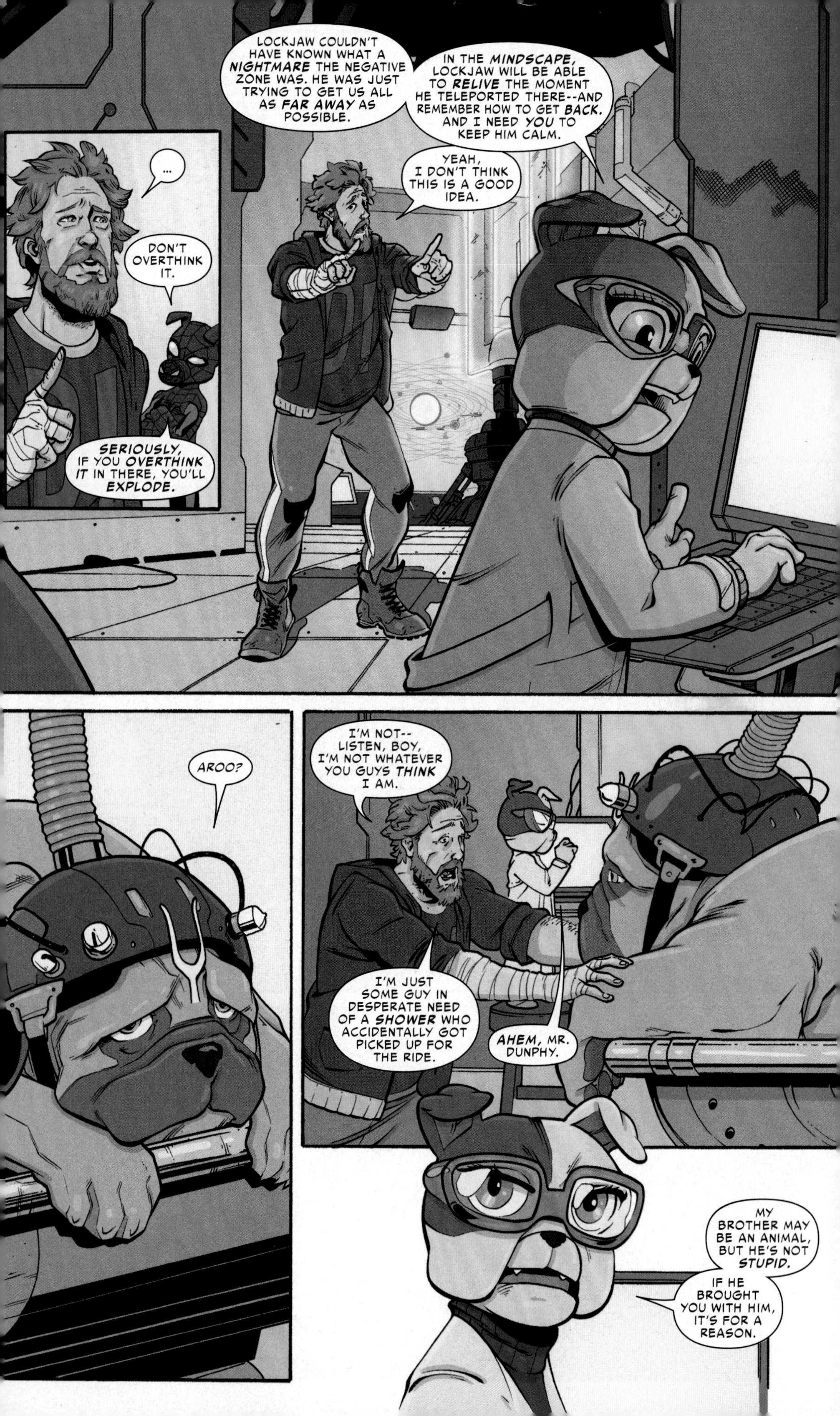

LOCKJAW COULDN'T HAVE KNOWN WHAT A NIGHTMARE THE NEGATIVE ZONE WAS. HE WAS JUST TRYING TO GET US ALL AS FAR AWAY AS POSSIBLE.
IN THE MINDSCAPE, LOCKJAW WILL BE ABLE TO RELIVE THE MOMENT HE TELEPORTED THERE--AND REMEMBER HOW TO GET BACK. AND I NEED YOU TO KEEP HIM CALM.
...
DON'T OVERTHINK IT.
SERIOUSLY, IF YOU OVERTHINK IT IN THERE, YOU'LL EXPLODE.
YEAH, I DON'T THINK THIS IS A GOOD IDEA.
AROO?
I'M NOT-- LISTEN, BOY, I'M NOT WHATEVER YOU GUYS THINK I AM.
I'M JUST SOME GUY IN DESPERATE NEED OF A SHOWER WHO ACCIDENTALLY GOT PICKED UP FOR THE RIDE.
AHEM, MR. DUNPHY.
MY BROTHER MAY BE AN ANIMAL, BUT HE'S NOT STUPID.
IF HE BROUGHT YOU WITH HIM, IT'S FOR A REASON.

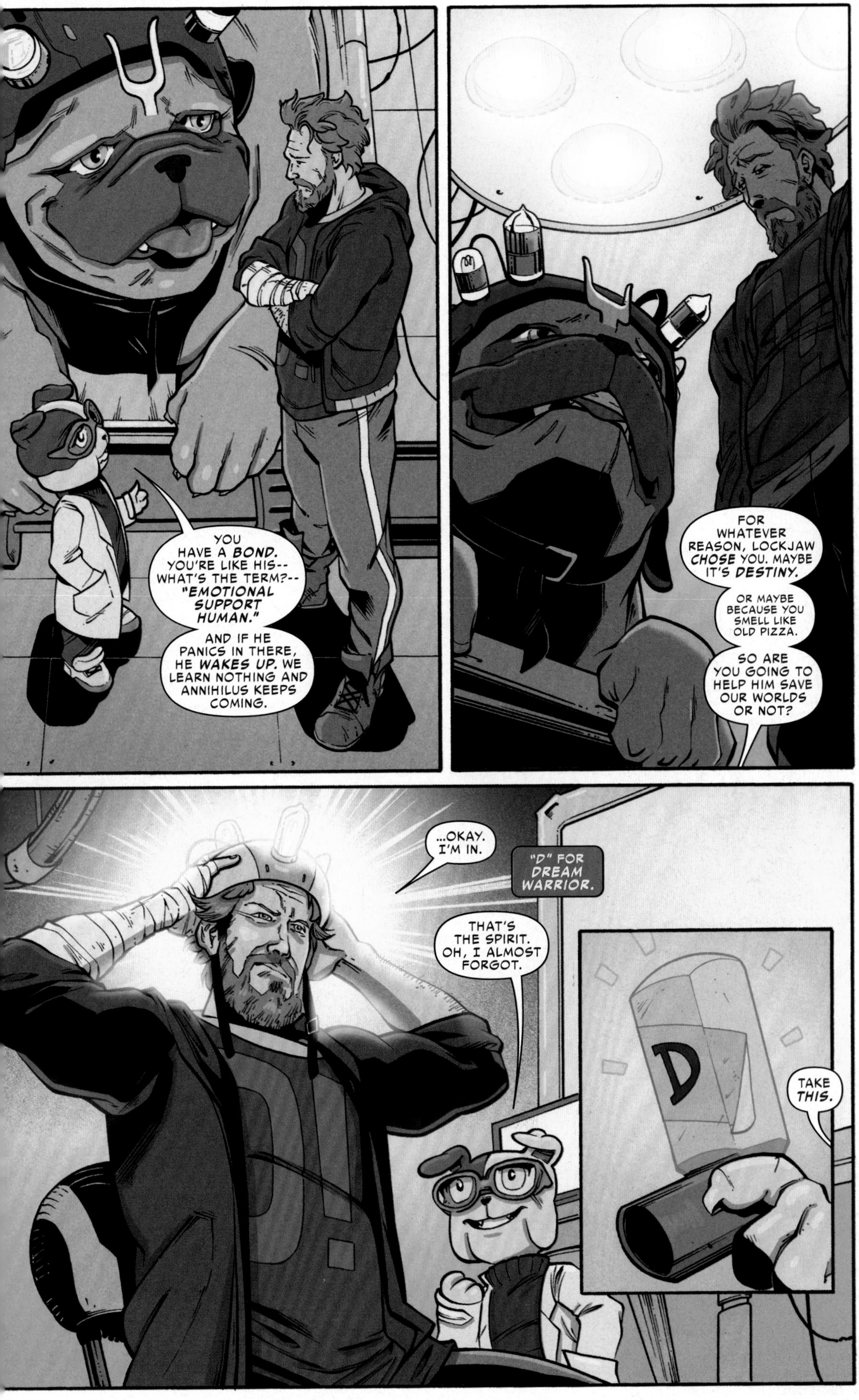

YOU HAVE A BOND. YOU'RE LIKE HIS-- WHAT'S THE TERM?-- "EMOTIONAL SUPPORT HUMAN."
AND IF HE PANICS IN THERE, HE WAKES UP. WE LEARN NOTHING AND ANNIHILUS KEEPS COMING.
FOR WHATEVER REASON, LOCKJAW CHOSE YOU. MAYBE IT'S DESTINY.
OR MAYBE BECAUSE YOU SMELL LIKE OLD PIZZA.
SO ARE YOU GOING TO HELP HIM SAVE OUR WORLDS OR NOT?
...OKAY. I'M IN.
"D" FOR DREAM WARRIOR.
THAT'S THE SPIRIT. OH, I ALMOST FORGOT.
D
TAKE THIS.

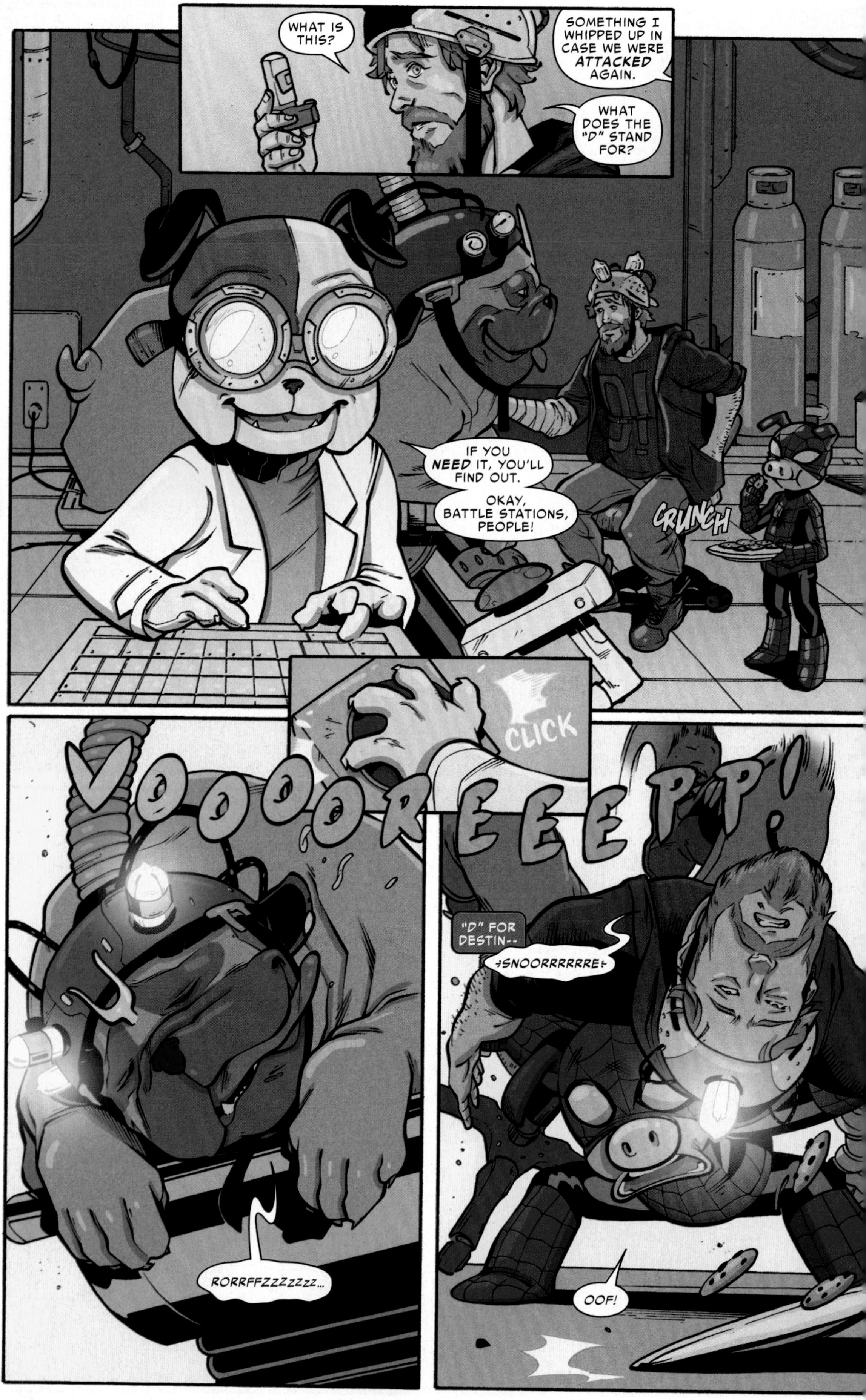
WHAT IS THIS?
SOMETHING I WHIPPED UP IN CASE WE WERE ATTACKED AGAIN.
WHAT DOES THE "D" STAND FOR?
IF YOU NEED IT, YOU'LL FIND OUT.
OKAY, BATTLE STATIONS, PEOPLE!
CRUNCH
CLICK
VOOOOREEEEPP!
RORRFFZZZZzzz...
"D" FOR DESTIN--
SNOORRRRRRE
OOF!

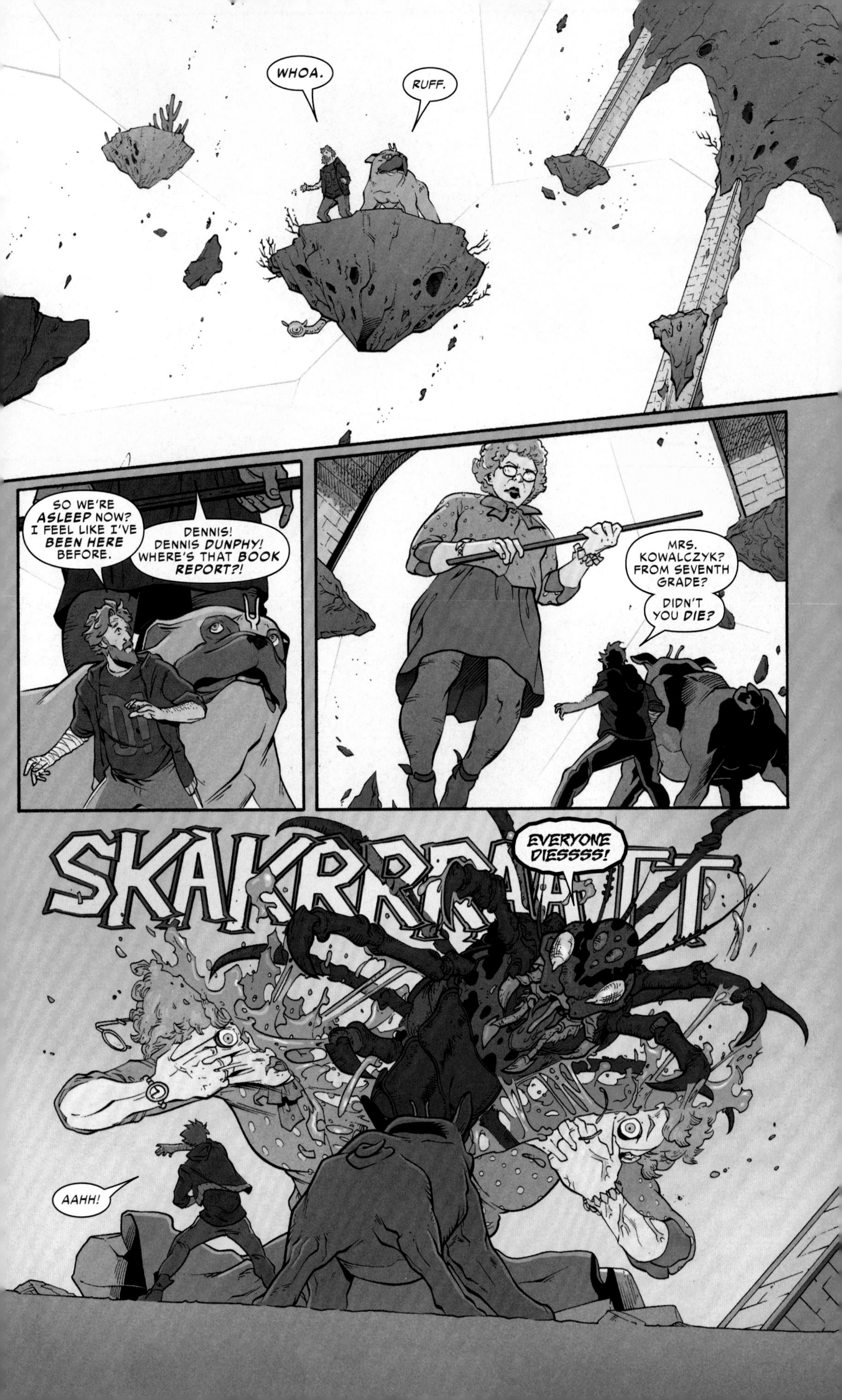
WHOA.
RUFF.
SO WE'RE ASLEEP NOW? I FEEL LIKE I'VE BEEN HERE BEFORE.
DENNIS! DENNIS DUNPHY! WHERE'S THAT BOOK REPORT?!
MRS. KOWALCZYK? FROM SEVENTH GRADE?
DIDN'T YOU DIE?
SKAKRRAATT
EVERYONE DIESSSS!
AAHH!

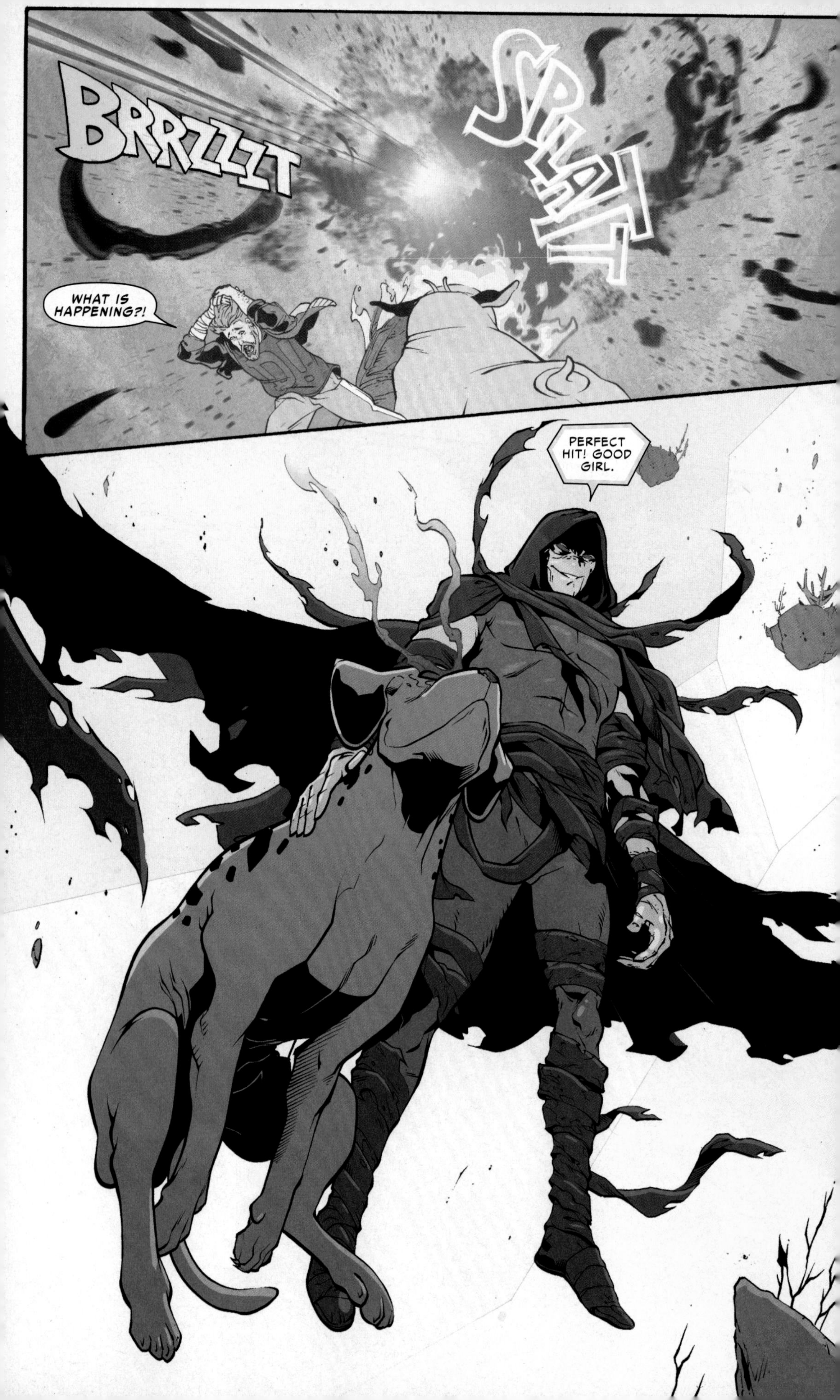
BRRZZZZT
SPLAT
WHAT IS HAPPENING?!
PERFECT HIT! GOOD GIRL.

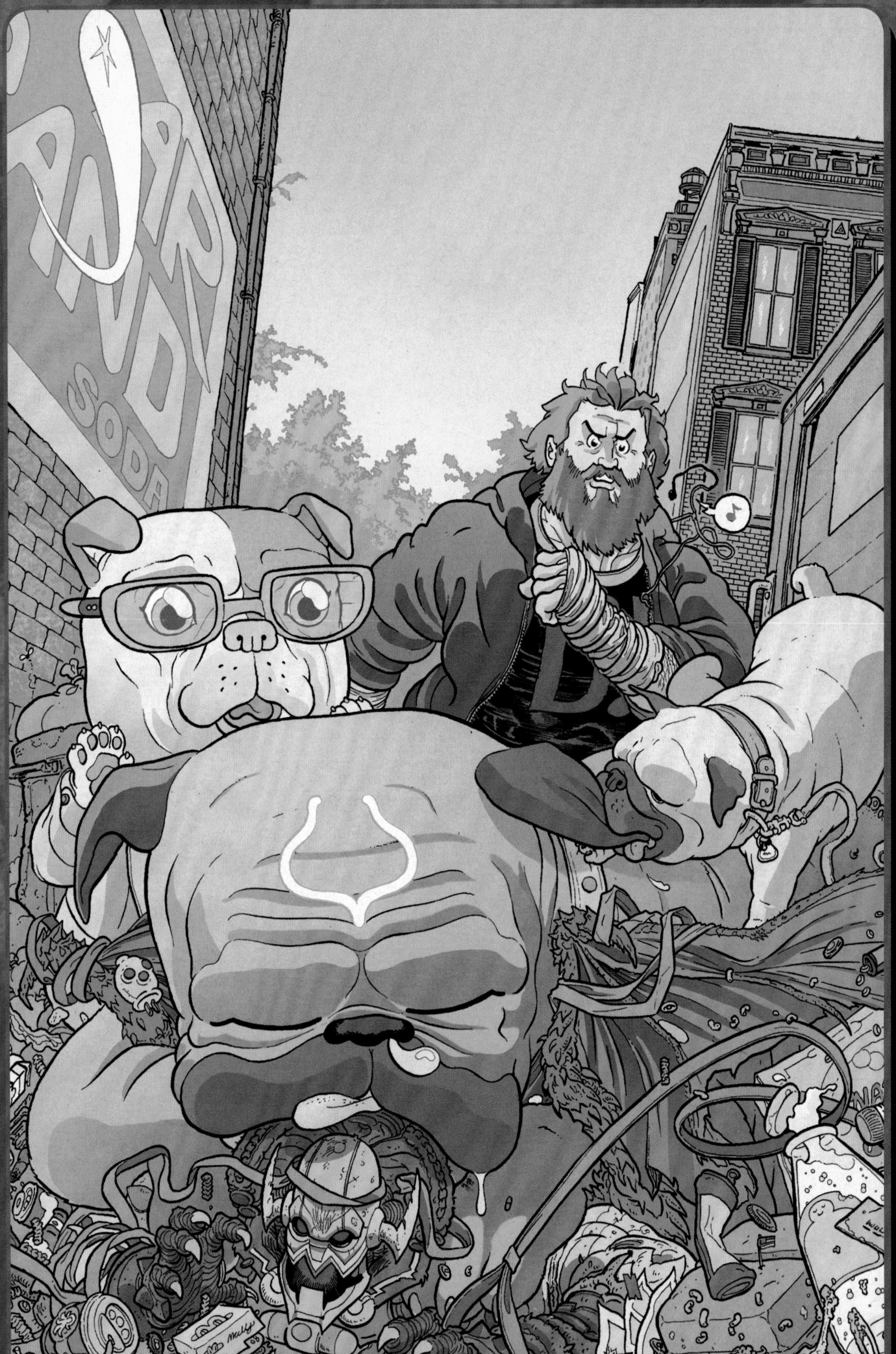
SODA

4

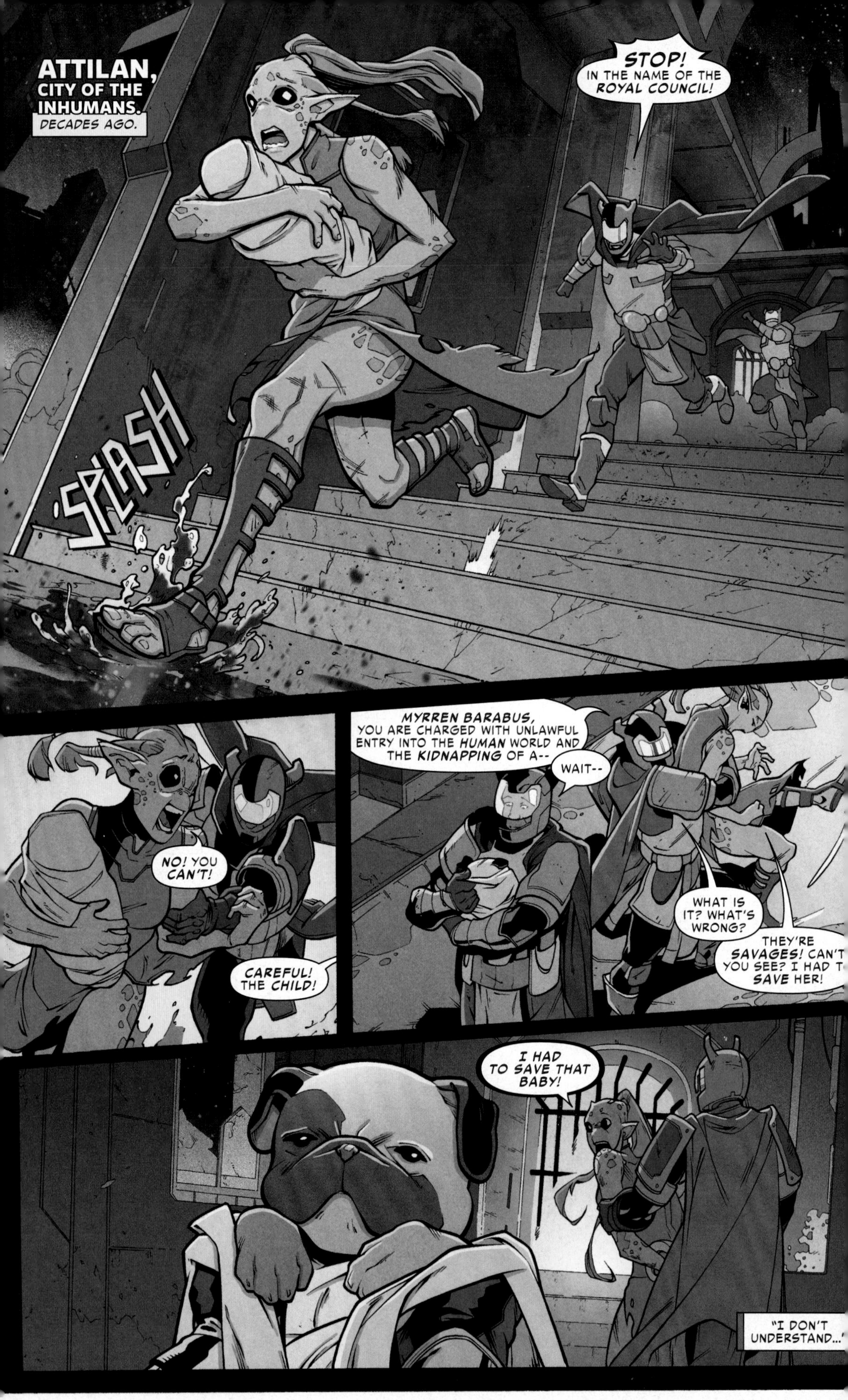
ATTILAN, CITY OF THE INHUMANS. DECADES AGO.
STOP! IN THE NAME OF THE ROYAL COUNCIL!
SPLASH
NO! YOU CAN'T!
CAREFUL! THE CHILD!
MYRREN BARABUS, YOU ARE CHARGED WITH UNLAWFUL ENTRY INTO THE HUMAN WORLD AND THE KIDNAPPING OF A--
WAIT--
WHAT IS IT? WHAT'S WRONG?
THEY'RE SAVAGES! CAN'T YOU SEE? I HAD T SAVE HER!
I HAD TO SAVE THAT BABY!
"I DON'T UNDERSTAND..."

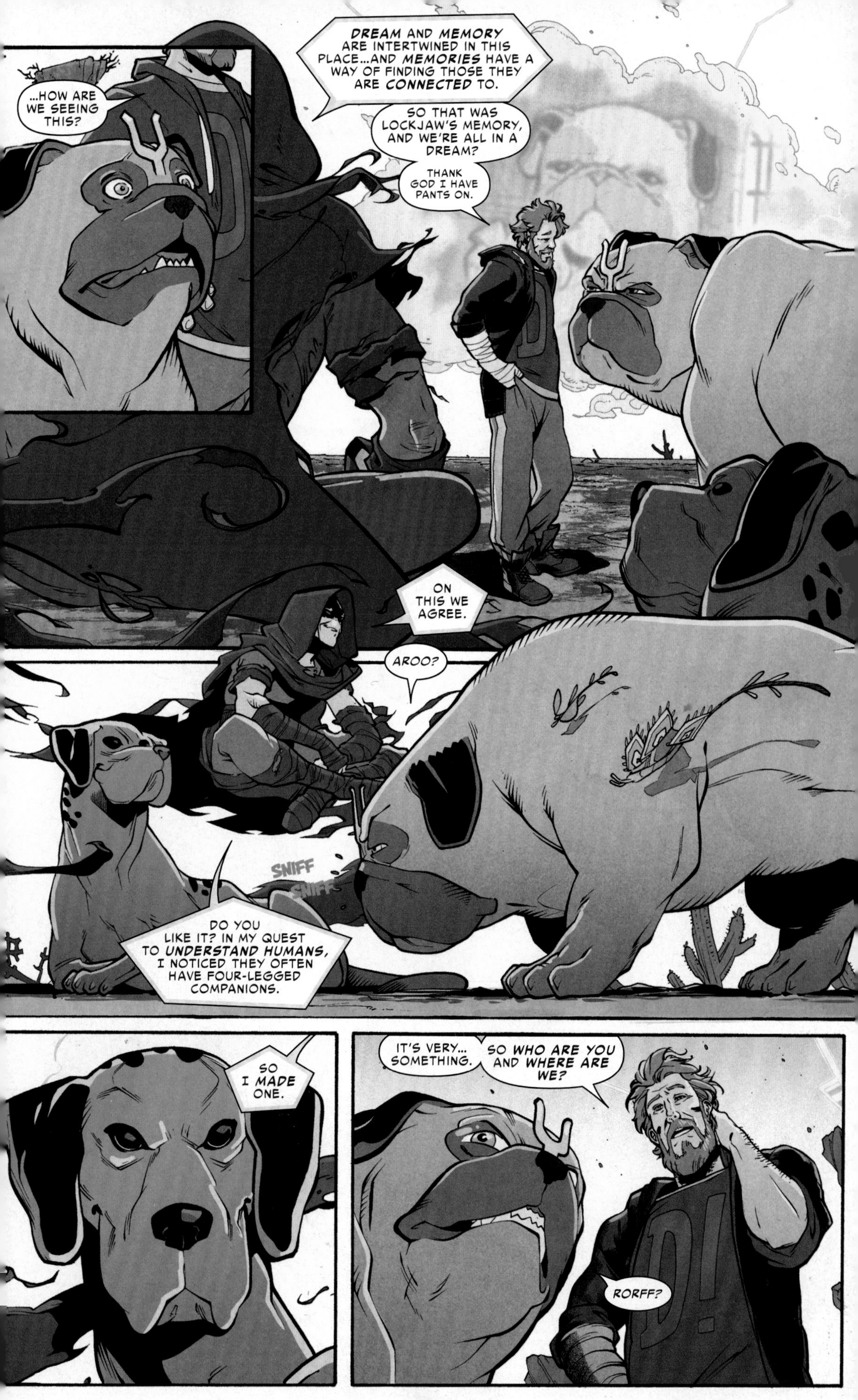

...HOW ARE WE SEEING THIS?
DREAM AND MEMORY ARE INTERTWINED IN THIS PLACE...AND MEMORIES HAVE A WAY OF FINDING THOSE THEY ARE CONNECTED TO.
SO THAT WAS LOCKJAW'S MEMORY, AND WE'RE ALL IN A DREAM?
THANK GOD I HAVE PANTS ON.
ON THIS WE AGREE.
AROO?
SNIFF
SNIFF
DO YOU LIKE IT? IN MY QUEST TO UNDERSTAND HUMANS, I NOTICED THEY OFTEN HAVE FOUR-LEGGED COMPANIONS.
SO I MADE ONE.
IT'S VERY... SOMETHING.
SO WHO ARE YOU AND WHERE ARE WE?
RORFF?

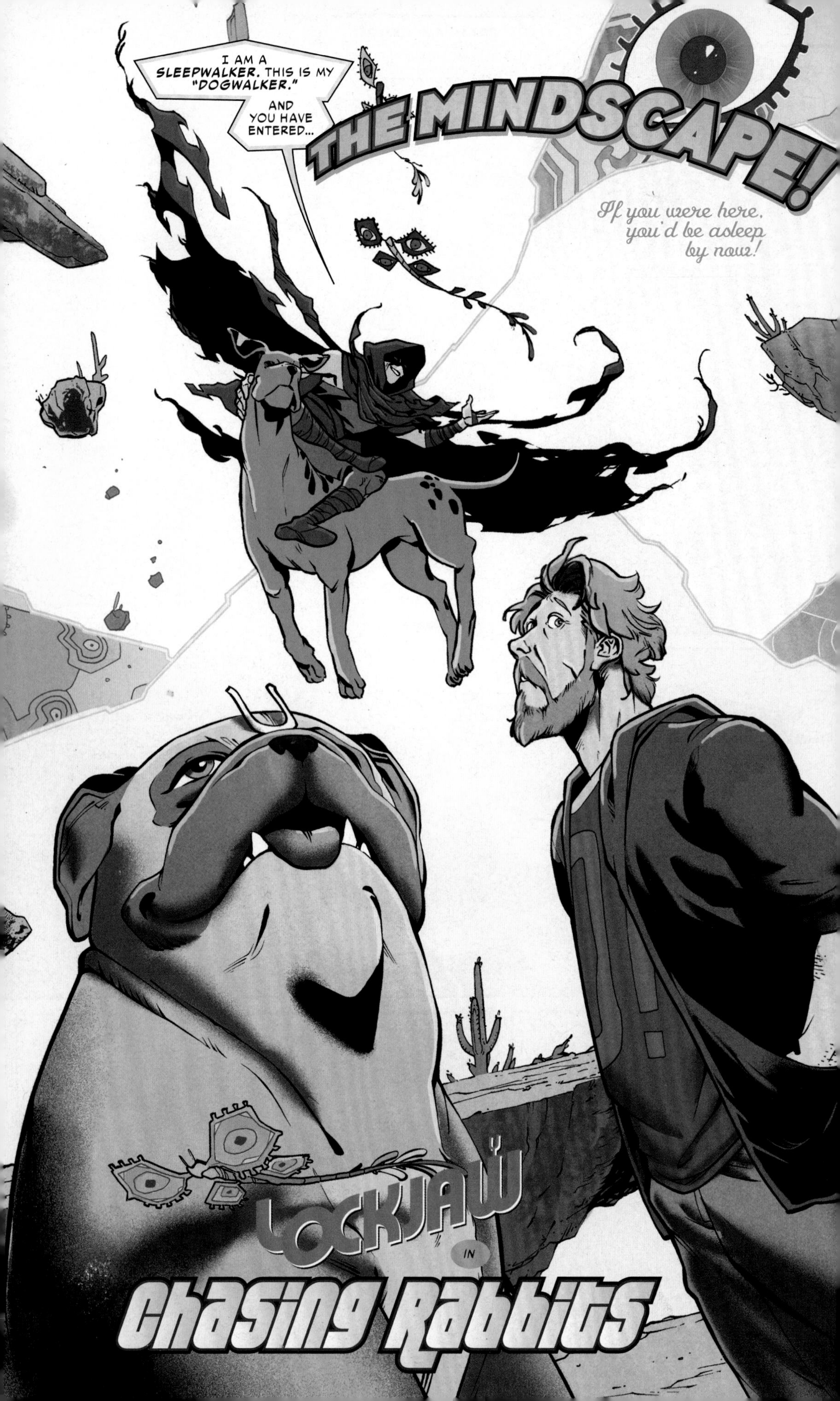

I AM A SLEEPWALKER. THIS IS MY "DOGWALKER."
AND YOU HAVE ENTERED...
THE MINDSCAPE!
If you were here, you'd be asleep by now!
LOCKJAW
IN
Chasing Rabbits

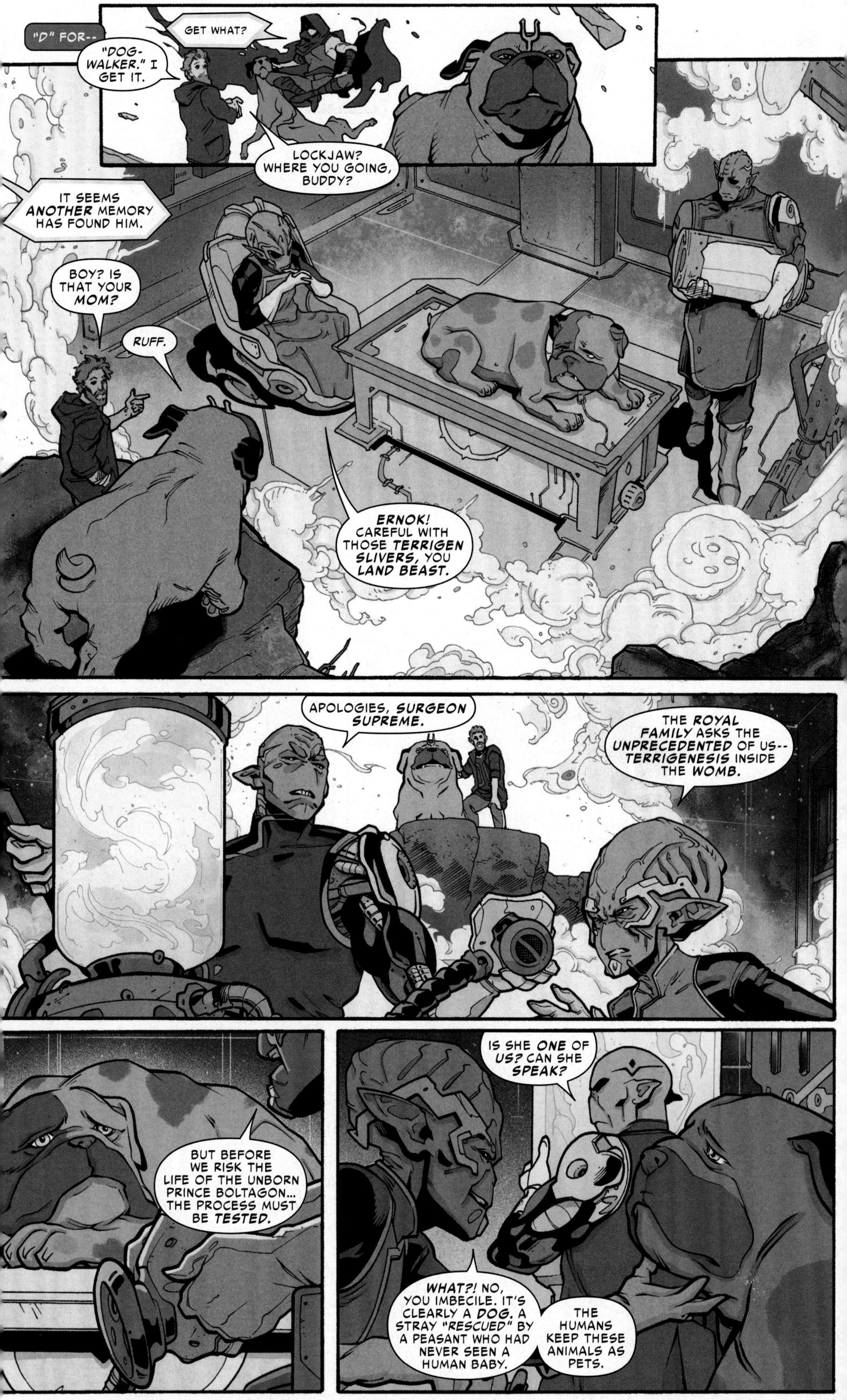
"D" FOR--
GET WHAT?
"DOG-WALKER." I GET IT.
LOCKJAW? WHERE YOU GOING, BUDDY?
IT SEEMS ANOTHER MEMORY HAS FOUND HIM.
BOY? IS THAT YOUR MOM?
RUFF.
ERNOK! CAREFUL WITH THOSE TERRIGEN SLIVERS, YOU LAND BEAST.
APOLOGIES, SURGEON SUPREME.
THE ROYAL FAMILY ASKS THE UNPRECEDENTED OF US--TERRIGENESIS INSIDE THE WOMB.
BUT BEFORE WE RISK THE LIFE OF THE UNBORN PRINCE BOLTAGON... THE PROCESS MUST BE TESTED.
IS SHE ONE OF US? CAN SHE SPEAK?
WHAT?! NO, YOU IMBECILE. IT'S CLEARLY A DOG. A STRAY "RESCUED" BY A PEASANT WHO HAD NEVER SEEN A HUMAN BABY.
THE HUMANS KEEP THESE ANIMALS AS PETS.

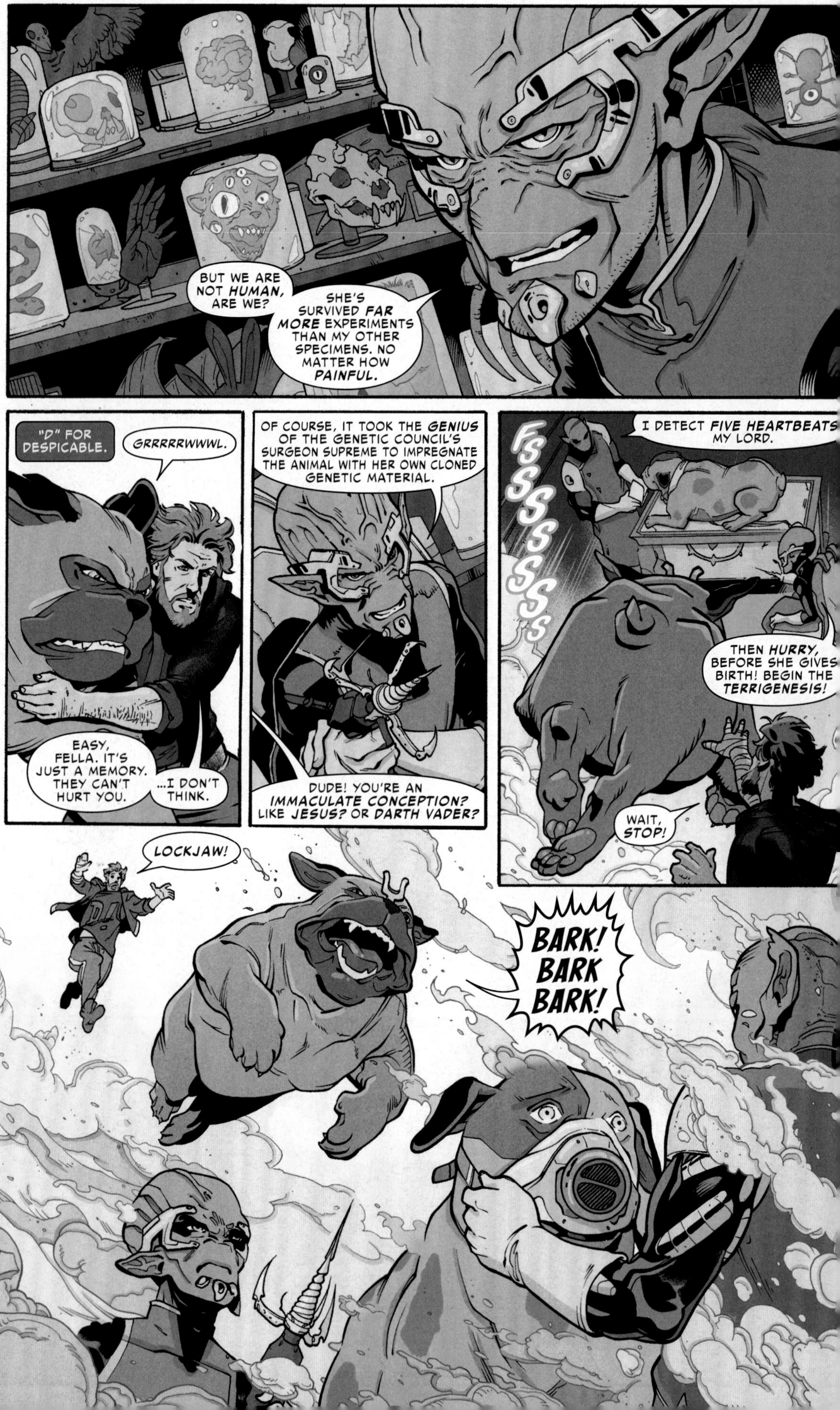
BUT WE ARE NOT *HUMAN*, ARE WE?
SHE'S SURVIVED *FAR MORE* EXPERIMENTS THAN MY OTHER SPECIMENS. NO MATTER HOW *PAINFUL*.
"D" FOR DESPICABLE.
GRRRRRWWWL.
EASY, FELLA. IT'S JUST A MEMORY. THEY CAN'T HURT YOU.
...I DON'T THINK.
OF COURSE, IT TOOK THE *GENIUS* OF THE GENETIC COUNCIL'S SURGEON SUPREME TO IMPREGNATE THE ANIMAL WITH HER OWN CLONED GENETIC MATERIAL.
DUDE! YOU'RE AN *IMMACULATE CONCEPTION?* LIKE *JESUS?* OR *DARTH VADER?*
FSSSSSSS
I DETECT *FIVE HEARTBEATS* MY LORD.
THEN *HURRY,* BEFORE SHE GIVES BIRTH! BEGIN THE *TERRIGENESIS!*
WAIT, *STOP!*
LOCKJAW!
BARK! BARK BARK!

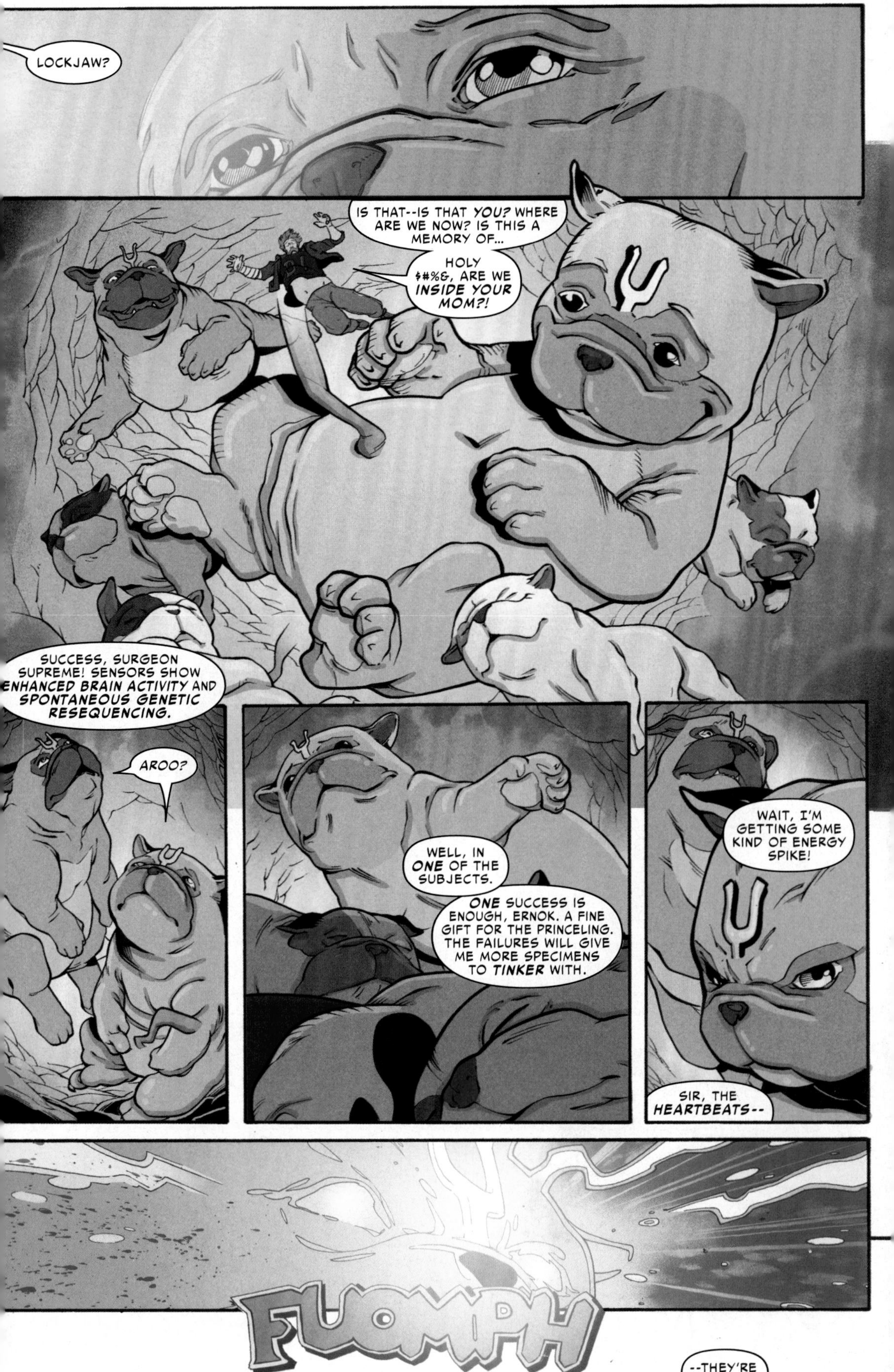
LOCKJAW?
IS THAT--IS THAT YOU? WHERE ARE WE NOW? IS THIS A MEMORY OF...
HOLY $#%&, ARE WE INSIDE YOUR MOM?!
SUCCESS, SURGEON SUPREME! SENSORS SHOW ENHANCED BRAIN ACTIVITY AND SPONTANEOUS GENETIC RESEQUENCING.
AROO?
WELL, IN ONE OF THE SUBJECTS.
ONE SUCCESS IS ENOUGH, ERNOK. A FINE GIFT FOR THE PRINCELING. THE FAILURES WILL GIVE ME MORE SPECIMENS TO TINKER WITH.
WAIT, I'M GETTING SOME KIND OF ENERGY SPIKE!
SIR, THE HEARTBEATS--
FLOMPH
--THEY'RE GONE.

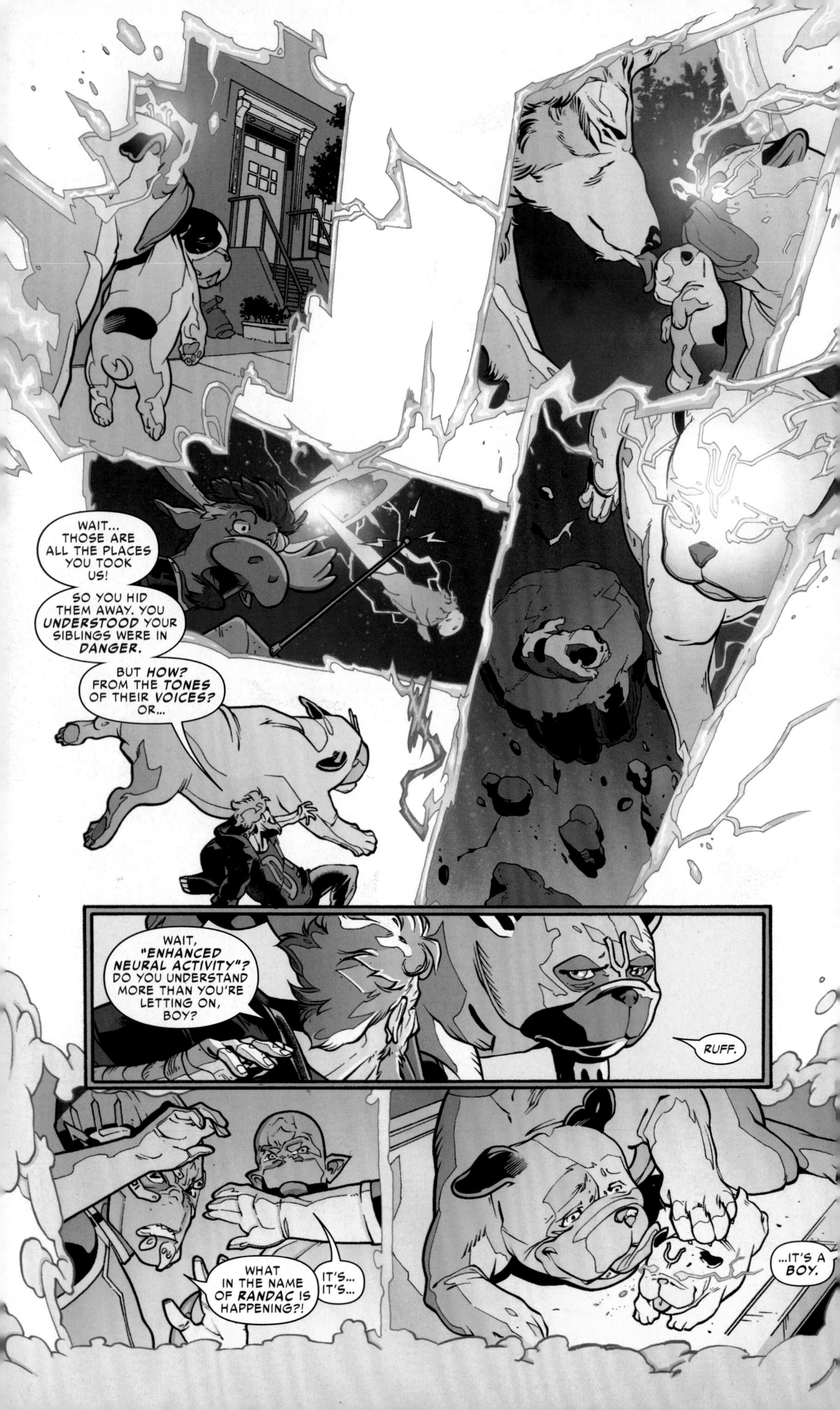

WAIT... THOSE ARE ALL THE PLACES YOU TOOK US!
SO YOU HID THEM AWAY. YOU UNDERSTOOD YOUR SIBLINGS WERE IN DANGER.
BUT HOW? FROM THE TONES OF THEIR VOICES? OR...
WAIT, "ENHANCED NEURAL ACTIVITY"? DO YOU UNDERSTAND MORE THAN YOU'RE LETTING ON, BOY?
RUFF.
WHAT IN THE NAME OF RANDAC IS HAPPENING?!
IT'S... IT'S...
...IT'S A BOY.

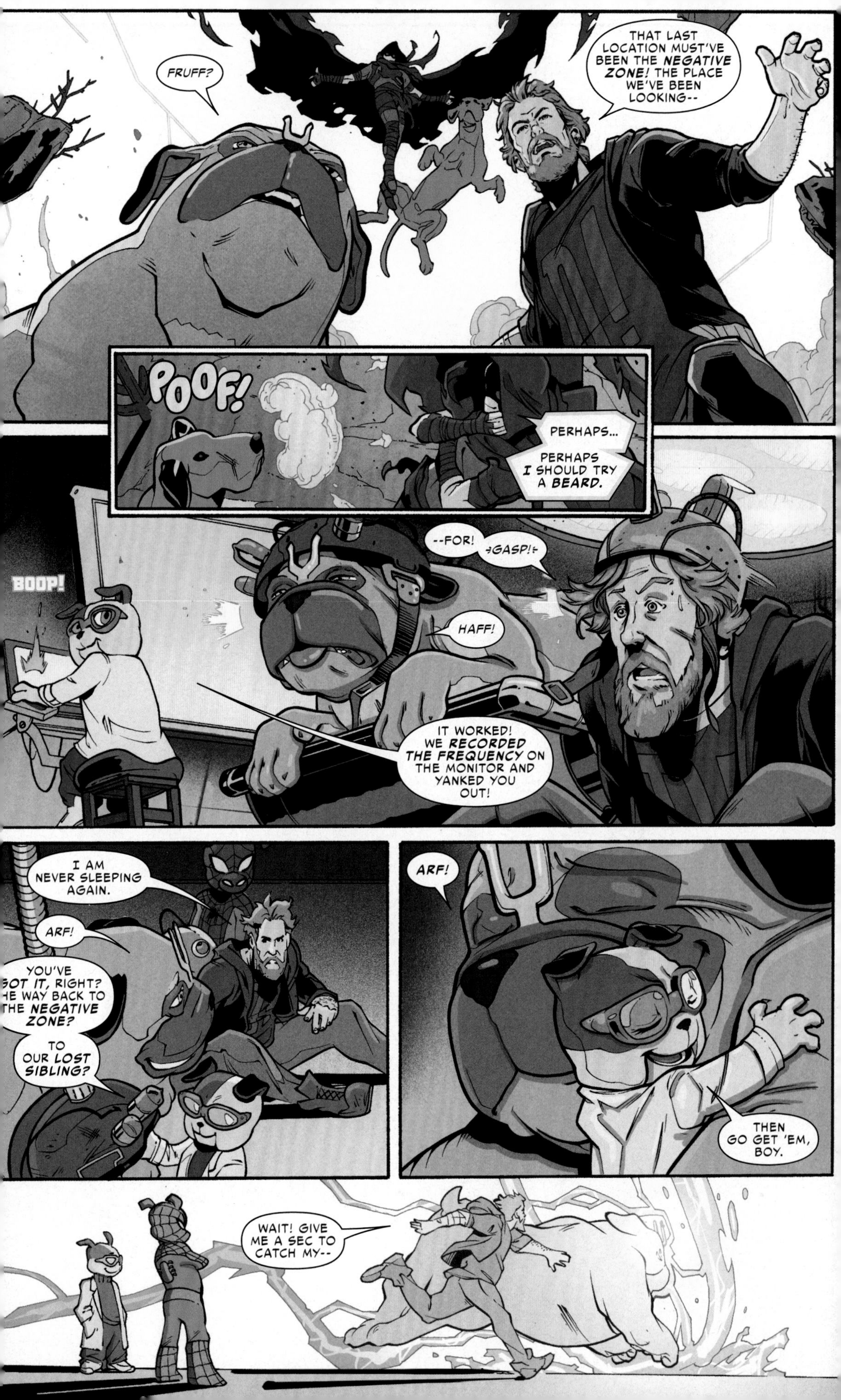
FRUFF?
THAT LAST LOCATION MUST'VE BEEN THE NEGATIVE ZONE! THE PLACE WE'VE BEEN LOOKING--
POOF!
PERHAPS...
PERHAPS I SHOULD TRY A BEARD.
BOOP!
--FOR!
GASP!
HAFF!
IT WORKED! WE RECORDED THE FREQUENCY ON THE MONITOR AND YANKED YOU OUT!
I AM NEVER SLEEPING AGAIN.
ARF!
YOU'VE GOT IT, RIGHT? THE WAY BACK TO THE NEGATIVE ZONE?
TO OUR LOST SIBLING?
ARF!
THEN GO GET 'EM, BOY.
WAIT! GIVE ME A SEC TO CATCH MY--

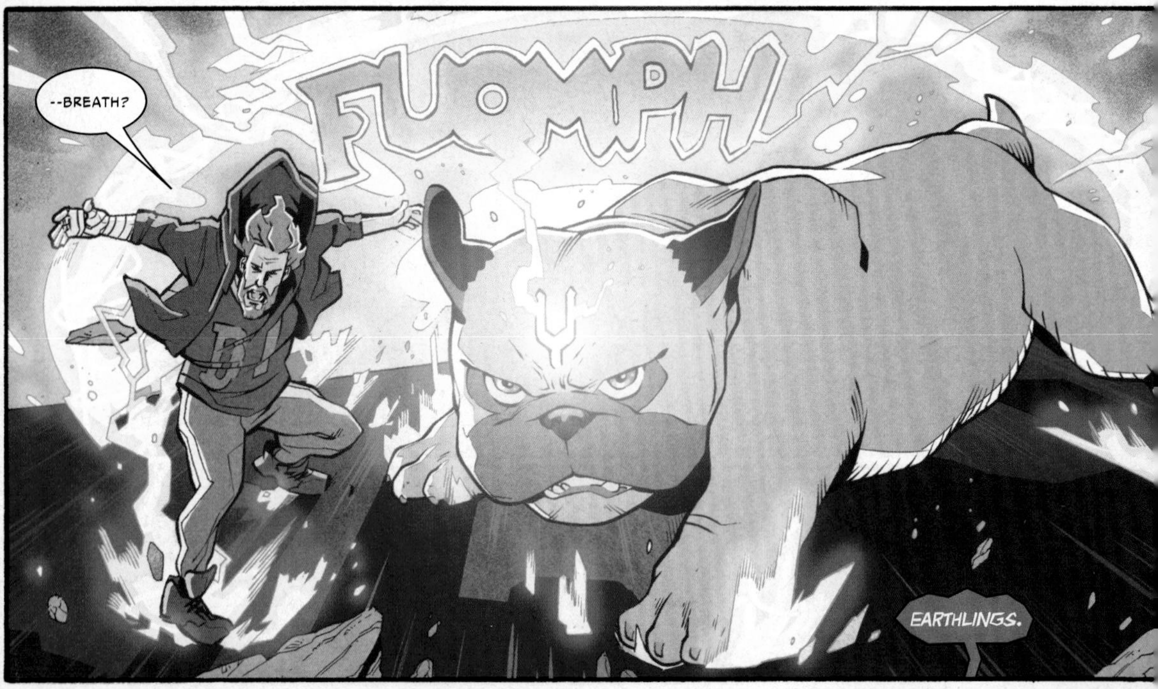
--BREATH?
FLOOMPH
EARTHLINGS.

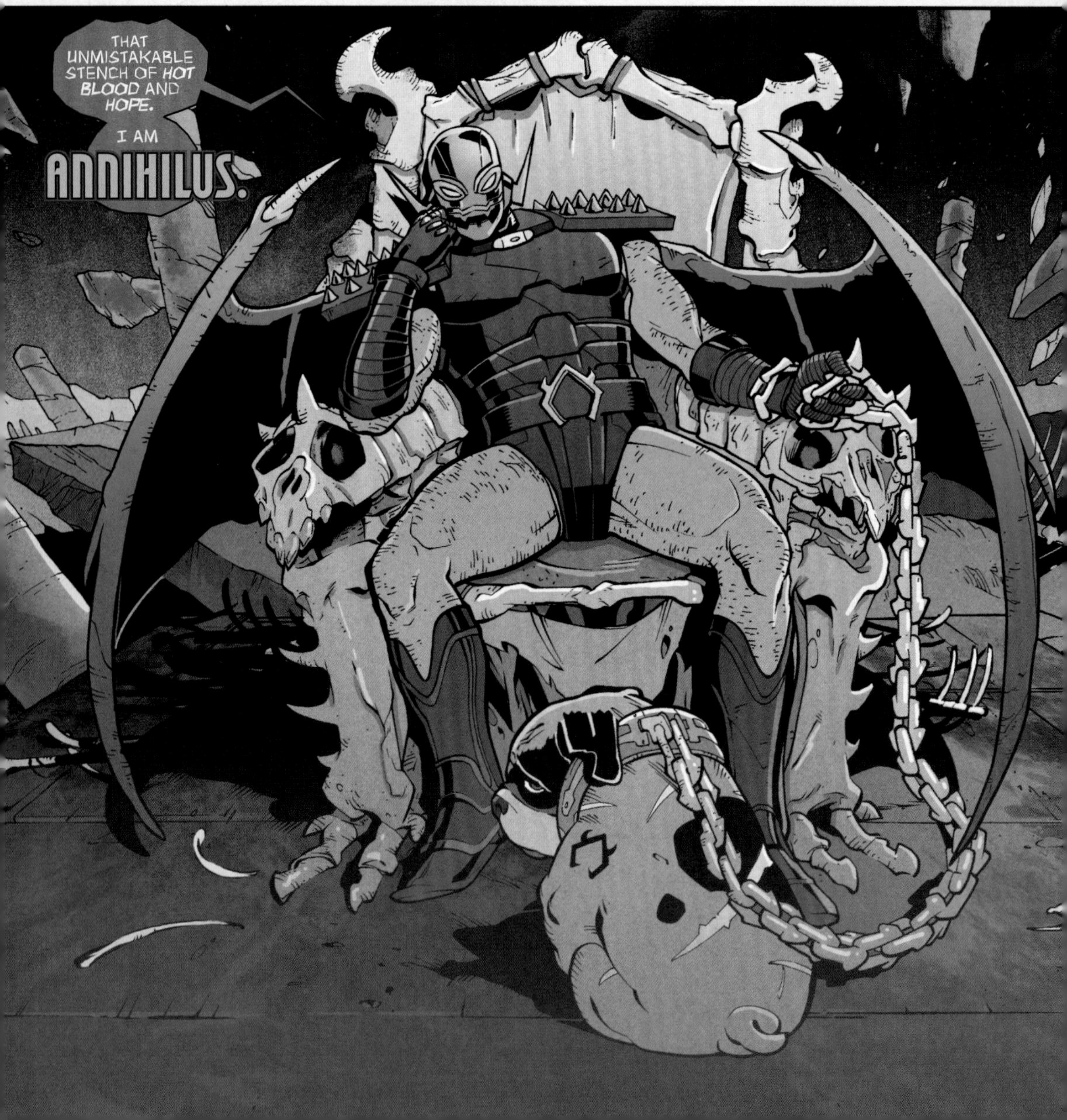
THAT UNMISTAKABLE STENCH OF HOT BLOOD AND HOPE.
I AM ANNIHILUS.

LET THERE BE DEATH.

VOOOOOORMP

RARRF!

KERPRSH

AAAH!

TYPICAL EARTHLING INTELLECT. THE VERY CREATURE I REQUIRE TO DESTROY YOUR WORLD, AND YOU BRING HIM TO MY DOORSTEP.

AND JUST AS MY LAST FOUNDLING IS STARTING TO WEAR OUT.

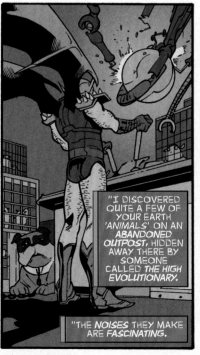

"I DISCOVERED QUITE A FEW OF YOUR EARTH 'ANIMALS' ON AN ABANDONED OUTPOST, HIDDEN AWAY THERE BY SOMEONE CALLED THE HIGH EVOLUTIONARY.

"THE NOISES THEY MAKE ARE FASCINATING.

"HIS MACHINERY HELPED ME UNLOCK THE GENETIC POTENTIAL OF THIS ONE. LATENT TELEPORTATION, BURIED DEEP IN ITS GENETIC CODE.

"OF COURSE, ACTIVATING IT TAKES QUITE A BIT OF TORTURE."

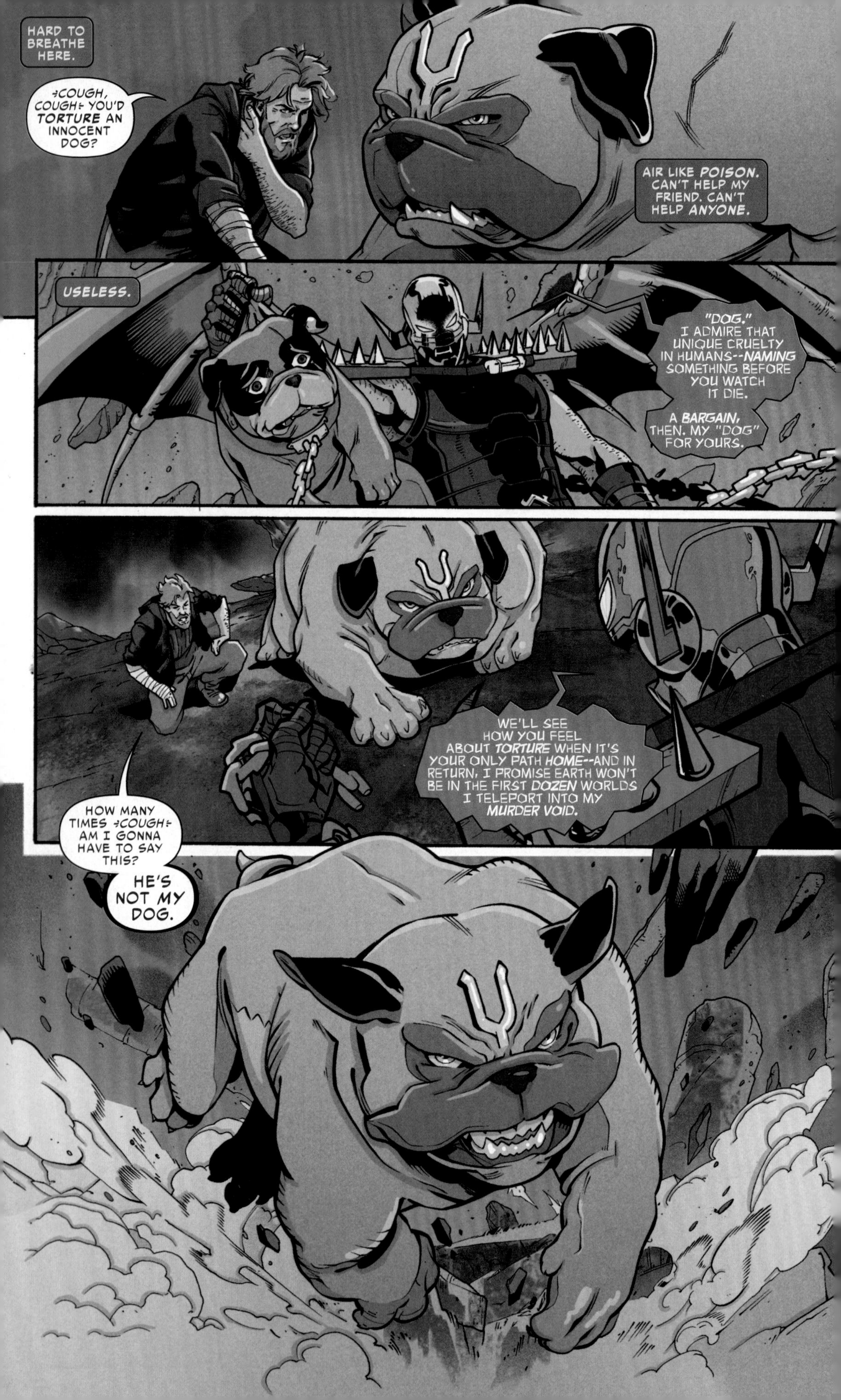
HARD TO BREATHE HERE.
-COUGH, COUGH- YOU'D TORTURE AN INNOCENT DOG?
AIR LIKE POISON. CAN'T HELP MY FRIEND. CAN'T HELP ANYONE.
USELESS.
"DOG." I ADMIRE THAT UNIQUE CRUELTY IN HUMANS--NAMING SOMETHING BEFORE YOU WATCH IT DIE.
A BARGAIN, THEN. MY "DOG" FOR YOURS.
WE'LL SEE HOW YOU FEEL ABOUT TORTURE WHEN IT'S YOUR ONLY PATH HOME--AND IN RETURN, I PROMISE EARTH WON'T BE IN THE FIRST DOZEN WORLDS I TELEPORT INTO MY MURDER VOID.
HOW MANY TIMES -COUGH- AM I GONNA HAVE TO SAY THIS?
HE'S NOT MY DOG.

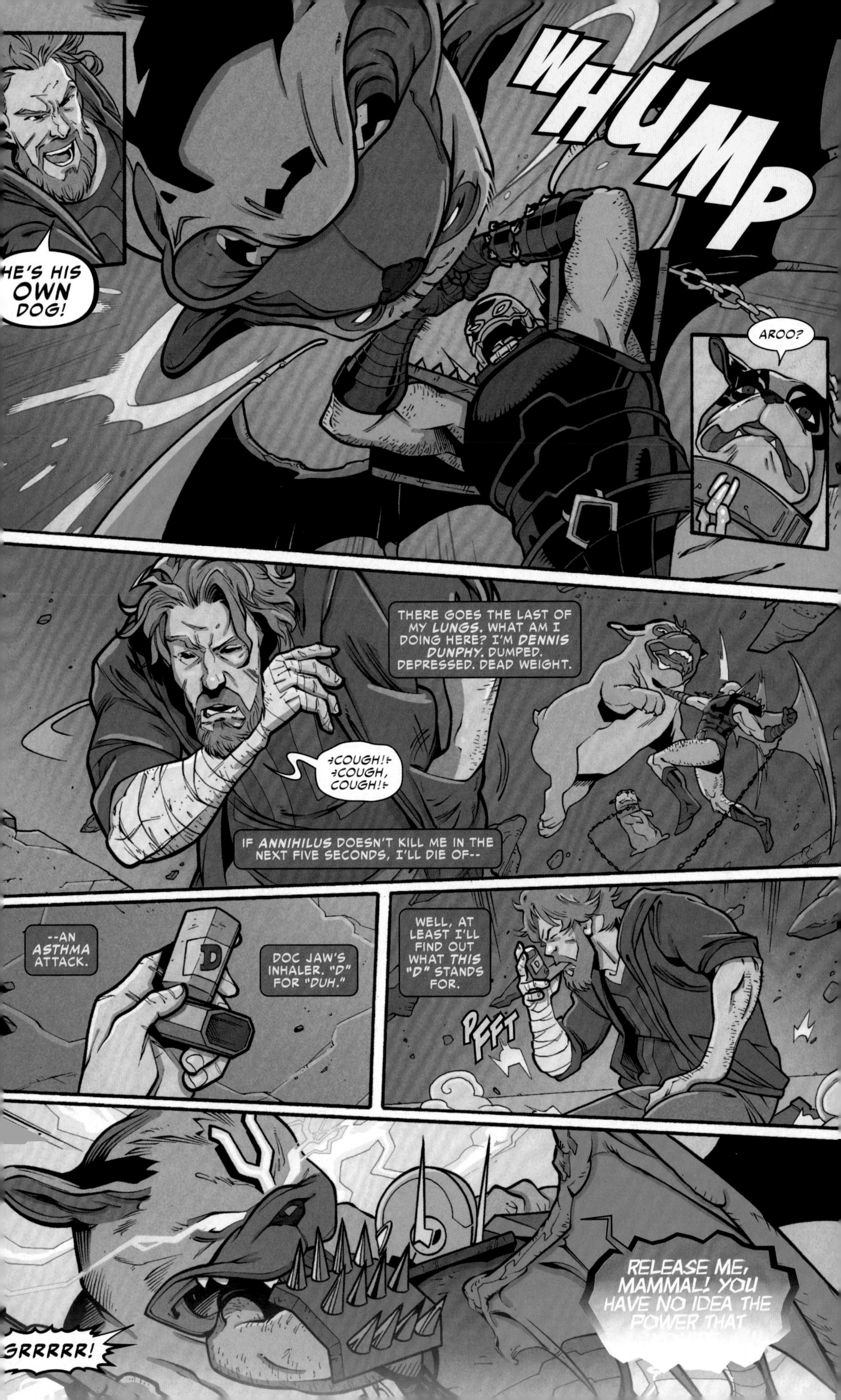

WHUMP
HE'S HIS OWN DOG!
AROO?
THERE GOES THE LAST OF MY LUNGS. WHAT AM I DOING HERE? I'M DENNIS DUNPHY. DUMPED. DEPRESSED. DEAD WEIGHT.
COUGH! COUGH, COUGH!
IF ANNIHILUS DOESN'T KILL ME IN THE NEXT FIVE SECONDS, I'LL DIE OF--
--AN ASTHMA ATTACK.
DOC JAW'S INHALER. "D" FOR "DUH."
WELL, AT LEAST I'LL FIND OUT WHAT THIS "D" STANDS FOR.
PFFT
GRRRRR!
RELEASE ME, MAMMAL! YOU HAVE NO IDEA THE POWER THAT

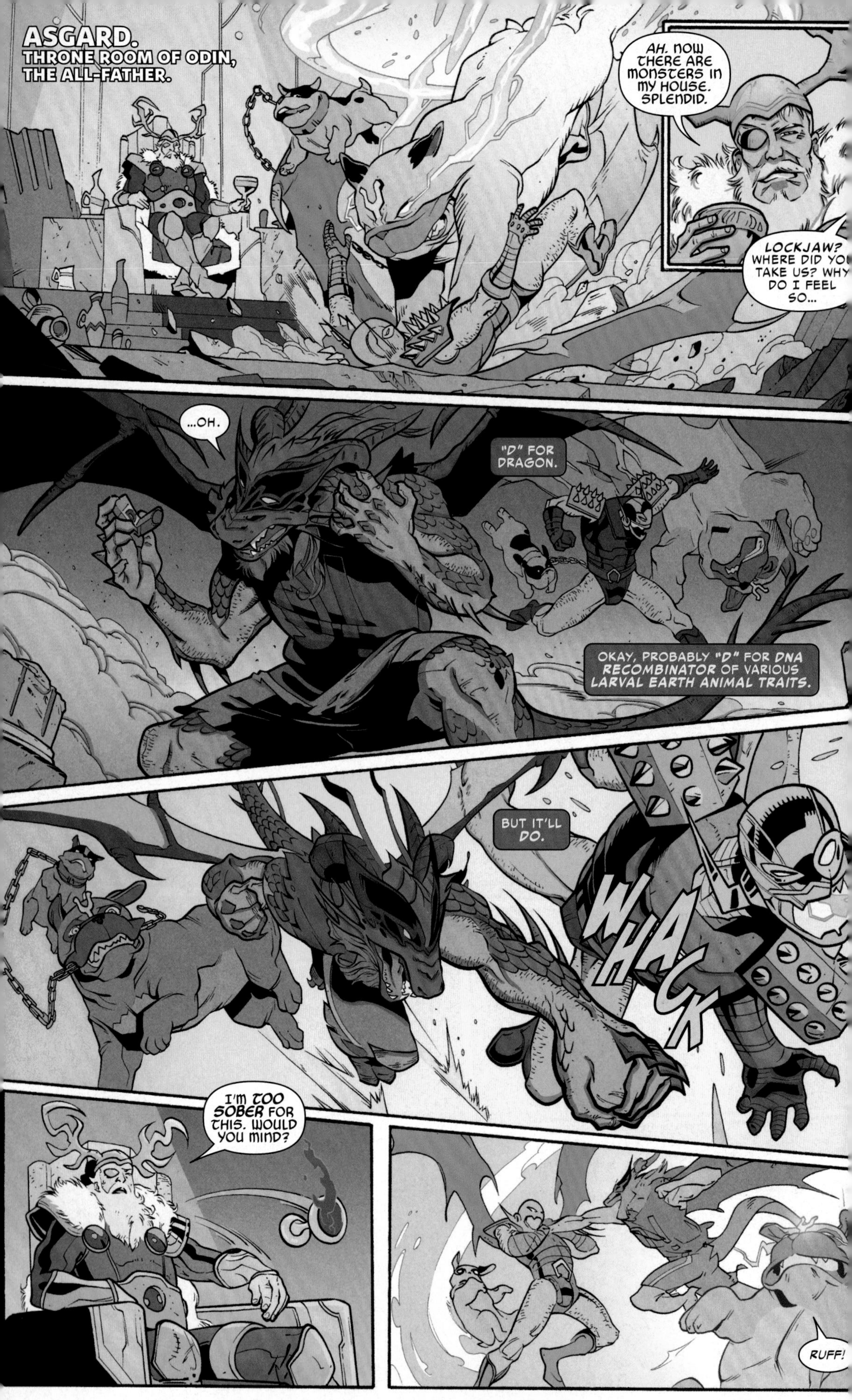
ASGARD.
THRONE ROOM OF ODIN, THE ALL-FATHER.
AH. NOW THERE ARE MONSTERS IN MY HOUSE. SPLENDID.
LOCKJAW? WHERE DID YOU TAKE US? WHY DO I FEEL SO...
...OH.
"D" FOR DRAGON.
OKAY, PROBABLY "D" FOR DNA RECOMBINATOR OF VARIOUS LARVAL EARTH ANIMAL TRAITS.
BUT IT'LL DO.
WHACK
I'M TOO SOBER FOR THIS. WOULD YOU MIND?
RUFF!

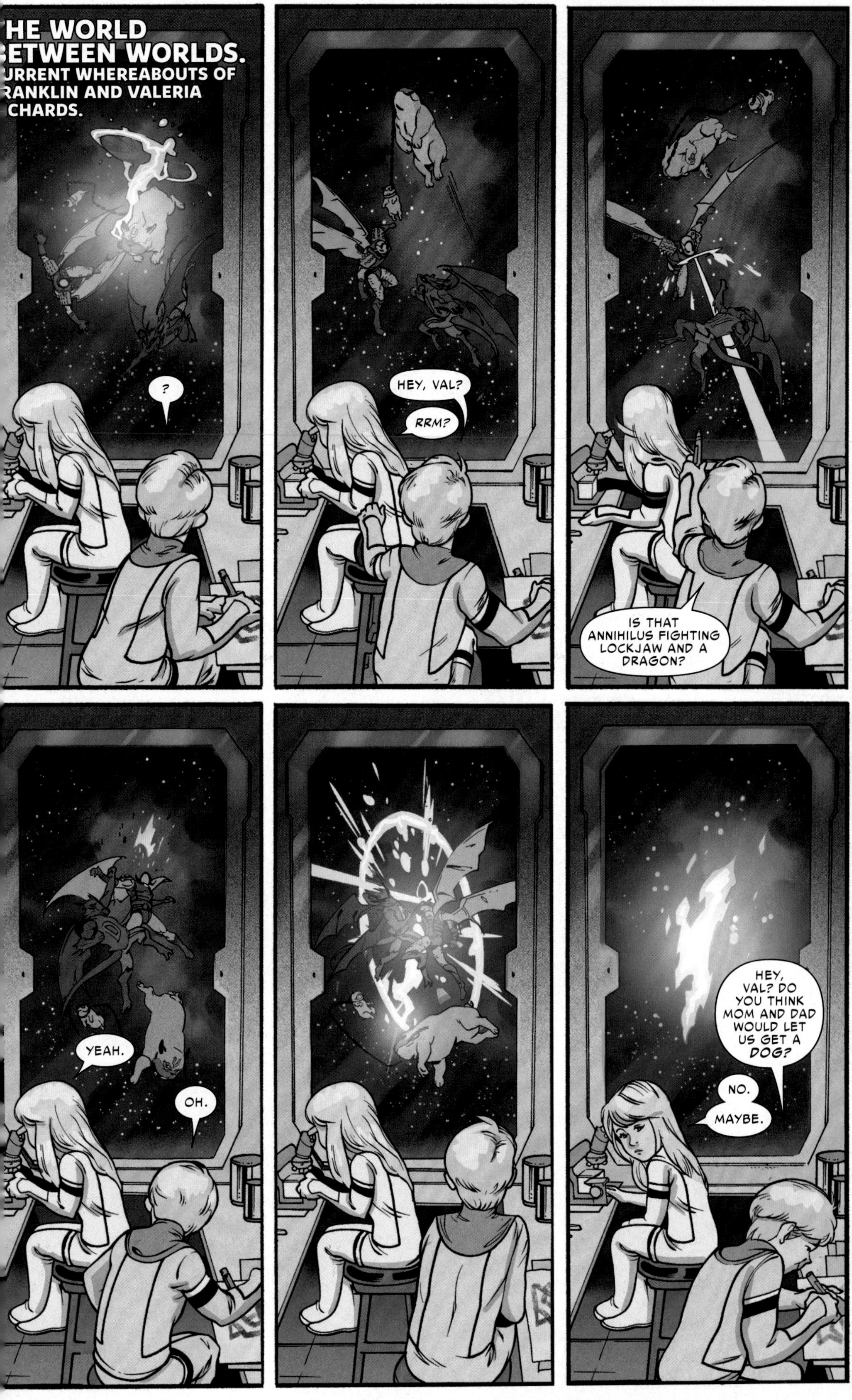

HE WORLD ETWEEN WORLDS.
URRENT WHEREABOUTS OF RANKLIN AND VALERIA CHARDS.
?
HEY, VAL?
RRM?
IS THAT ANNIHILUS FIGHTING LOCKJAW AND A DRAGON?
YEAH.
OH.
HEY, VAL? DO YOU THINK MOM AND DAD WOULD LET US GET A DOG?
NO.
MAYBE.

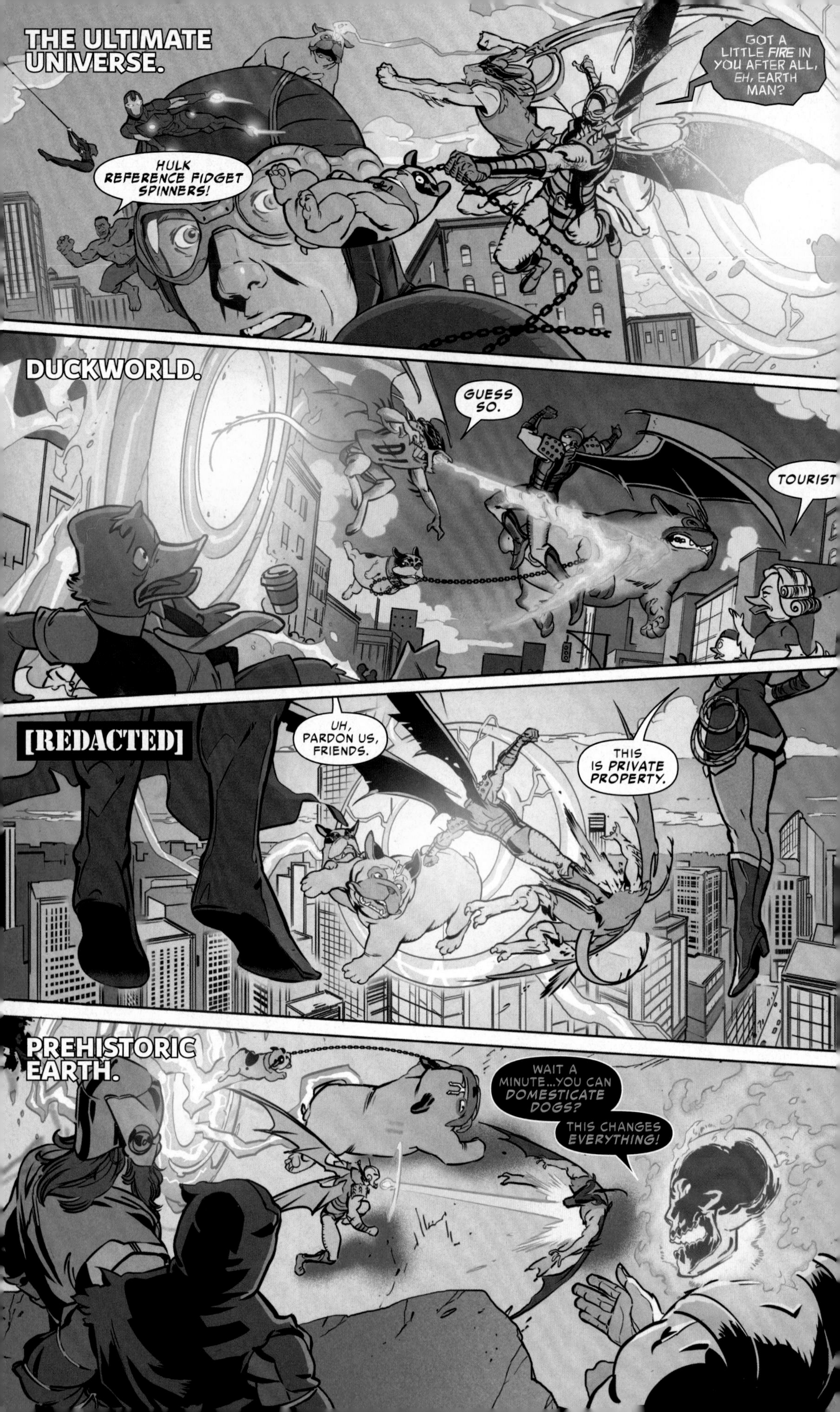
THE ULTIMATE UNIVERSE.
GOT A LITTLE *FIRE* IN YOU AFTER ALL, *EH*, EARTH MAN?
HULK REFERENCE FIDGET SPINNERS!
DUCKWORLD.
GUESS SO.
TOURIST
[REDACTED]
UH, PARDON US, FRIENDS.
THIS IS *PRIVATE PROPERTY.*
PREHISTORIC EARTH.
WAIT A MINUTE...YOU CAN *DOMESTICATE DOGS?*
THIS CHANGES *EVERYTHING!*

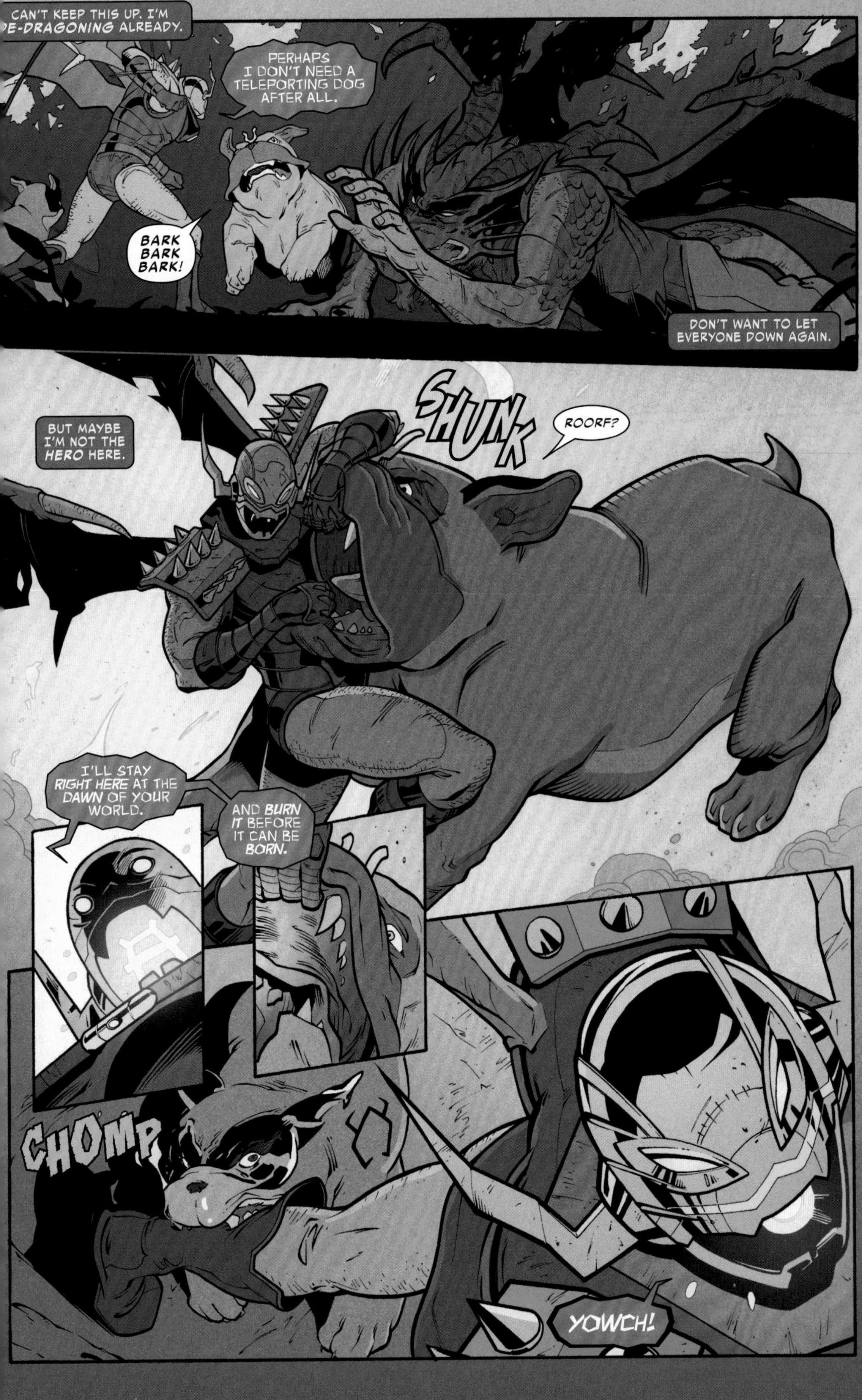

CAN'T KEEP THIS UP. I'M DE-DRAGONING ALREADY.
PERHAPS I DON'T NEED A TELEPORTING DOG AFTER ALL.
BARK BARK BARK!
DON'T WANT TO LET EVERYONE DOWN AGAIN.
BUT MAYBE I'M NOT THE HERO HERE.
SHUNK
ROORF?
I'LL STAY RIGHT HERE AT THE DAWN OF YOUR WORLD.
AND BURN IT BEFORE IT CAN BE BORN.
CHOMP
YOWCH!

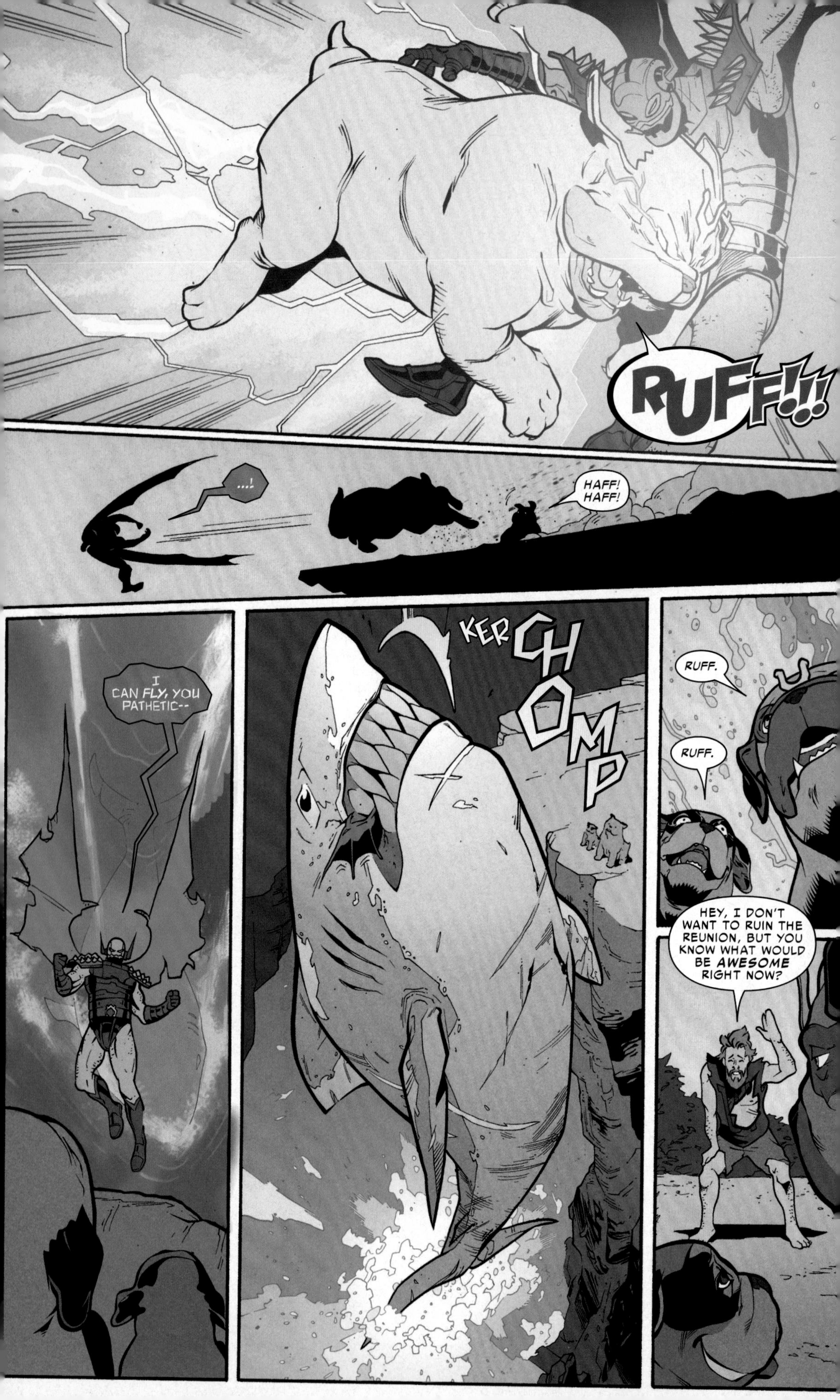
RUFF!!!
...!
HAFF! HAFF!
I CAN FLY, YOU PATHETIC--
KERCHOMP
RUFF.
RUFF.
HEY, I DON'T WANT TO RUIN THE REUNION, BUT YOU KNOW WHAT WOULD BE AWESOME RIGHT NOW?

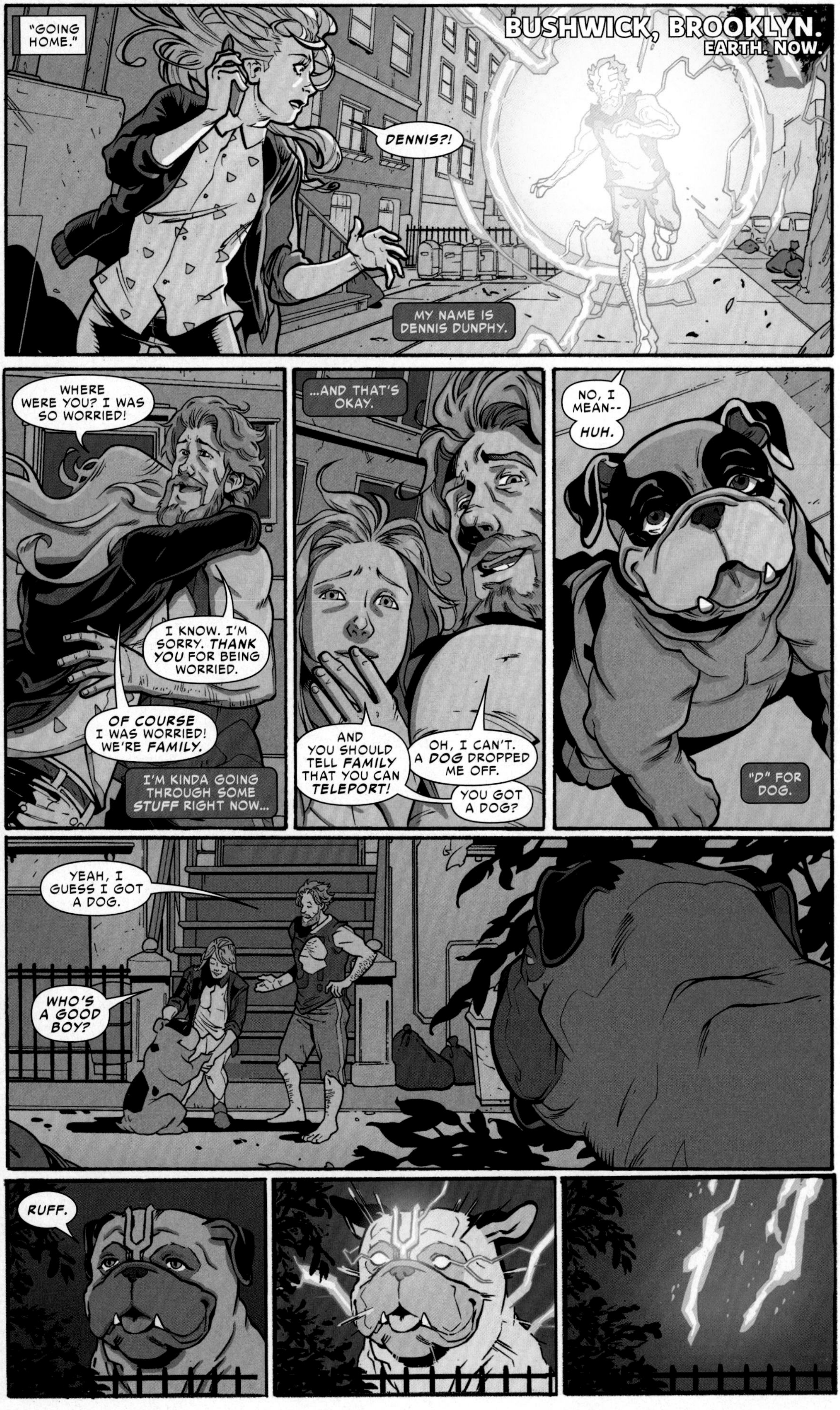
"GOING HOME."
BUSHWICK, BROOKLYN.
EARTH. NOW.
DENNIS?!
MY NAME IS DENNIS DUNPHY.
WHERE WERE YOU? I WAS SO WORRIED!
I KNOW. I'M SORRY. THANK YOU FOR BEING WORRIED.
OF COURSE I WAS WORRIED! WE'RE FAMILY.
I'M KINDA GOING THROUGH SOME STUFF RIGHT NOW...
...AND THAT'S OKAY.
AND YOU SHOULD TELL FAMILY THAT YOU CAN TELEPORT!
OH, I CAN'T. A DOG DROPPED ME OFF.
YOU GOT A DOG?
NO, I MEAN-- HUH.
"D" FOR DOG.
YEAH, I GUESS I GOT A DOG.
WHO'S A GOOD BOY?
RUFF.

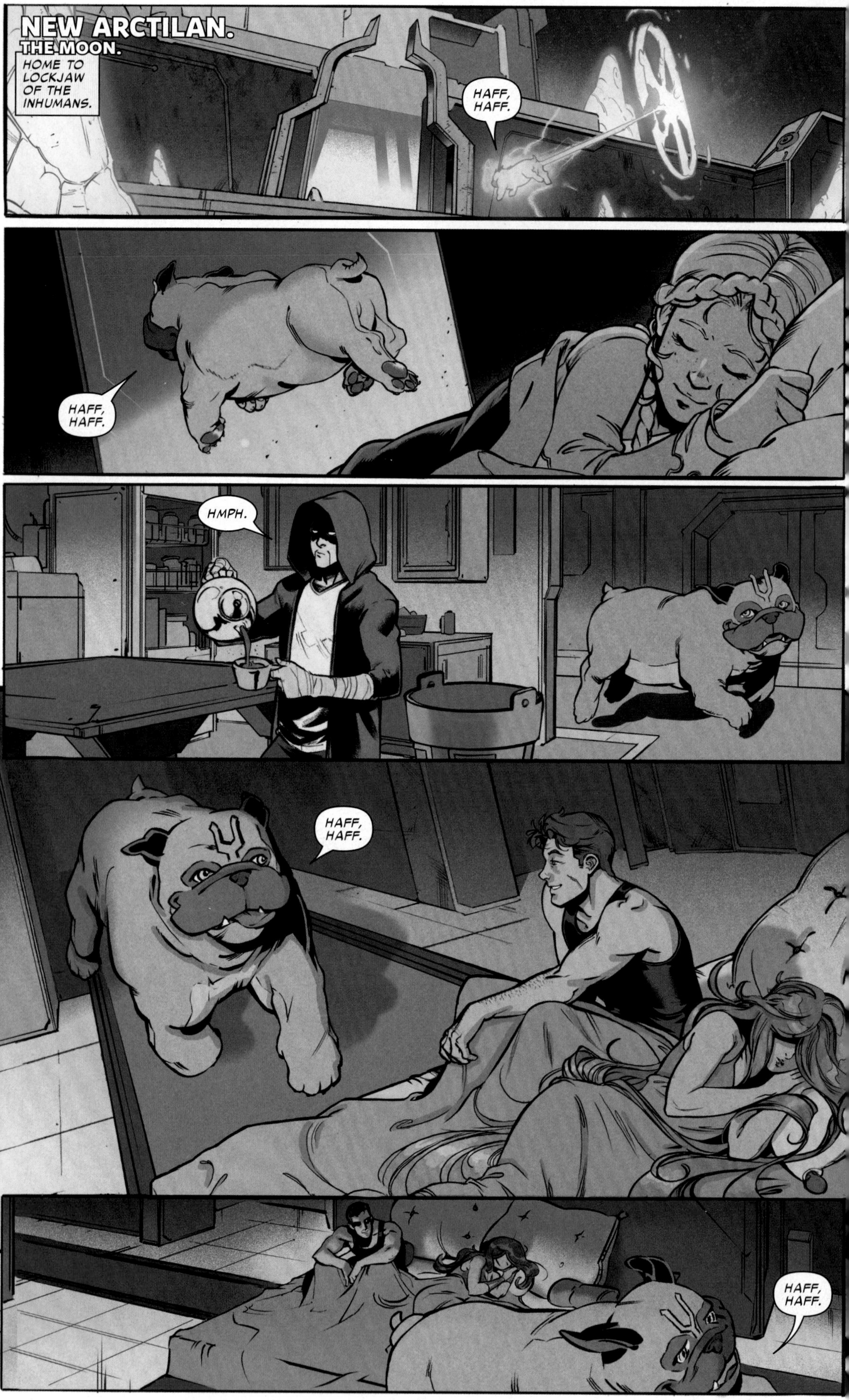
NEW ARCTILAN.
THE MOON.
HOME TO LOCKJAW OF THE INHUMANS.
HAFF, HAFF.
HAFF, HAFF.
HMPH.
HAFF, HAFF.
HAFF, HAFF.

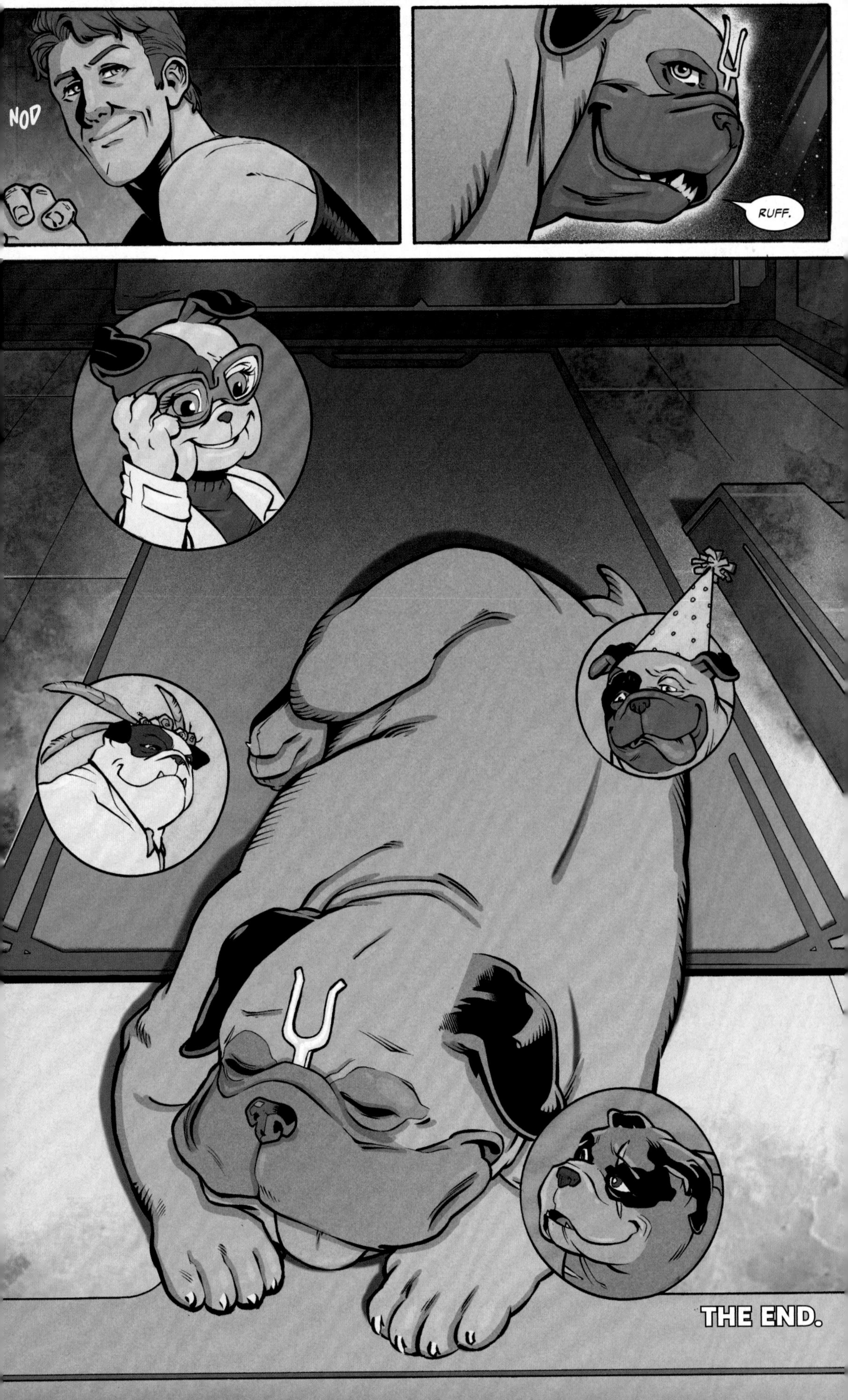
NOD
RUFF.
THE END.

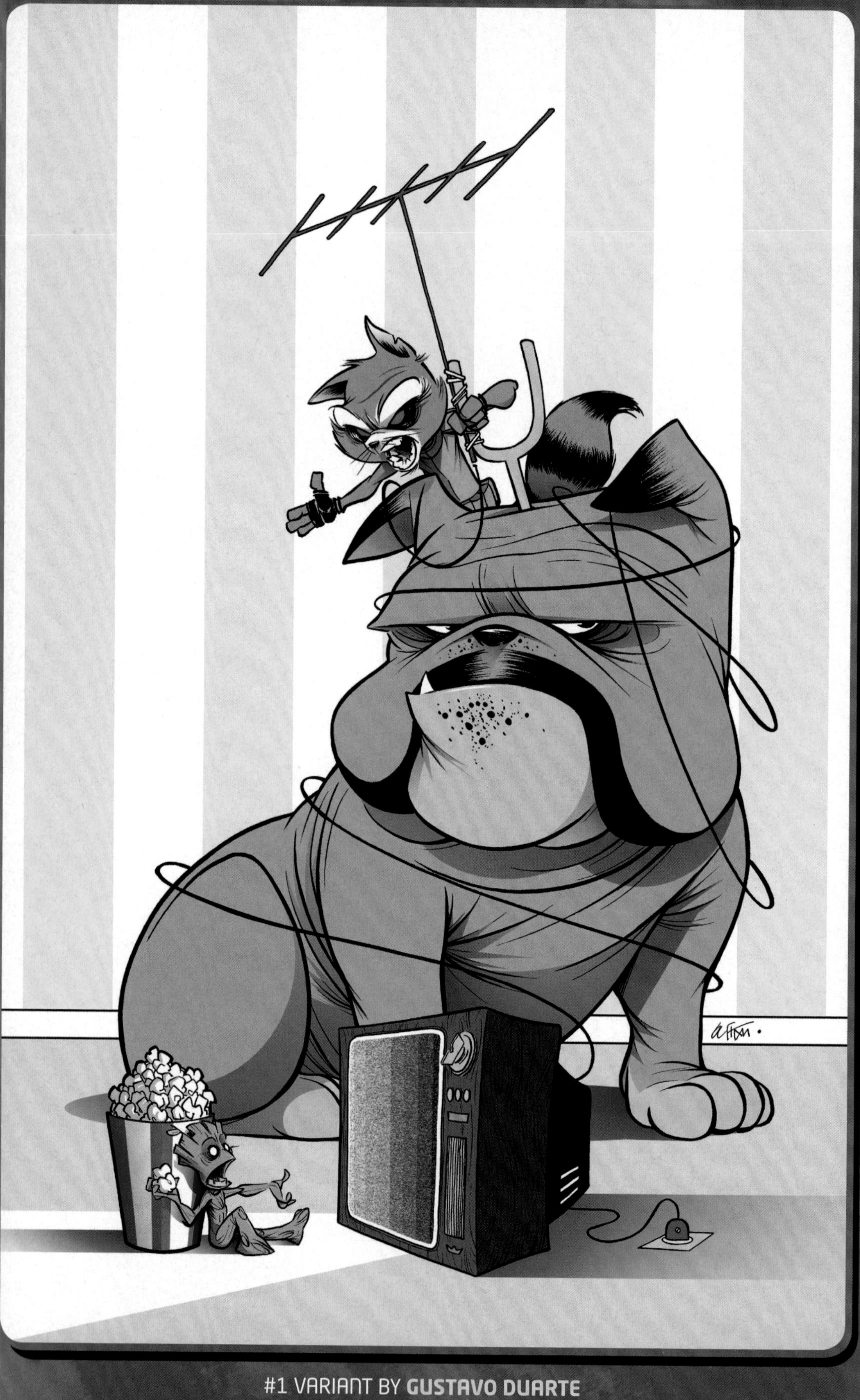

#1 VARIANT BY **GUSTAVO DUARTE**

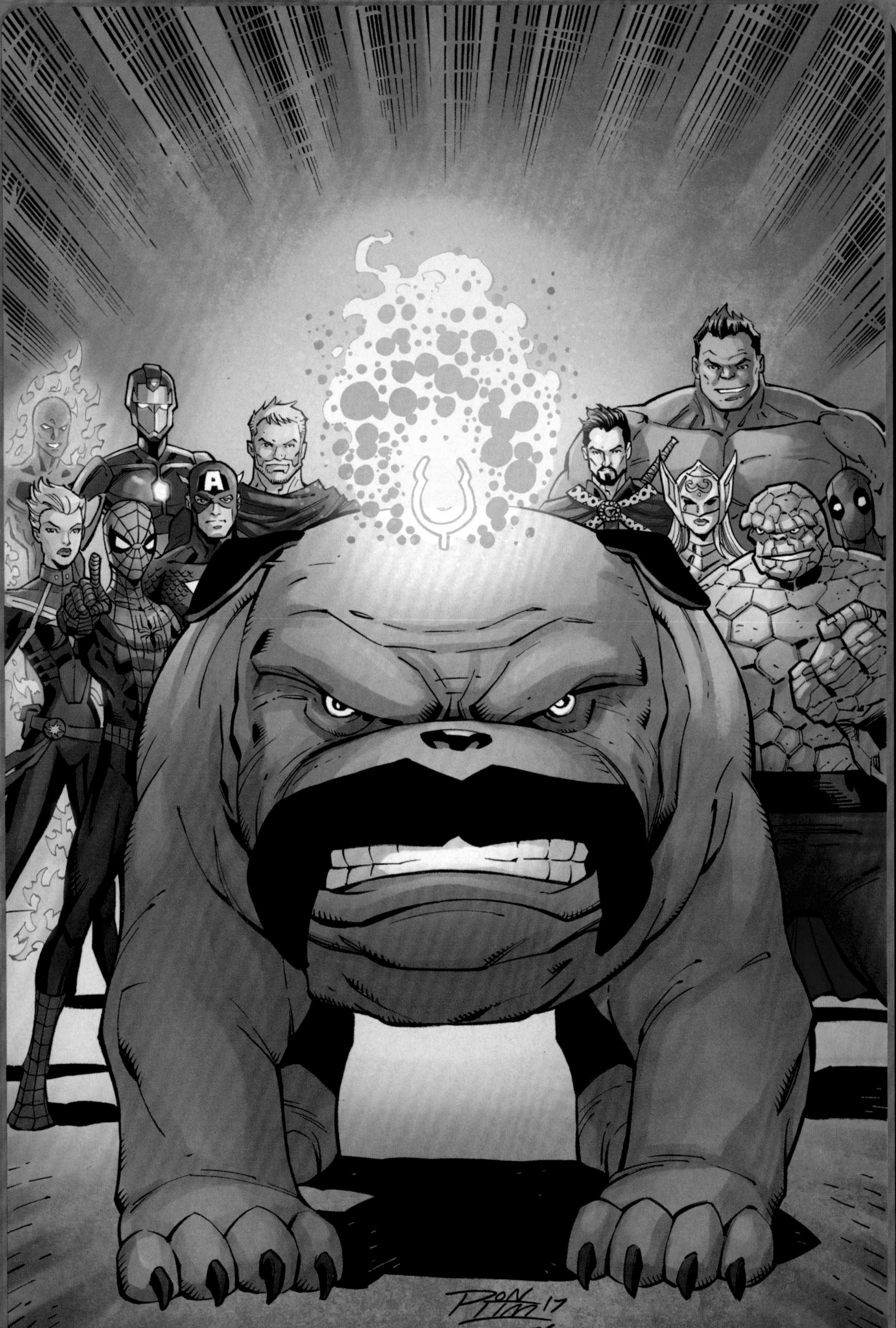

RON LIM 17
S. HANNA

#1 VARIANT BY **RON LIM, SCOTT HANNA & JIM CAMPBELL**

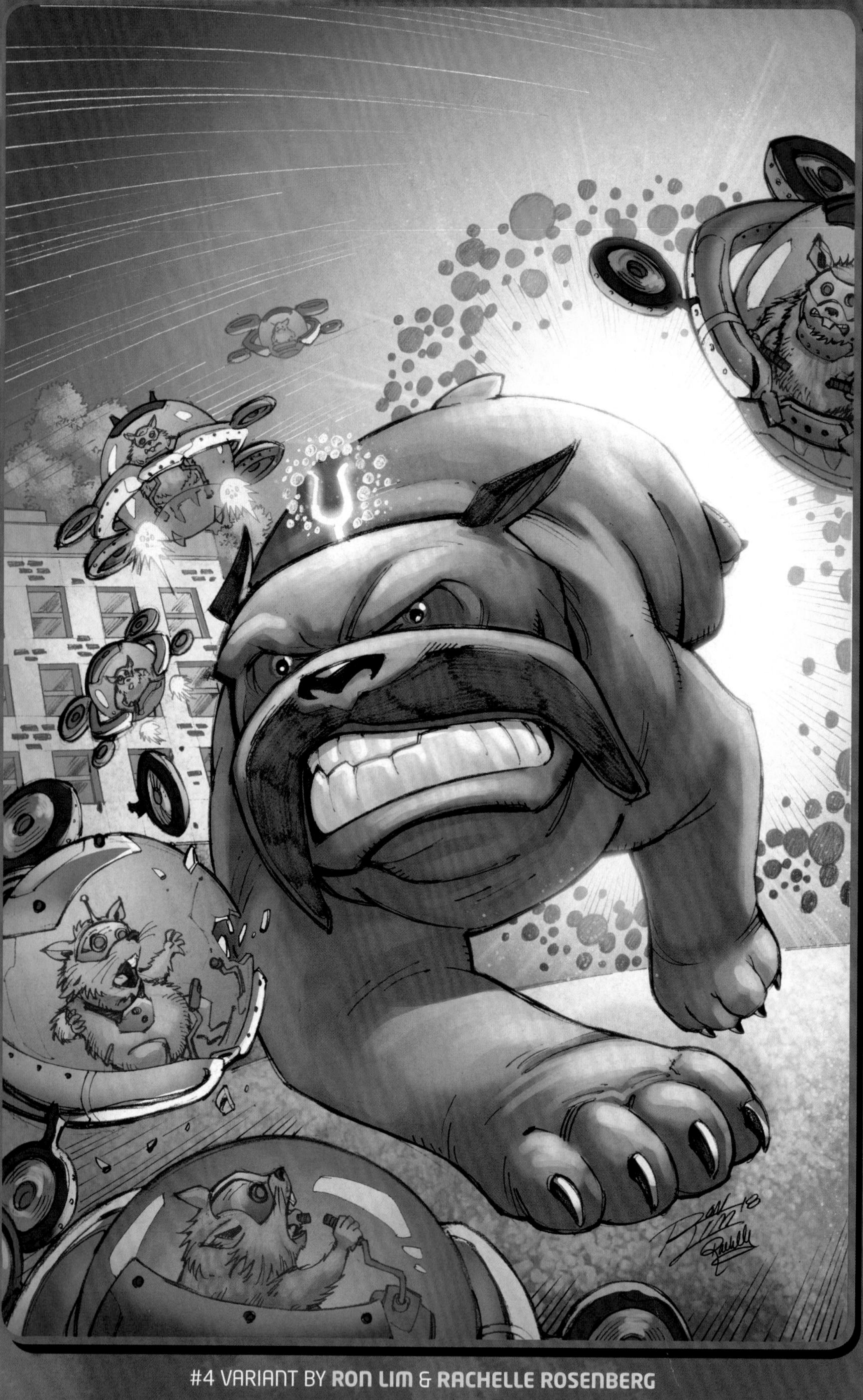

#4 VARIANT BY **RON LIM & RACHELLE ROSENBERG**

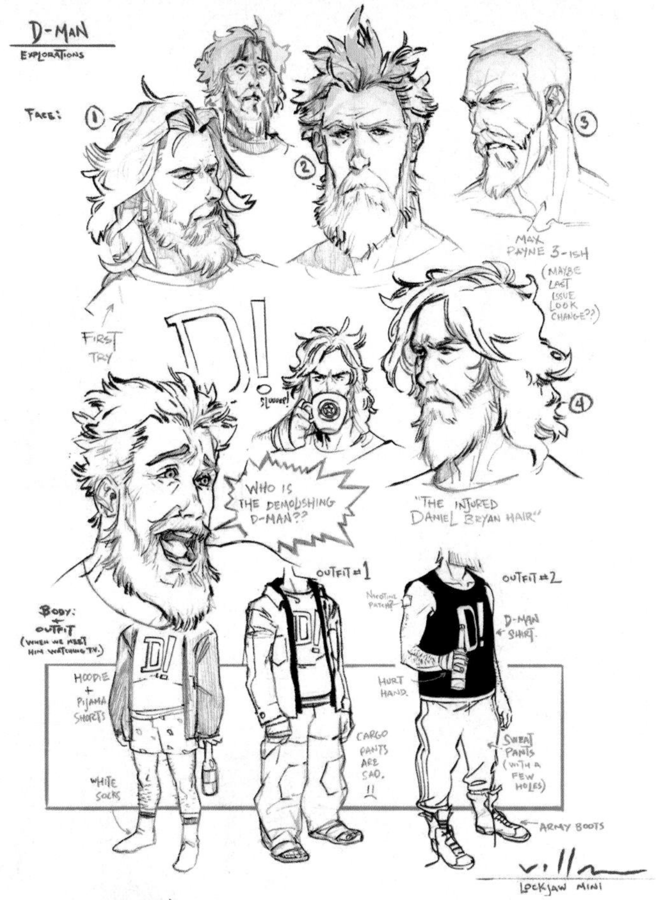
D-MAN
EXPLORATIONS
FACE:
1
2
3
MAX PAYNE 3-ISH
(MAYBE LAST ISSUE LOOK CHANGE??)
FIRST TRY
D!
4
"THE INJURED DANIEL BRYAN HAIR"
WHO IS THE DEMOLISHING D-MAN??
OUTFIT #1
OUTFIT #2
NICOTINE PATCH?
D-MAN SHIRT
BODY: OUTFIT (WHEN WE MEET HIM WATCHING TV.)
HOODIE + PIJAMA SHORTS
HURT HAND.
CARGO PANTS ARE SAD. !!
SWEAT PANTS (WITH A FEW HOLES)
WHITE SOCKS
ARMY BOOTS
villa
LOCKJAW MINI

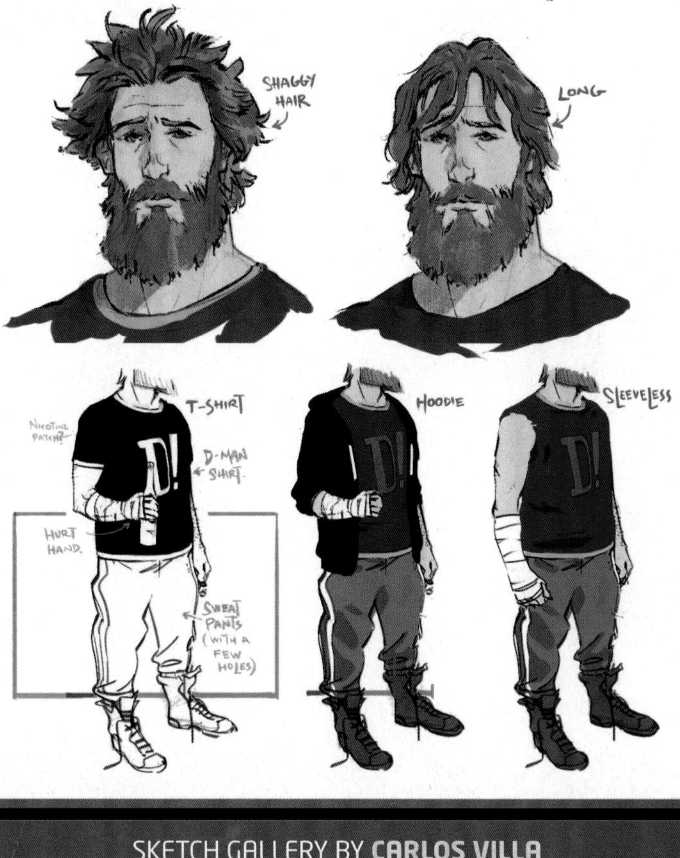
SHAGGY HAIR
LONG
T-SHIRT
HOODIE
SLEEVELESS
NICOTINE PATCH?
D-MAN SHIRT.
HURT HAND.
SWEAT PANTS (WITH A FEW HOLES)

SKETCH GALLERY BY **CARLOS VILLA**

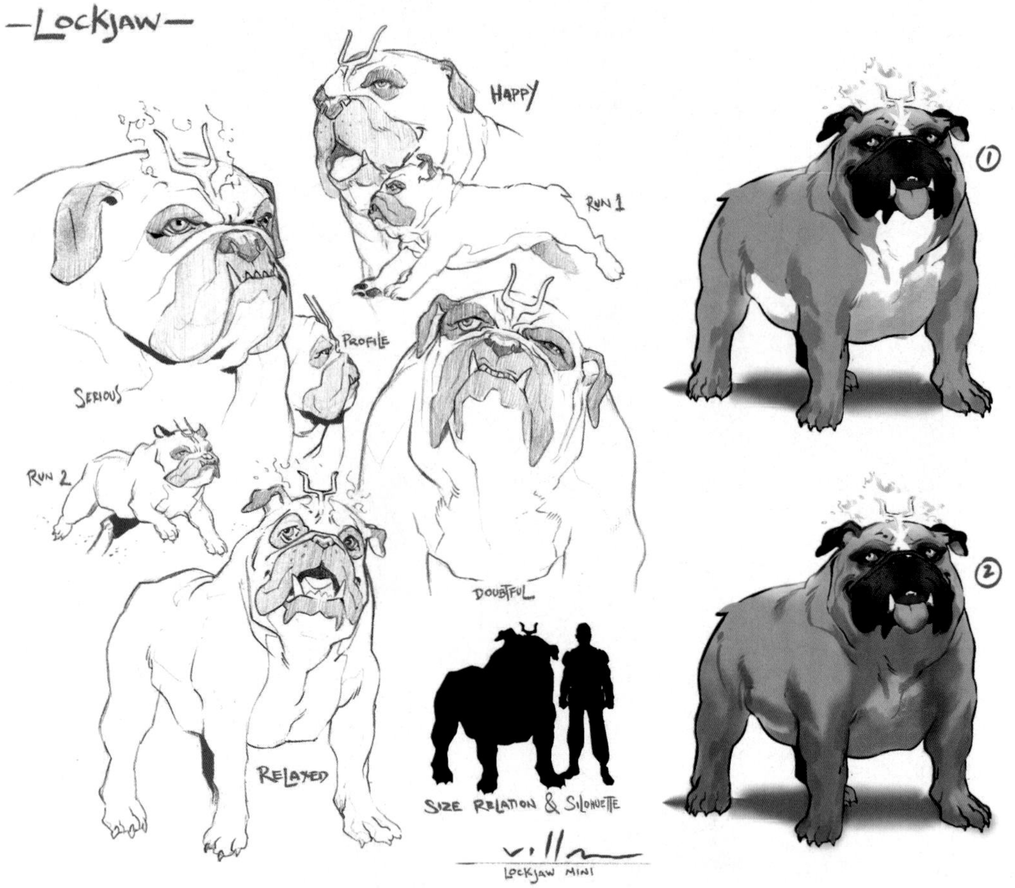
-LOCKJAW-
HAPPY
RUN 1
SERIOUS
PROFILE
RUN 2
DOUBTFUL
RELAXED
SIZE RELATION & SILOUETTE
LOCKJAW MINI
1
2

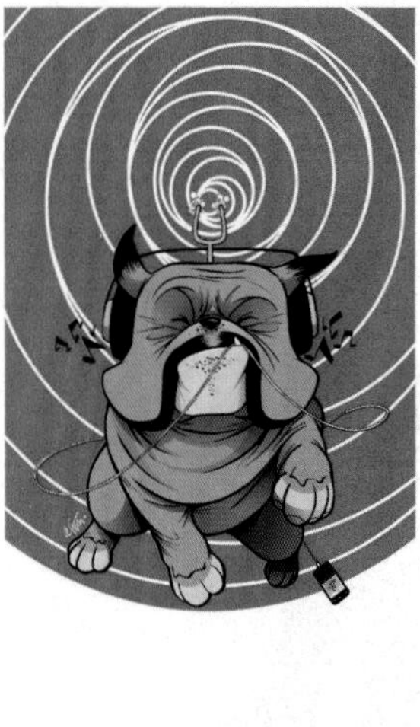

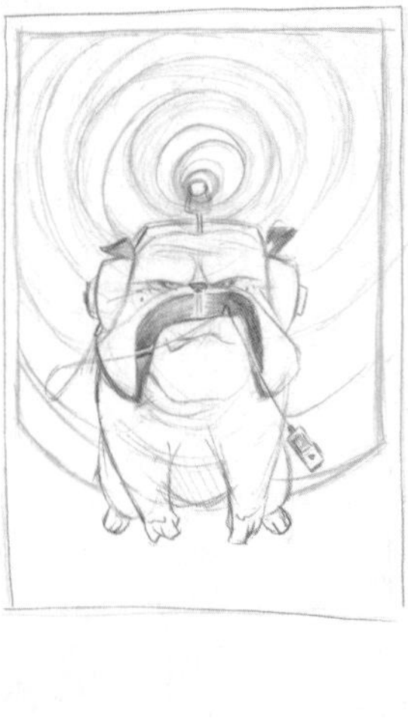

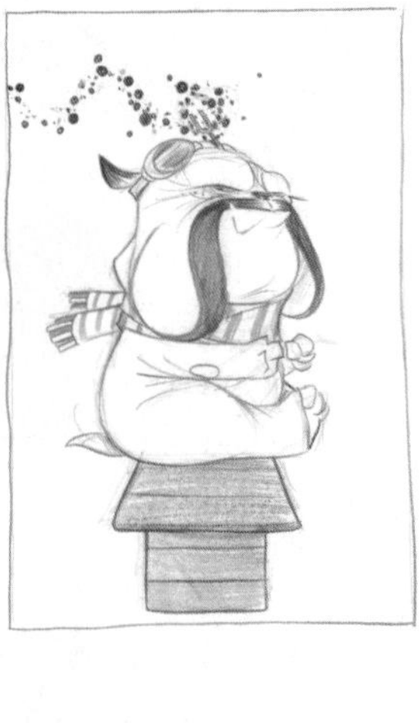

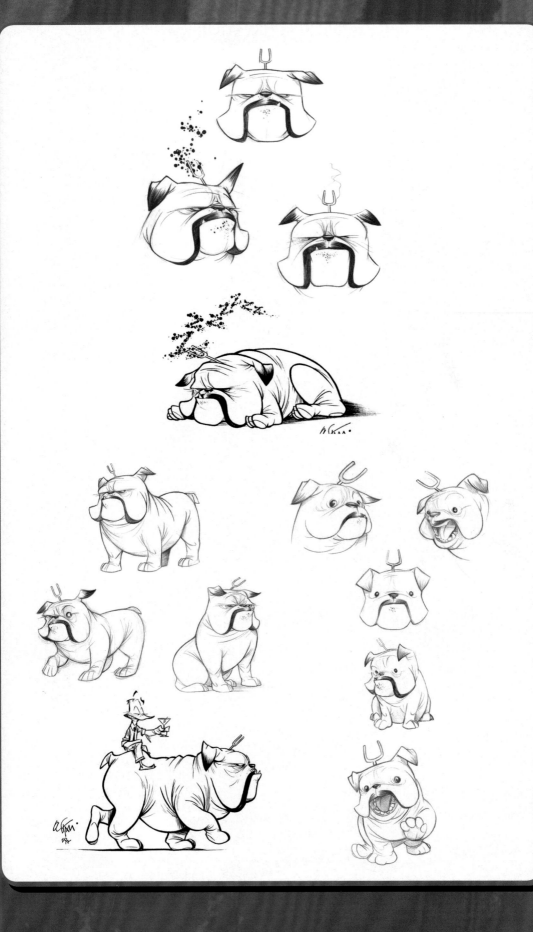

WITH LOCKJAW BEING IGNORED BY THE INHUMAN ROYAL FAMILY, HE DECIDES TO VISIT EARTH AND RUNS INTO THE EVER-LOVIN' BLUE-EYED THING!

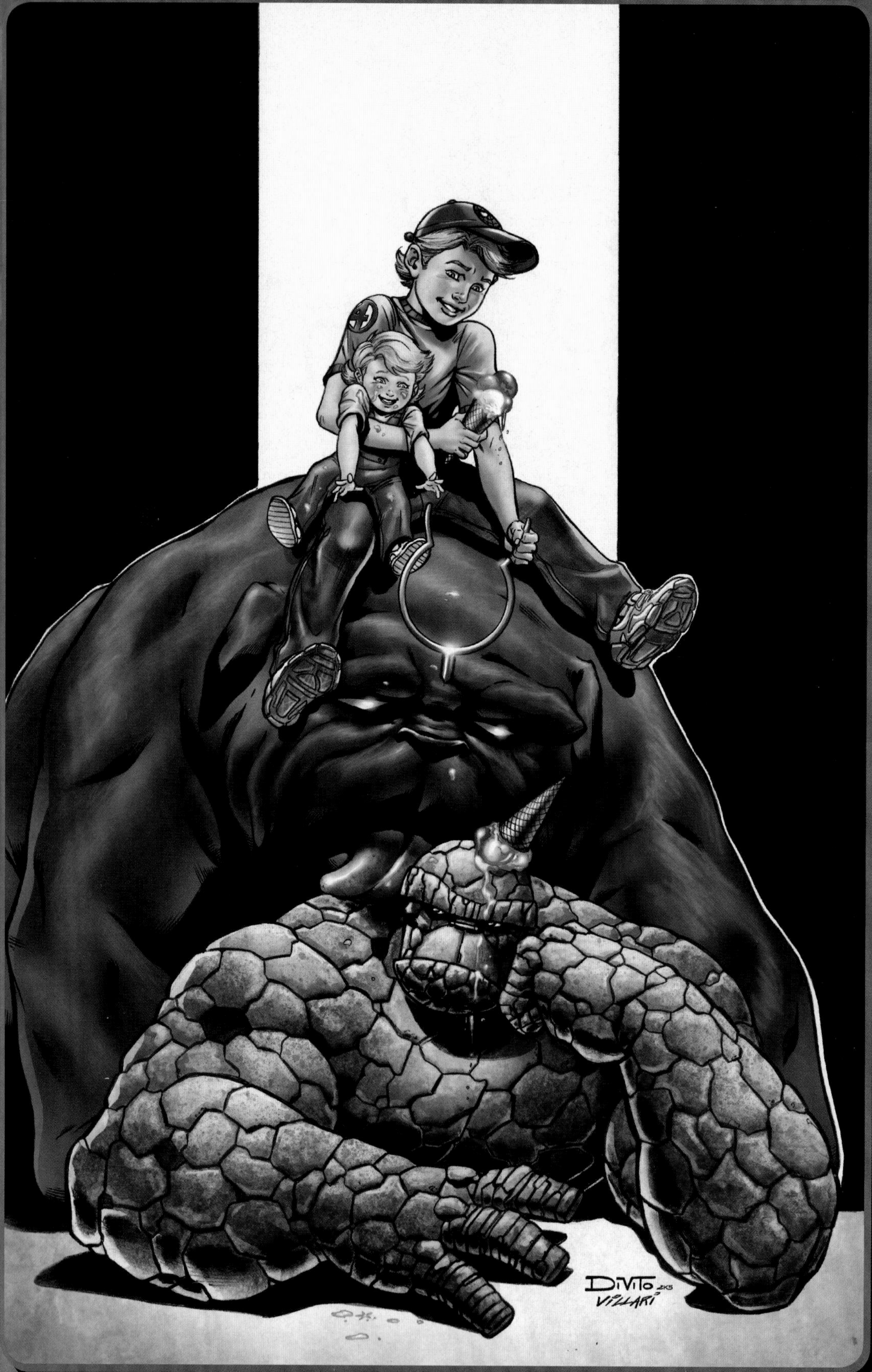
DiVito 2K5
Villari

THE THING #4

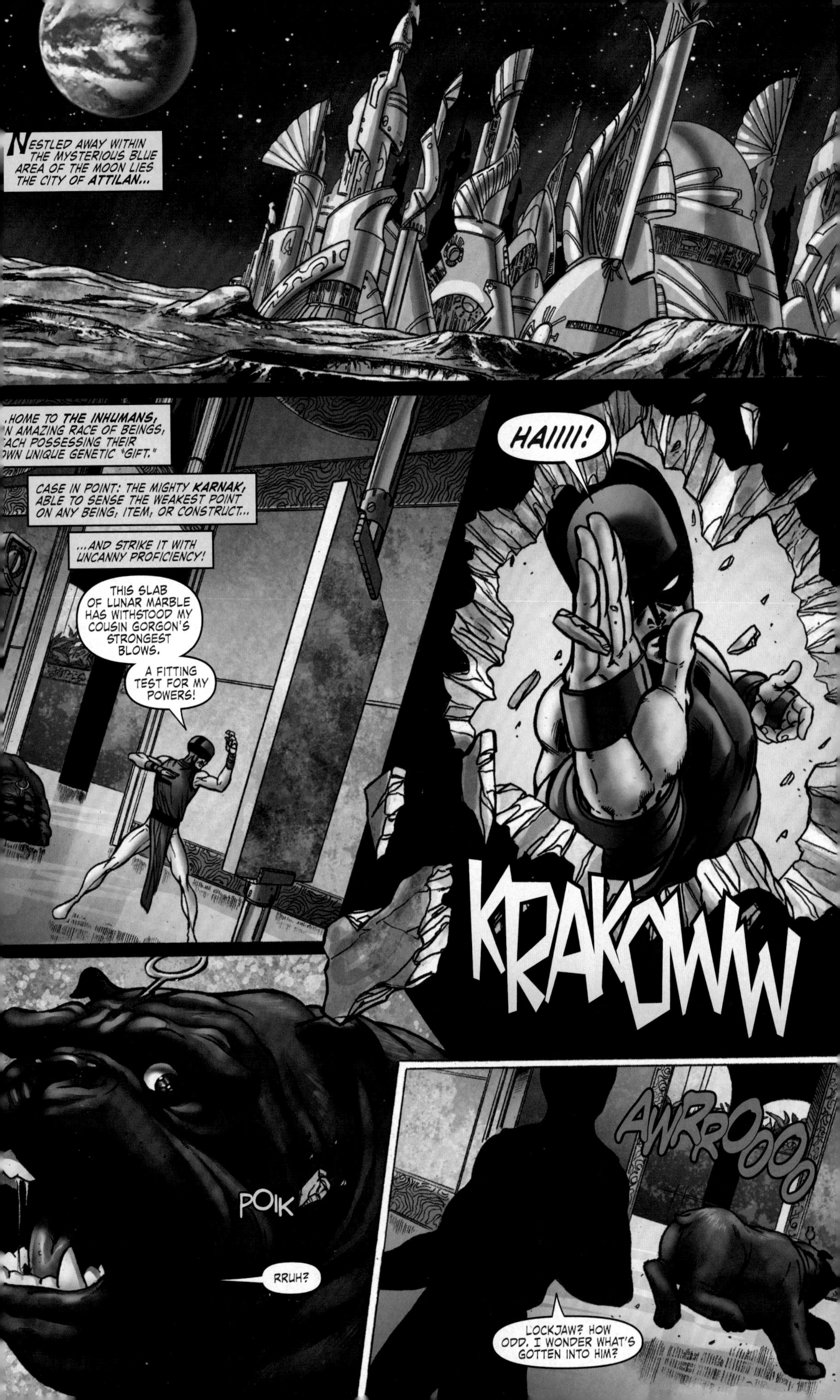

NESTLED AWAY WITHIN THE MYSTERIOUS BLUE AREA OF THE MOON LIES THE CITY OF ATTILAN...
...HOME TO THE INHUMANS, AN AMAZING RACE OF BEINGS, EACH POSSESSING THEIR OWN UNIQUE GENETIC "GIFT."
CASE IN POINT: THE MIGHTY KARNAK, ABLE TO SENSE THE WEAKEST POINT ON ANY BEING, ITEM, OR CONSTRUCT...
...AND STRIKE IT WITH UNCANNY PROFICIENCY!
THIS SLAB OF LUNAR MARBLE HAS WITHSTOOD MY COUSIN GORGON'S STRONGEST BLOWS.
A FITTING TEST FOR MY POWERS!
HAIIII!
KRAKOWW
POIK
RRUH?
AWRROOOO
LOCKJAW? HOW ODD. I WONDER WHAT'S GOTTEN INTO HIM?

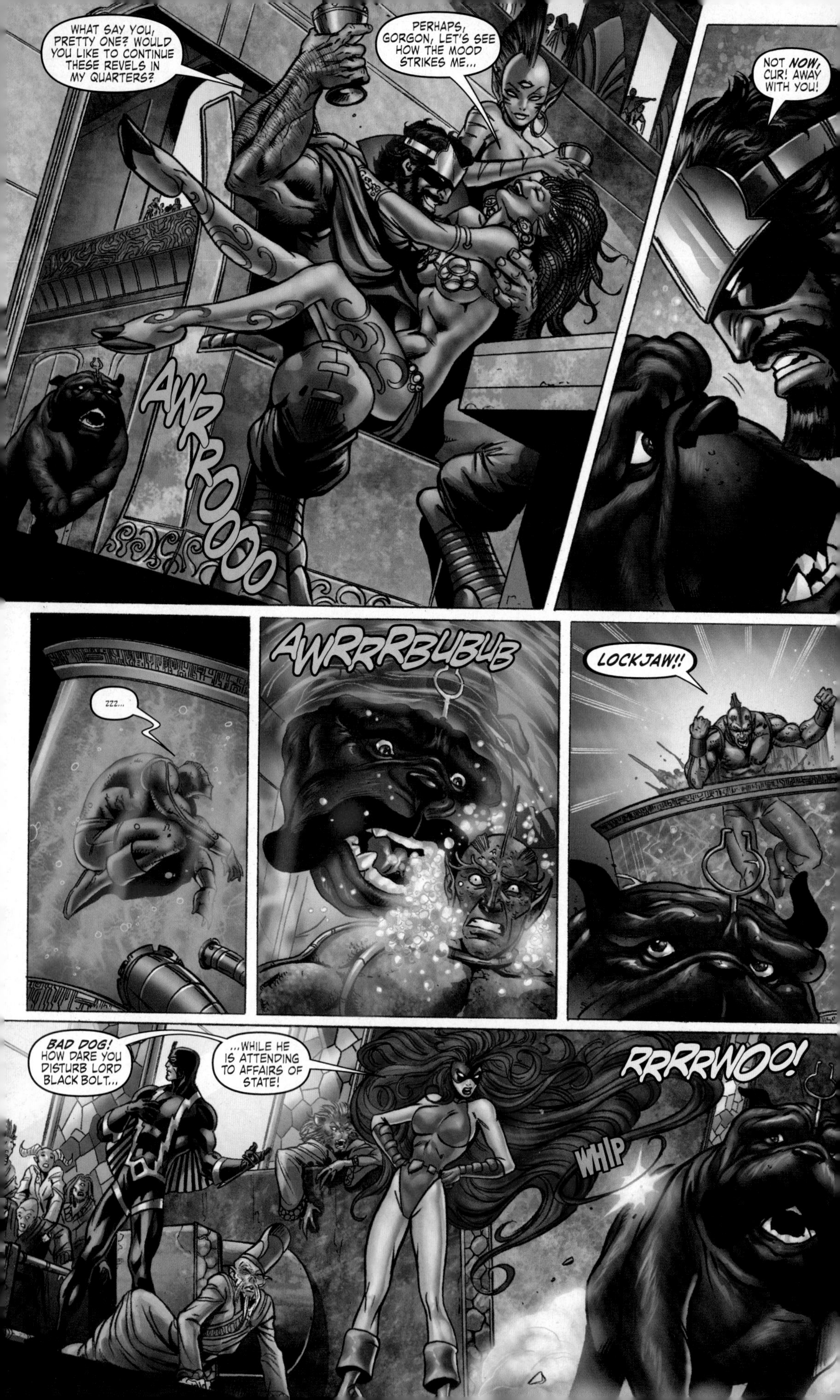
WHAT SAY YOU, PRETTY ONE? WOULD YOU LIKE TO CONTINUE THESE REVELS IN MY QUARTERS?
PERHAPS, GORGON, LET'S SEE HOW THE MOOD STRIKES ME...
AWRROOOO
NOT NOW, CUR! AWAY WITH YOU!
ZZZ...
AWRRRBUBUB
LOCKJAW!!
BAD DOG! HOW DARE YOU DISTURB LORD BLACK BOLT...
...WHILE HE IS ATTENDING TO AFFAIRS OF STATE!
RRRRWOO!
WHIP

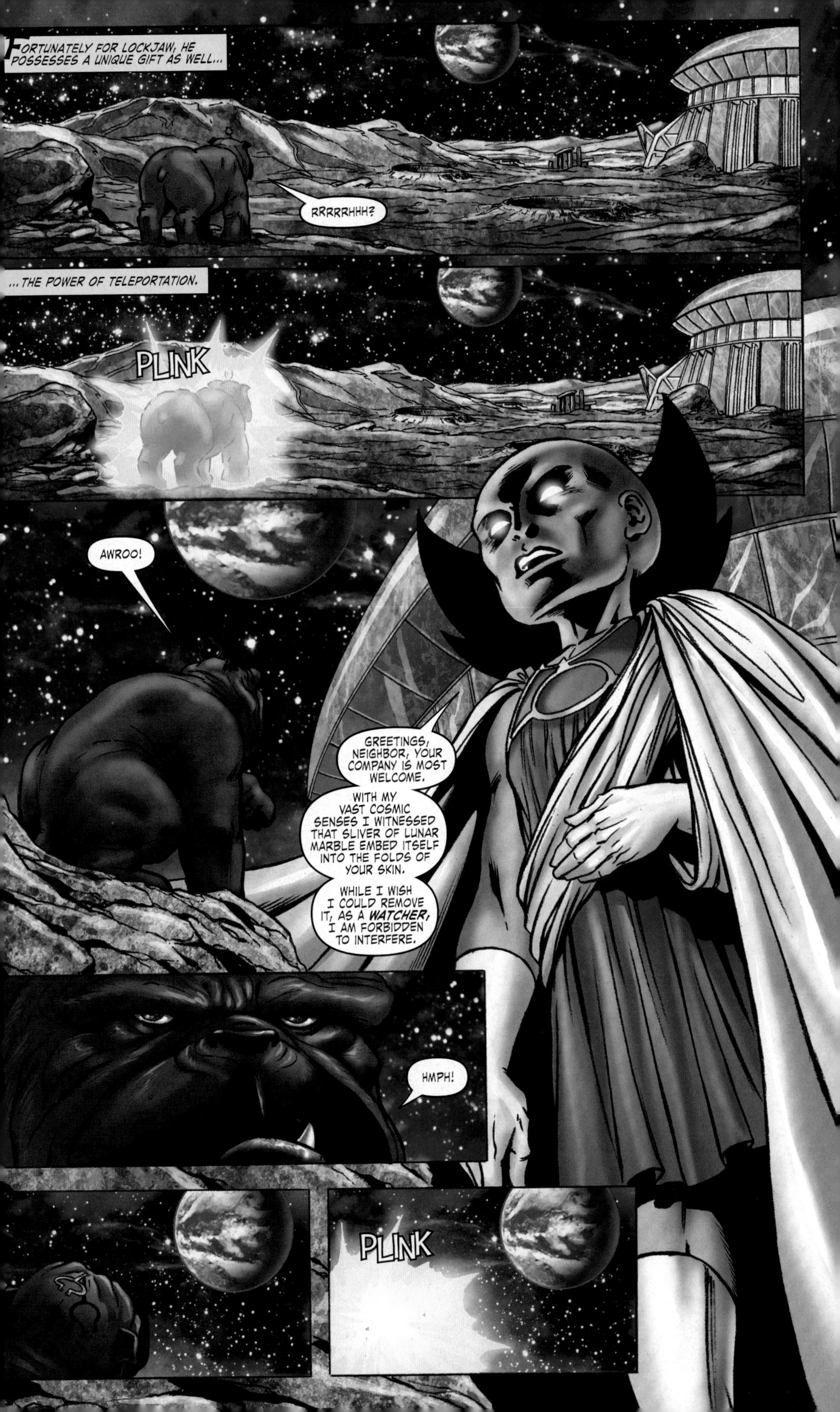
FORTUNATELY FOR LOCKJAW, HE POSSESSES A UNIQUE GIFT AS WELL...
RRRRRHHH?
...THE POWER OF TELEPORTATION.
PLINK
AWROO!
GREETINGS, NEIGHBOR, YOUR COMPANY IS MOST WELCOME.
WITH MY VAST COSMIC SENSES I WITNESSED THAT SLIVER OF LUNAR MARBLE EMBED ITSELF INTO THE FOLDS OF YOUR SKIN.
WHILE I WISH I COULD REMOVE IT, AS A *WATCHER,* I AM FORBIDDEN TO INTERFERE.
HMPH!
PLINK

PAWS & FAST-FORWARD

DAN SLOTT
STORY

ANDREA DIVITO
ARTIST

LAURA VILLARI
COLORS

DAVE LANPHEAR
LETTERS

SCHMIDT, LAZER & SITTERSON
ASSISTANT EDITORS

TOM BREVOORT
EDITOR

JOE QUESADA
EDITOR IN CHIEF

DAN BUCKLEY
PUBLISHER

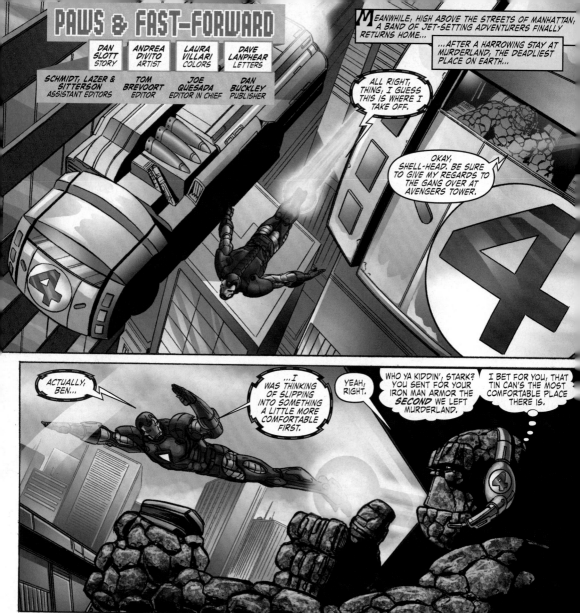

MEANWHILE, HIGH ABOVE THE STREETS OF MANHATTAN, A BAND OF JET-SETTING ADVENTURERS FINALLY RETURNS HOME...

...AFTER A HARROWING STAY AT MURDERLAND, THE DEADLIEST PLACE ON EARTH...

ALL RIGHT, THING, I GUESS THIS IS WHERE I TAKE OFF.

OKAY, SHELL-HEAD. BE SURE TO GIVE MY REGARDS TO THE GANG OVER AT AVENGERS TOWER.

ACTUALLY, BEN...

...I WAS THINKING OF SLIPPING INTO SOMETHING A LITTLE MORE COMFORTABLE FIRST.

YEAH, RIGHT.

WHO YA KIDDIN', STARK? YOU SENT FOR YOUR IRON MAN ARMOR THE SECOND WE LEFT MURDERLAND.

I BET FOR YOU, THAT TIN CAN'S THE MOST COMFORTABLE PLACE THERE IS.

AND I GUESS FER ME, EVEN THOUGH I'M SOME BIG-SHOT BILLIONAIRE NOW, I'M MORE COMFORTABLE HERE, AMONGST THE HOI POLLOI.

POOR GUYS, THEY SURE BEEN THROUGH A LOT. WHEN ARCADE KIDNAPPED ME AND ALL A' THEIR RICH BOSSES...

...WE DIDN'T REALIZE THAT THEY GOT SNATCHED TOO!

WELL, NOT TILL STARK AND I FOUND 'EM IN A ROOM UNDER MURDERLAND...WRAPPED UP LIKE BIRTHDAY PRESENTS!

BUNNY?!

MR. GRIMM, THANK GOODNESS!

LET US OUT!

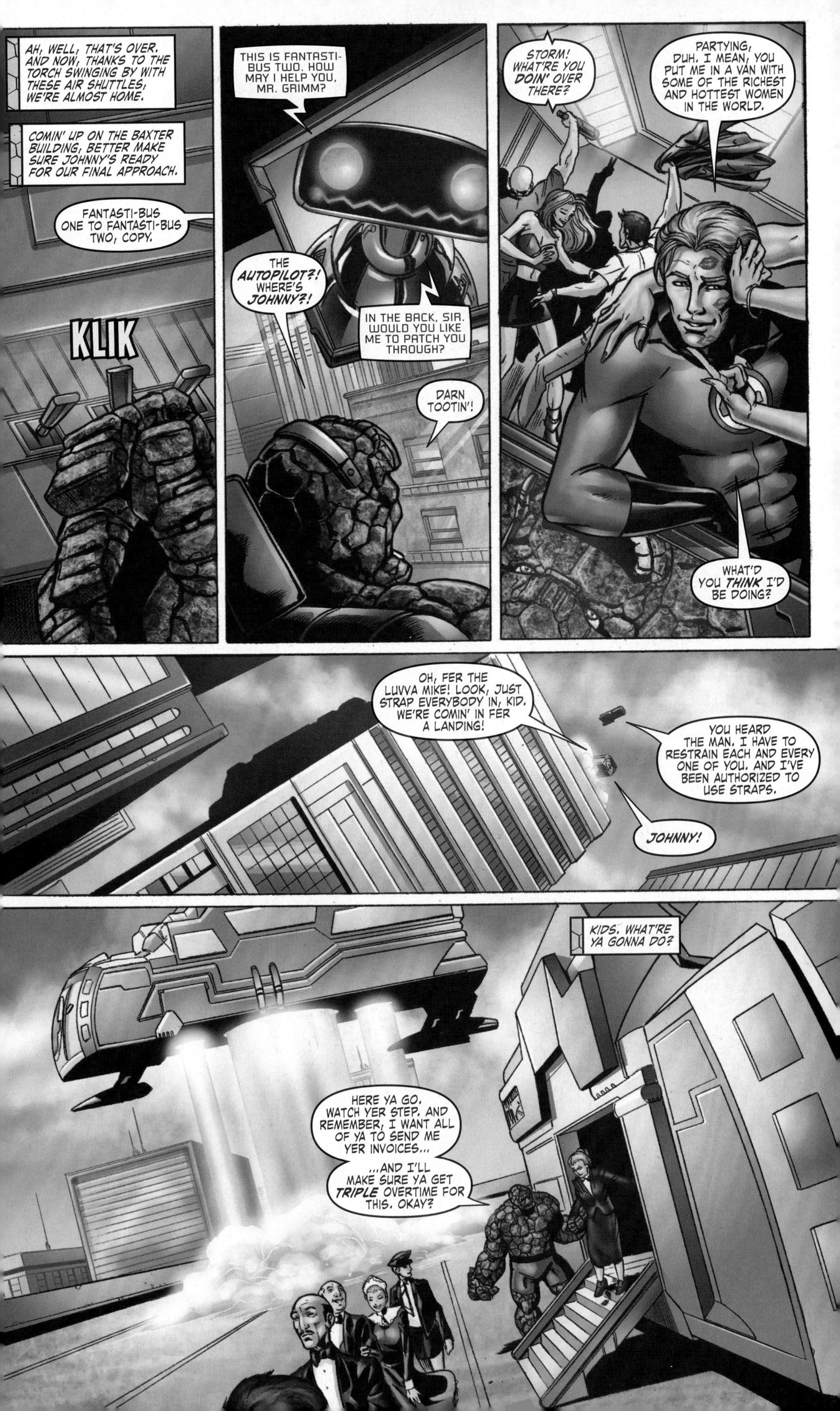
AH, WELL, THAT'S OVER. AND NOW, THANKS TO THE TORCH SWINGING BY WITH THESE AIR SHUTTLES, WE'RE ALMOST HOME.
COMIN' UP ON THE BAXTER BUILDING, BETTER MAKE SURE JOHNNY'S READY FOR OUR FINAL APPROACH.
FANTASTI-BUS ONE TO FANTASTI-BUS TWO, COPY.
KLIK
THIS IS FANTASTI-BUS TWO. HOW MAY I HELP YOU, MR. GRIMM?
THE AUTOPILOT?! WHERE'S JOHNNY?!
IN THE BACK, SIR. WOULD YOU LIKE ME TO PATCH YOU THROUGH?
DARN TOOTIN'!
STORM! WHAT'RE YOU DOIN' OVER THERE?
PARTYING, DUH. I MEAN, YOU PUT ME IN A VAN WITH SOME OF THE RICHEST AND HOTTEST WOMEN IN THE WORLD.
WHAT'D YOU THINK I'D BE DOING?
OH, FER THE LUVVA MIKE! LOOK, JUST STRAP EVERYBODY IN, KID. WE'RE COMIN' IN FER A LANDING!
YOU HEARD THE MAN. I HAVE TO RESTRAIN EACH AND EVERY ONE OF YOU. AND I'VE BEEN AUTHORIZED TO USE STRAPS.
JOHNNY!
KIDS. WHAT'RE YA GONNA DO?
HERE YA GO. WATCH YER STEP. AND REMEMBER, I WANT ALL OF YA TO SEND ME YER INVOICES...
...AND I'LL MAKE SURE YA GET TRIPLE OVERTIME FOR THIS. OKAY?

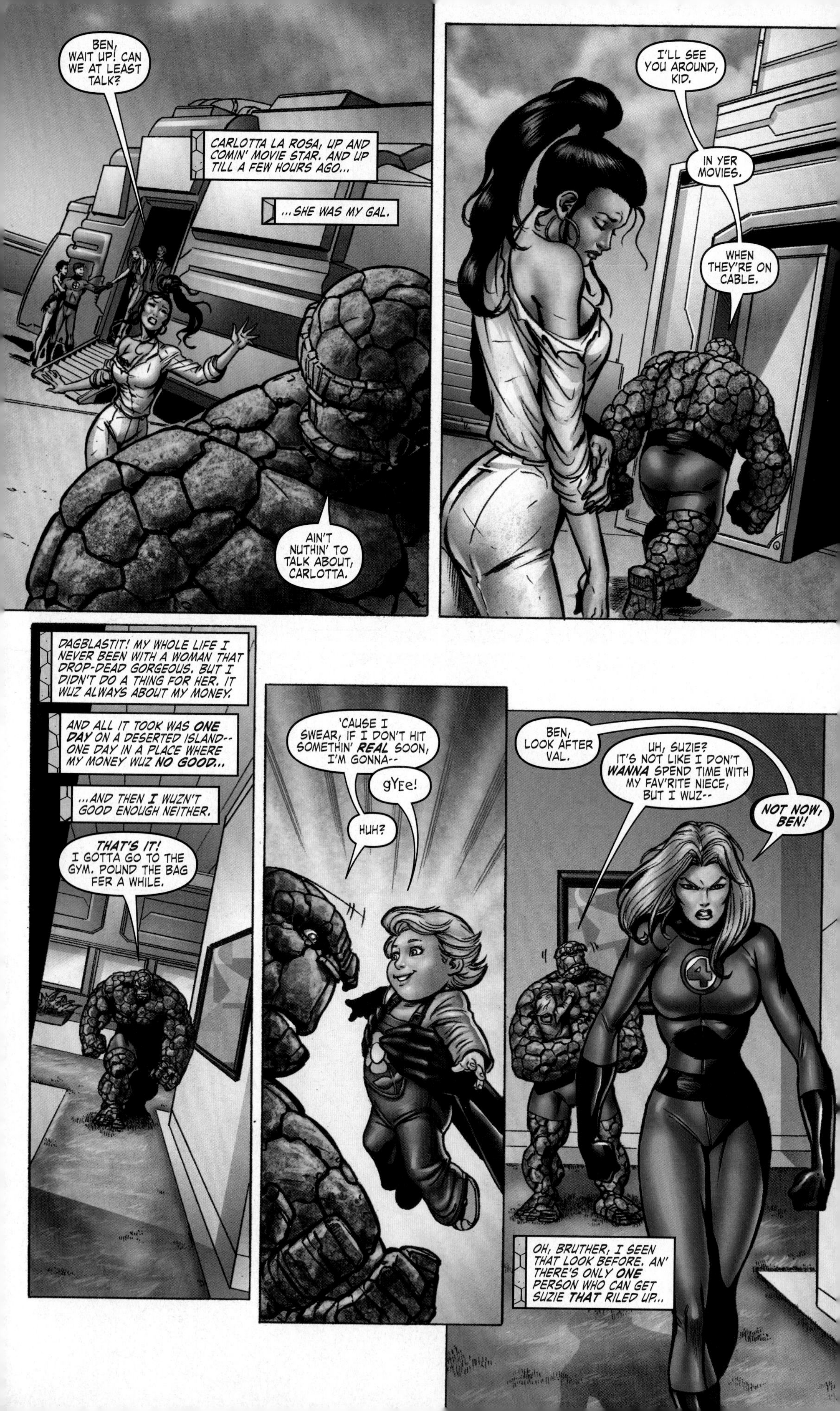
BEN, WAIT UP! CAN WE AT LEAST TALK?
CARLOTTA LA ROSA, UP AND COMIN' MOVIE STAR. AND UP TILL A FEW HOURS AGO...
...SHE WAS MY GAL.
AIN'T NUTHIN' TO TALK ABOUT, CARLOTTA.
I'LL SEE YOU AROUND, KID.
IN YER MOVIES.
WHEN THEY'RE ON CABLE.
DAGBLASTIT! MY WHOLE LIFE I NEVER BEEN WITH A WOMAN THAT DROP-DEAD GORGEOUS. BUT I DIDN'T DO A THING FOR HER. IT WUZ ALWAYS ABOUT MY MONEY.
AND ALL IT TOOK WAS ONE DAY ON A DESERTED ISLAND-- ONE DAY IN A PLACE WHERE MY MONEY WUZ NO GOOD...
...AND THEN I WUZN'T GOOD ENOUGH NEITHER.
THAT'S IT! I GOTTA GO TO THE GYM. POUND THE BAG FER A WHILE.
'CAUSE I SWEAR, IF I DON'T HIT SOMETHIN' REAL SOON, I'M GONNA--
gYEe!
HUH?
BEN, LOOK AFTER VAL.
UH, SUZIE? IT'S NOT LIKE I DON'T WANNA SPEND TIME WITH MY FAV'RITE NIECE, BUT I WUZ--
NOT NOW, BEN!
OH, BRUTHER, I SEEN THAT LOOK BEFORE. AN' THERE'S ONLY ONE PERSON WHO CAN GET SUZIE THAT RILED UP...

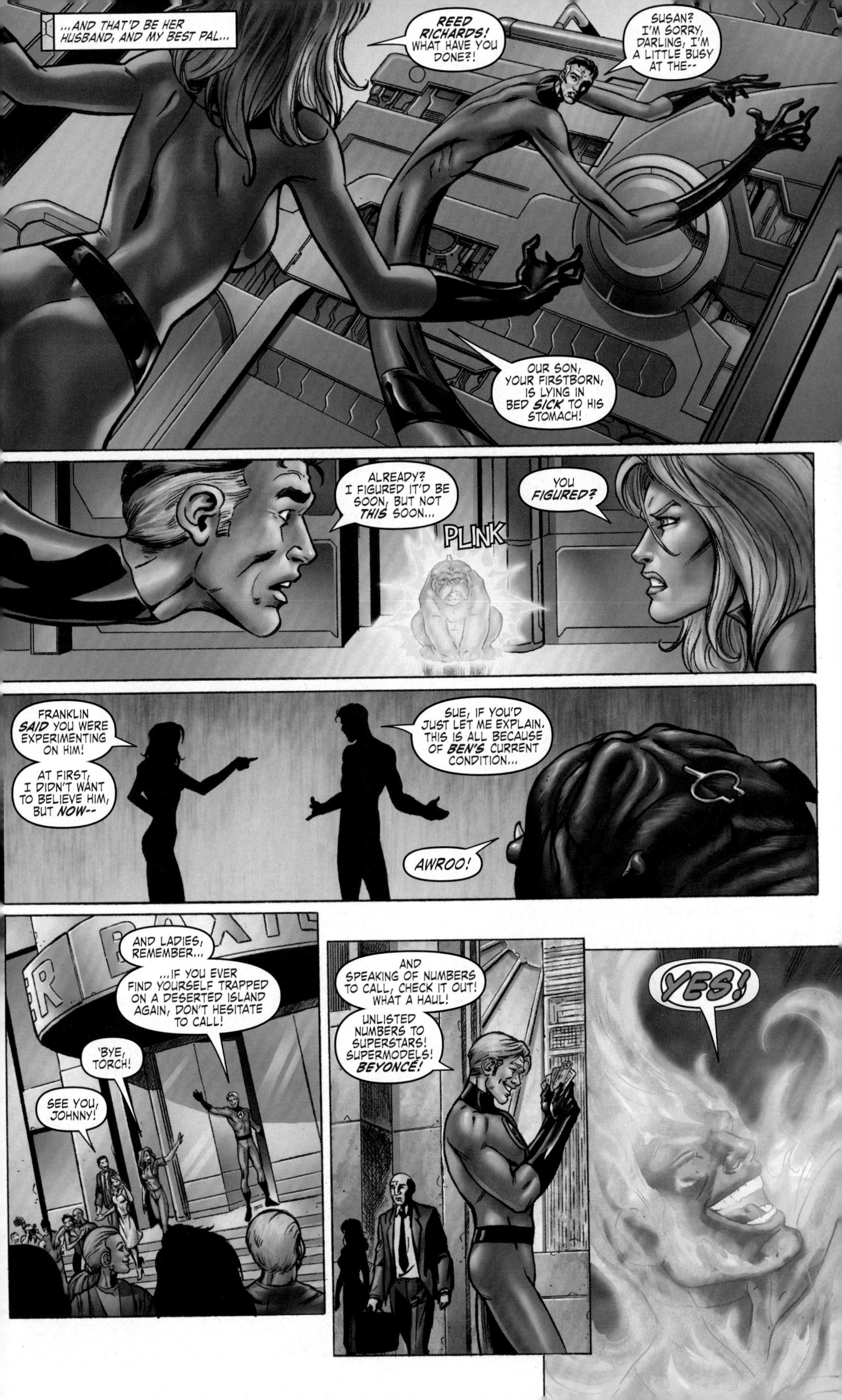
...AND THAT'D BE HER HUSBAND, AND MY BEST PAL...
REED RICHARDS! WHAT HAVE YOU DONE?!
SUSAN? I'M SORRY, DARLING, I'M A LITTLE BUSY AT THE--
OUR SON, YOUR FIRSTBORN, IS LYING IN BED SICK TO HIS STOMACH!
ALREADY? I FIGURED IT'D BE SOON, BUT NOT THIS SOON...
PLINK
YOU FIGURED?
FRANKLIN SAID YOU WERE EXPERIMENTING ON HIM!
AT FIRST, I DIDN'T WANT TO BELIEVE HIM, BUT NOW--
SUE, IF YOU'D JUST LET ME EXPLAIN. THIS IS ALL BECAUSE OF BEN'S CURRENT CONDITION...
AWROO!
AND LADIES, REMEMBER...
...IF YOU EVER FIND YOURSELF TRAPPED ON A DESERTED ISLAND AGAIN, DON'T HESITATE TO CALL!
'BYE, TORCH!
SEE YOU, JOHNNY!
AND SPEAKING OF NUMBERS TO CALL, CHECK IT OUT! WHAT A HAUL!
UNLISTED NUMBERS TO SUPERSTARS! SUPERMODELS! BEYONCÉ!
YES!

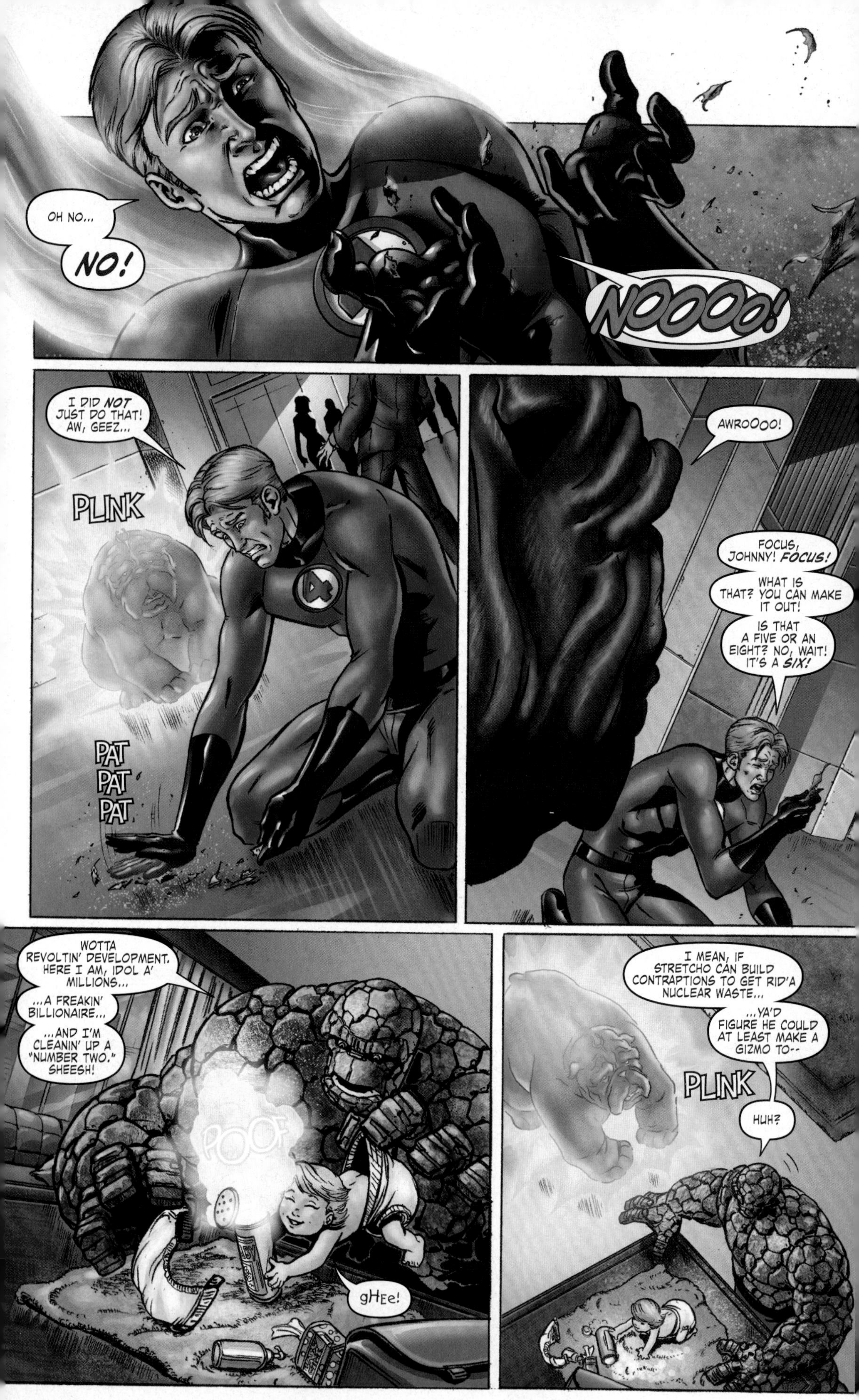

OH NO...
NO!
NOOOOo!
I DID NOT JUST DO THAT! AW, GEEZ...
PLINK
PAT PAT PAT
AWROOOO!
FOCUS, JOHNNY! FOCUS!
WHAT IS THAT? YOU CAN MAKE IT OUT!
IS THAT A FIVE OR AN EIGHT? NO, WAIT! IT'S A SIX!
WOTTA REVOLTIN' DEVELOPMENT. HERE I AM, IDOL A' MILLIONS...
...A FREAKIN' BILLIONAIRE...
...AND I'M CLEANIN' UP A "NUMBER TWO." SHEESH!
POOF
gHEe!
I MEAN, IF STRETCHO CAN BUILD CONTRAPTIONS TO GET RID'A NUCLEAR WASTE...
...YA'D FIGURE HE COULD AT LEAST MAKE A GIZMO TO--
PLINK
HUH?

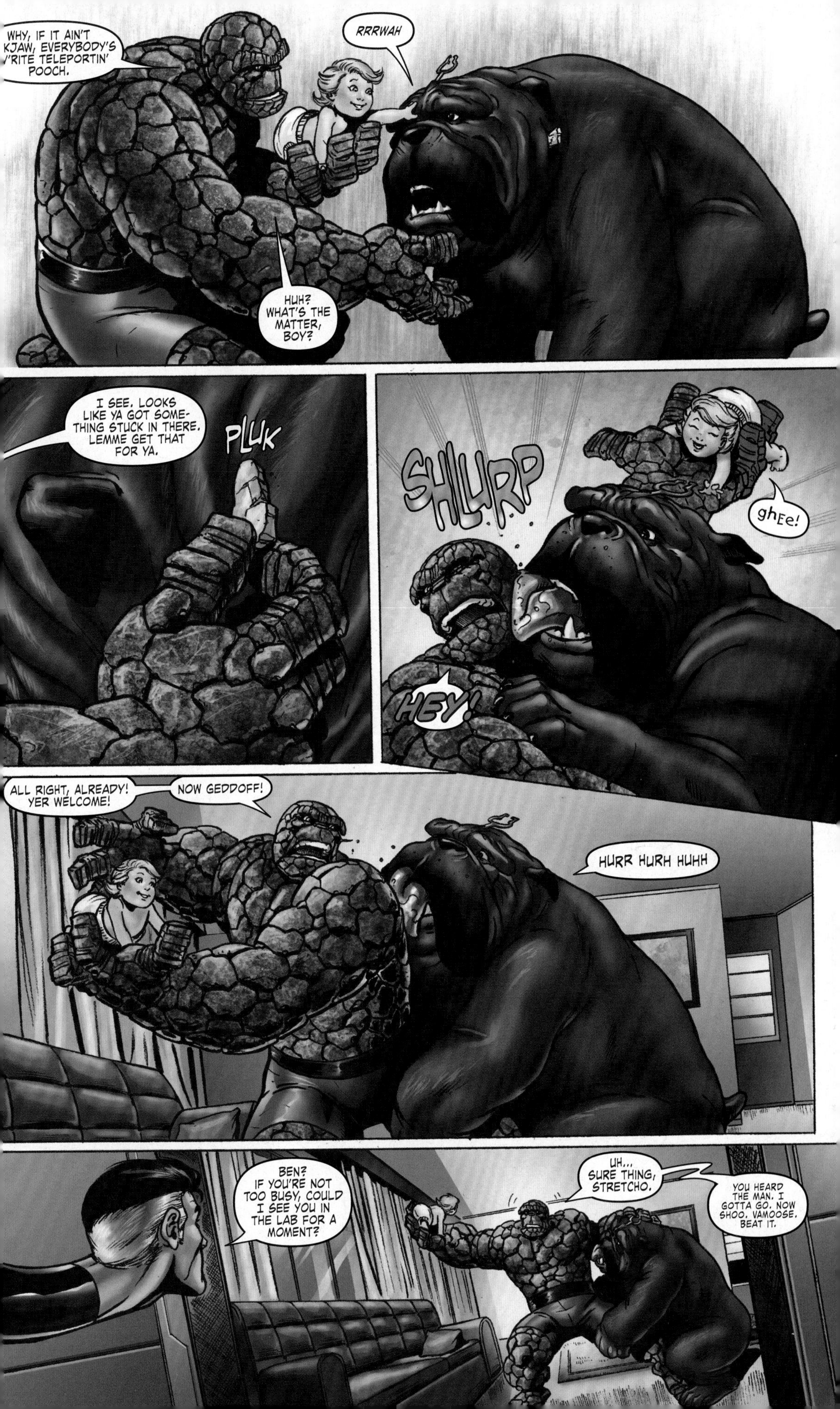
WHY, IF IT AIN'T
KJAW, EVERYBODY'S
'RITE TELEPORTIN'
POOCH.
RRRWAH
HUH? WHAT'S THE MATTER, BOY?
I SEE. LOOKS LIKE YA GOT SOMETHING STUCK IN THERE. LEMME GET THAT FOR YA.
PLUK
SHLURP
ghEe!
HEY!
ALL RIGHT, ALREADY! YER WELCOME!
NOW GEDDOFF!
HURR HURH HUHH
BEN? IF YOU'RE NOT TOO BUSY, COULD I SEE YOU IN THE LAB FOR A MOMENT?
UH... SURE THING, STRETCHO.
YOU HEARD THE MAN. I GOTTA GO. NOW SHOO. VAMOOSE. BEAT IT.

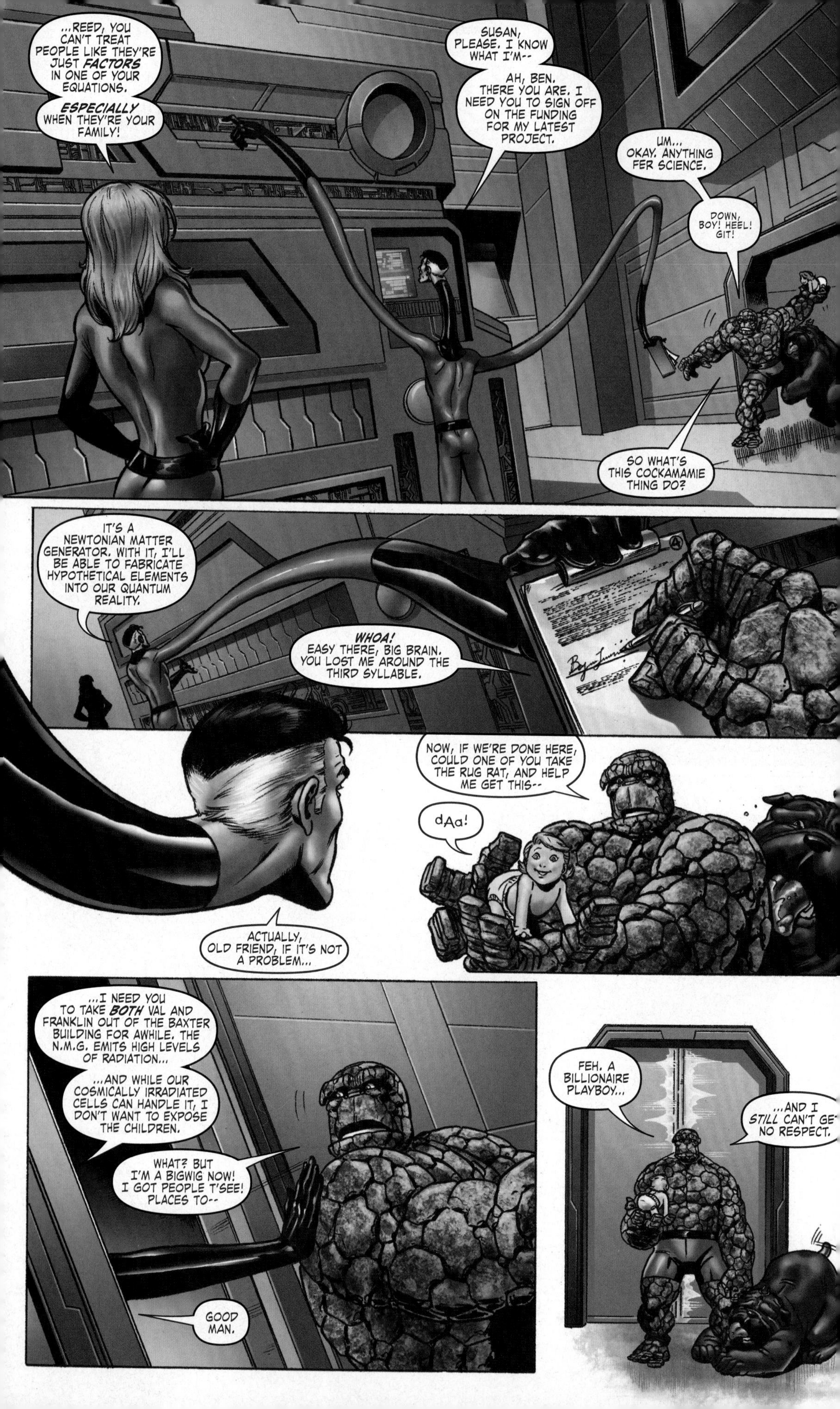
...REED, YOU CAN'T TREAT PEOPLE LIKE THEY'RE JUST *FACTORS* IN ONE OF YOUR EQUATIONS.
ESPECIALLY WHEN THEY'RE YOUR FAMILY!
SUSAN, PLEASE. I KNOW WHAT I'M--
AH, BEN. THERE YOU ARE. I NEED YOU TO SIGN OFF ON THE FUNDING FOR MY LATEST PROJECT.
UM... OKAY. ANYTHING FER SCIENCE.
DOWN, BOY! HEEL! GIT!
SO WHAT'S THIS COCKAMAMIE THING DO?
IT'S A NEWTONIAN MATTER GENERATOR. WITH IT, I'LL BE ABLE TO FABRICATE HYPOTHETICAL ELEMENTS INTO OUR QUANTUM REALITY.
WHOA! EASY THERE, BIG BRAIN. YOU LOST ME AROUND THE THIRD SYLLABLE.
NOW, IF WE'RE DONE HERE, COULD ONE OF YOU TAKE THE RUG RAT, AND HELP ME GET THIS--
dAa!
ACTUALLY, OLD FRIEND, IF IT'S NOT A PROBLEM...
...I NEED YOU TO TAKE *BOTH* VAL AND FRANKLIN OUT OF THE BAXTER BUILDING FOR AWHILE. THE N.M.G. EMITS HIGH LEVELS OF RADIATION...
...AND WHILE OUR COSMICALLY IRRADIATED CELLS CAN HANDLE IT, I DON'T WANT TO EXPOSE THE CHILDREN.
WHAT? BUT I'M A BIGWIG NOW! I GOT PEOPLE T'SEE! PLACES TO--
GOOD MAN.
FEH. A BILLIONAIRE PLAYBOY...
...AND I *STILL* CAN'T GE NO RESPECT.

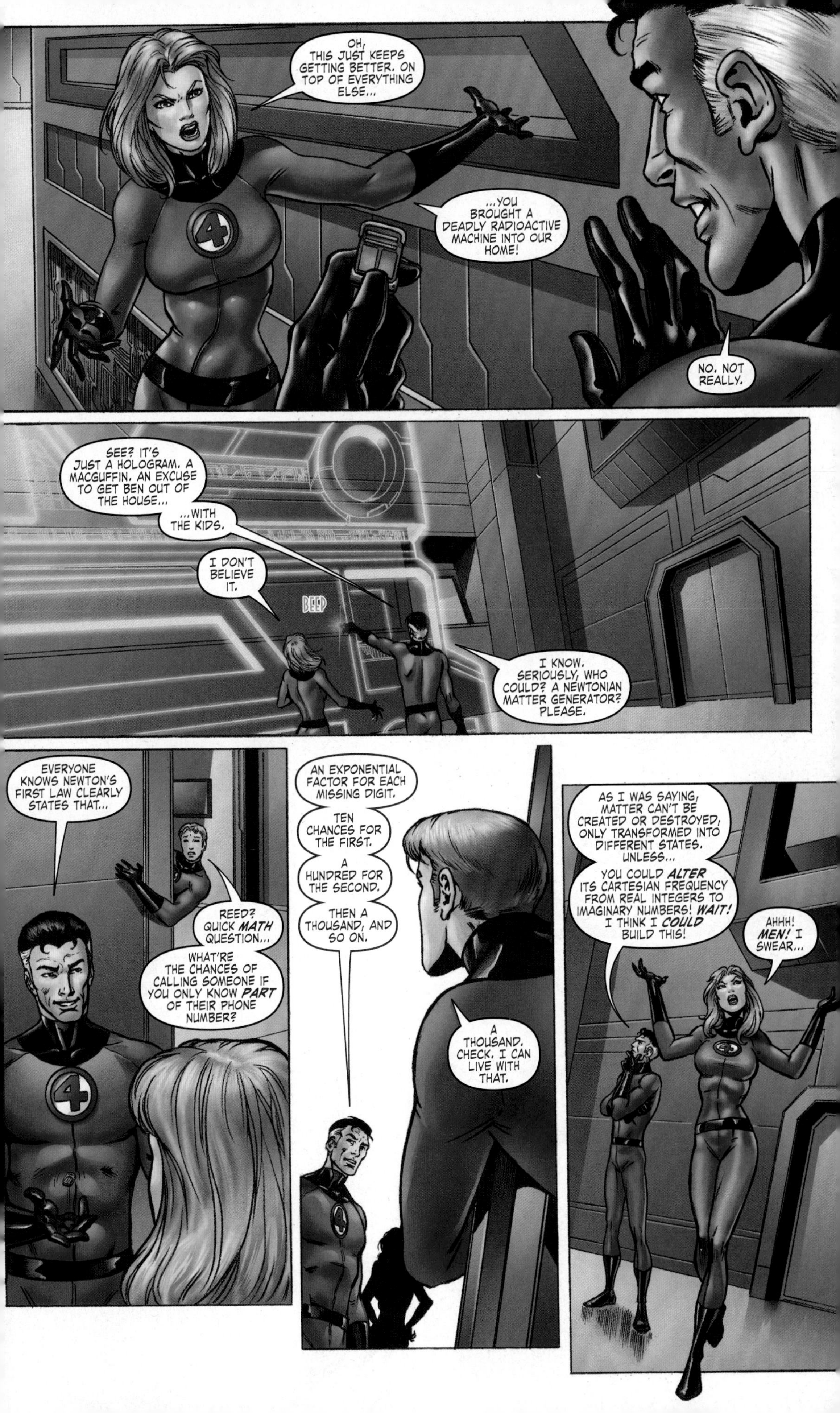
OH, THIS JUST KEEPS GETTING BETTER. ON TOP OF EVERYTHING ELSE...
...YOU BROUGHT A DEADLY RADIOACTIVE MACHINE INTO OUR HOME!
NO. NOT REALLY.
SEE? IT'S JUST A HOLOGRAM. A MACGUFFIN. AN EXCUSE TO GET BEN OUT OF THE HOUSE...
...WITH THE KIDS.
I DON'T BELIEVE IT.
BEEP
I KNOW. SERIOUSLY, WHO COULD? A NEWTONIAN MATTER GENERATOR? PLEASE.
EVERYONE KNOWS NEWTON'S FIRST LAW CLEARLY STATES THAT...
REED? QUICK MATH QUESTION...
WHAT'RE THE CHANCES OF CALLING SOMEONE IF YOU ONLY KNOW PART OF THEIR PHONE NUMBER?
AN EXPONENTIAL FACTOR FOR EACH MISSING DIGIT.
TEN CHANCES FOR THE FIRST.
A HUNDRED FOR THE SECOND.
THEN A THOUSAND, AND SO ON.
A THOUSAND. CHECK. I CAN LIVE WITH THAT.
AS I WAS SAYING, MATTER CAN'T BE CREATED OR DESTROYED, ONLY TRANSFORMED INTO DIFFERENT STATES. UNLESS...
YOU COULD ALTER ITS CARTESIAN FREQUENCY FROM REAL INTEGERS TO IMAGINARY NUMBERS! WAIT! I THINK I COULD BUILD THIS!
AHHH! MEN! I SWEAR...

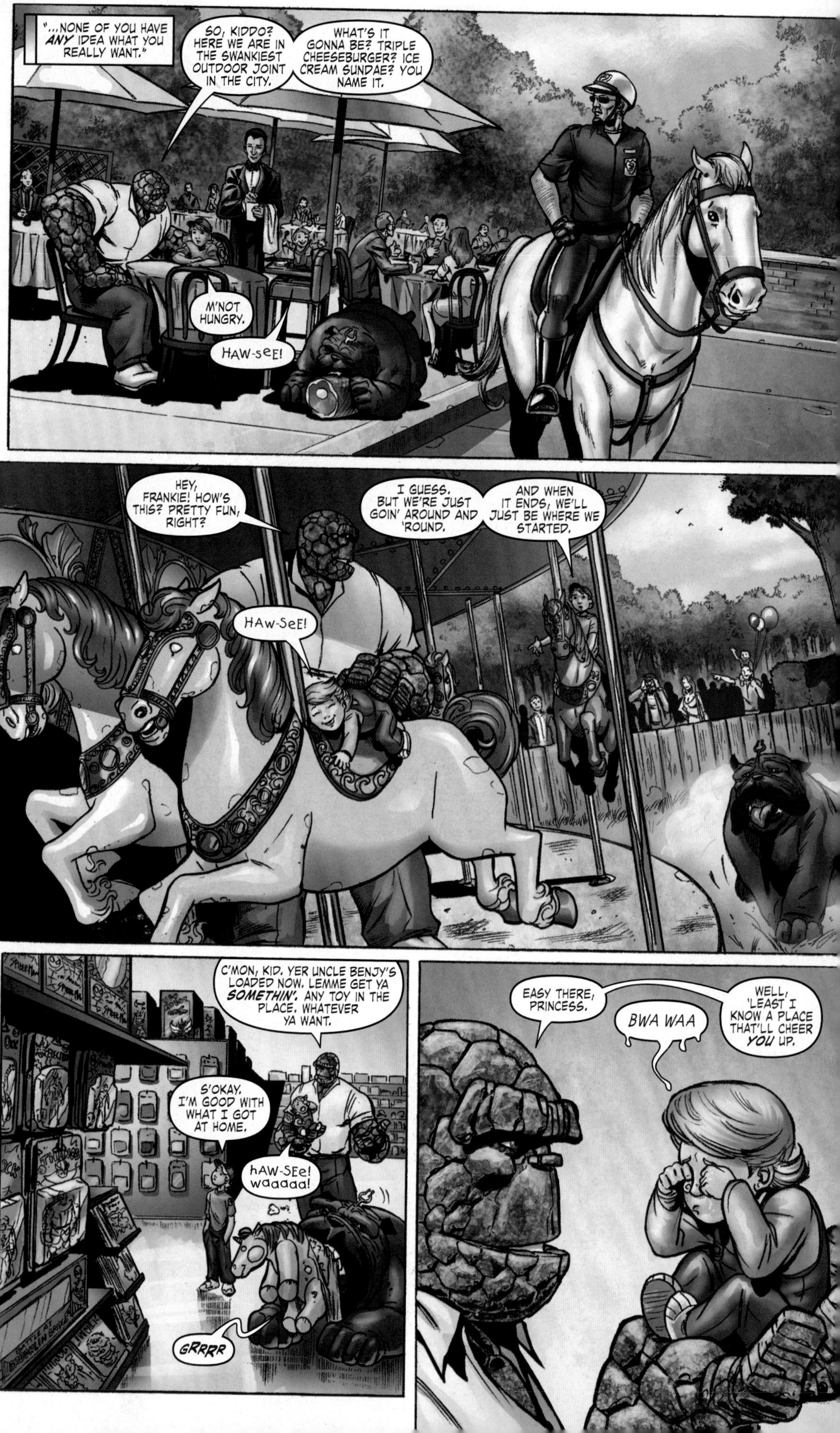
"...NONE OF YOU HAVE *ANY* IDEA WHAT YOU REALLY WANT."
SO, KIDDO? HERE WE ARE IN THE SWANKIEST OUTDOOR JOINT IN THE CITY.
WHAT'S IT GONNA BE? TRIPLE CHEESEBURGER? ICE CREAM SUNDAE? YOU NAME IT.
M'NOT HUNGRY.
HAW-SEE!
HEY, FRANKIE! HOW'S THIS? PRETTY FUN, RIGHT?
I GUESS. BUT WE'RE JUST GOIN' AROUND AND 'ROUND.
AND WHEN IT ENDS, WE'LL JUST BE WHERE WE STARTED.
HAW-SEE!
C'MON, KID. YER UNCLE BENJY'S LOADED NOW. LEMME GET YA *SOMETHIN'*. ANY TOY IN THE PLACE. WHATEVER YA WANT.
S'OKAY. I'M GOOD WITH WHAT I GOT AT HOME.
HAW-SEE! waaaaa!
GRRRR
EASY THERE, PRINCESS.
BWA WAA
WELL, 'LEAST I KNOW A PLACE THAT'LL CHEER *YOU* UP.

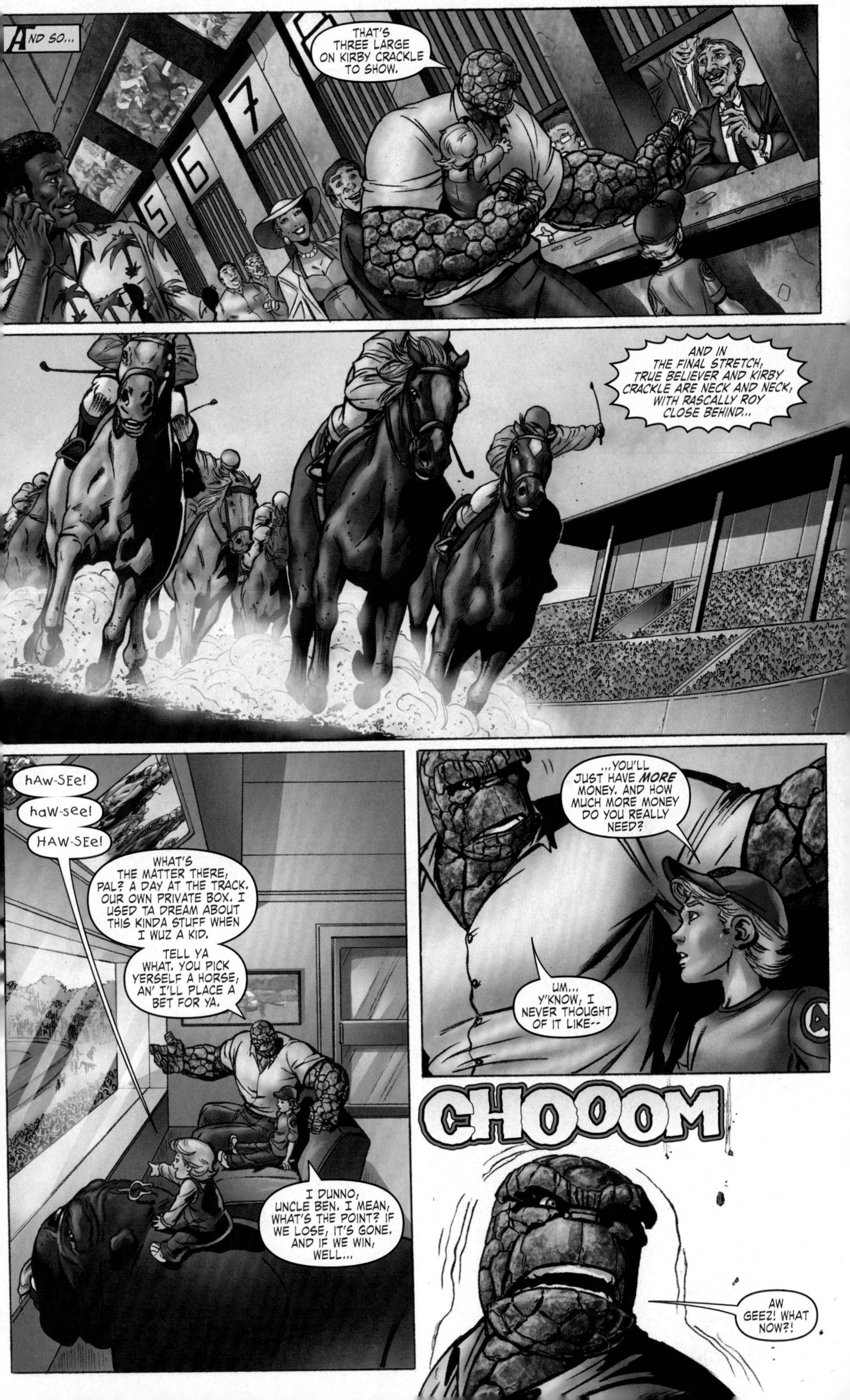
AND SO...
THAT'S THREE LARGE ON KIRBY CRACKLE TO SHOW.
AND IN THE FINAL STRETCH, TRUE BELIEVER AND KIRBY CRACKLE ARE NECK AND NECK, WITH RASCALLY ROY CLOSE BEHIND...
hAW-SEe!
haW-see!
HAW-SEe!
WHAT'S THE MATTER THERE, PAL? A DAY AT THE TRACK. OUR OWN PRIVATE BOX. I USED TA DREAM ABOUT THIS KINDA STUFF WHEN I WUZ A KID.
TELL YA WHAT. YOU PICK YERSELF A HORSE, AN' I'LL PLACE A BET FOR YA.
I DUNNO, UNCLE BEN. I MEAN, WHAT'S THE POINT? IF WE LOSE, IT'S GONE. AND IF WE WIN, WELL...
...YOU'LL JUST HAVE MORE MONEY. AND HOW MUCH MORE MONEY DO YOU REALLY NEED?
UM... Y'KNOW, I NEVER THOUGHT OF IT LIKE--
CHOOOM
AW GEEZ! WHAT NOW?!

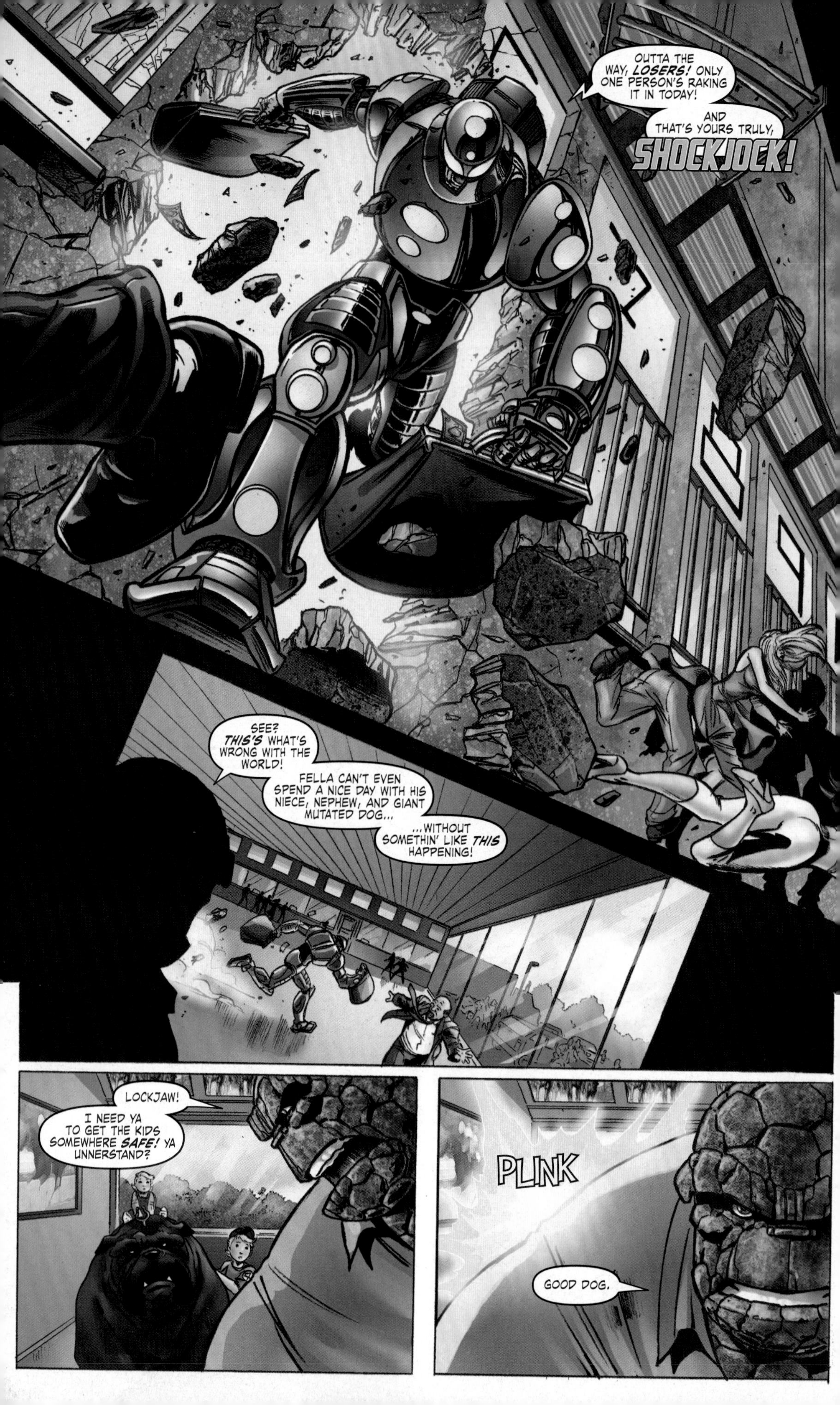

OUTTA THE WAY, LOSERS! ONLY ONE PERSON'S RAKING IT IN TODAY!
AND THAT'S YOURS TRULY,
SHOCKJOCK!
SEE? THIS'S WHAT'S WRONG WITH THE WORLD!
FELLA CAN'T EVEN SPEND A NICE DAY WITH HIS NIECE, NEPHEW, AND GIANT MUTATED DOG...
...WITHOUT SOMETHIN' LIKE THIS HAPPENING!
LOCKJAW!
I NEED YA TO GET THE KIDS SOMEWHERE SAFE! YA UNNERSTAND?
PLINK
GOOD DOG.

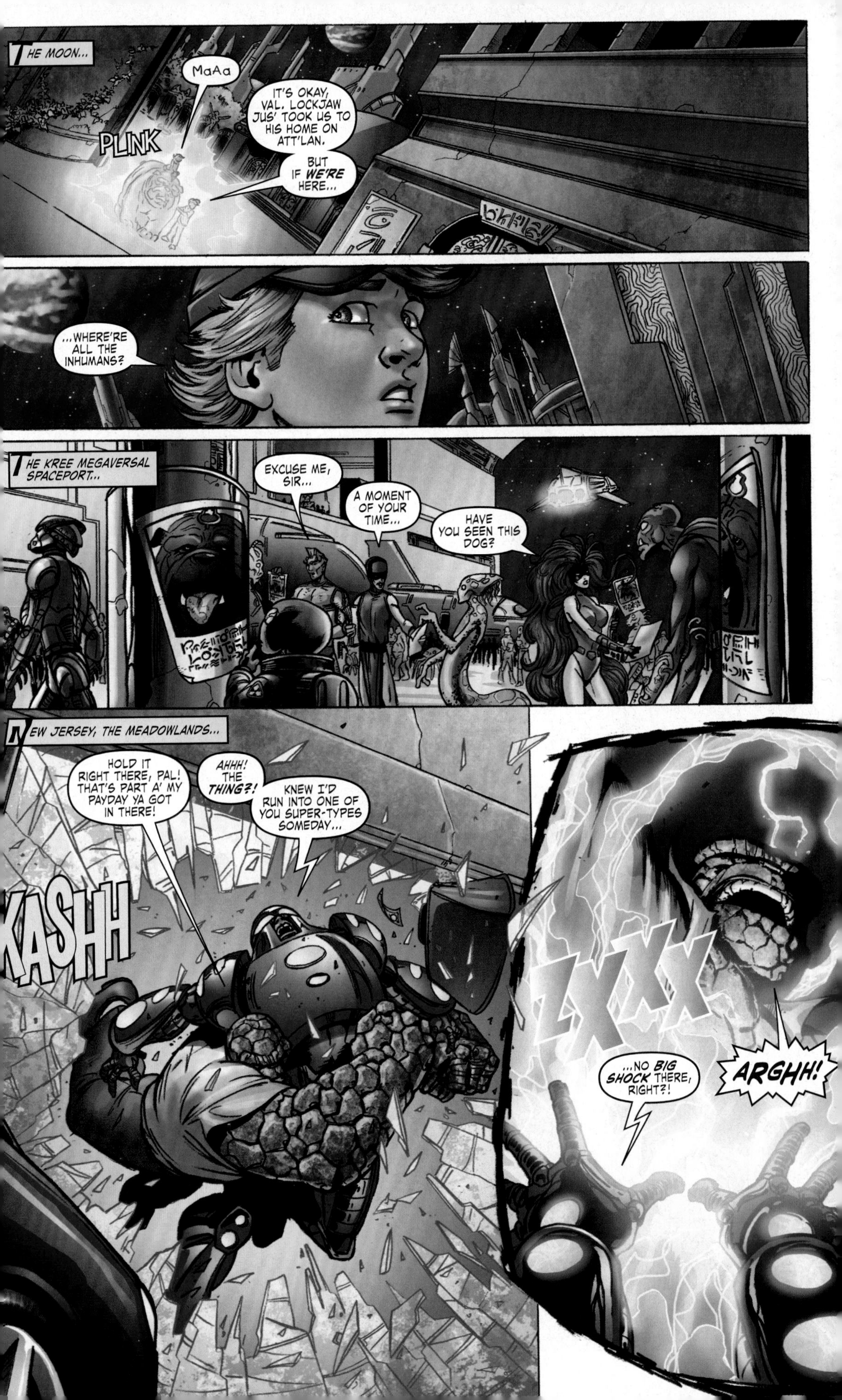
THE MOON...
MaAa
PLINK
IT'S OKAY, VAL. LOCKJAW JUS' TOOK US TO HIS HOME ON ATT'LAN.
BUT IF WE'RE HERE...
...WHERE'RE ALL THE INHUMANS?
THE KREE MEGAVERSAL SPACEPORT...
EXCUSE ME, SIR...
A MOMENT OF YOUR TIME...
HAVE YOU SEEN THIS DOG?
NEW JERSEY, THE MEADOWLANDS...
HOLD IT RIGHT THERE, PAL! THAT'S PART A' MY PAYDAY YA GOT IN THERE!
AHHH! THE THING?!
KNEW I'D RUN INTO ONE OF YOU SUPER-TYPES SOMEDAY...
KASHH
ZXXX
...NO BIG SHOCK THERE, RIGHT?!
ARGHH!

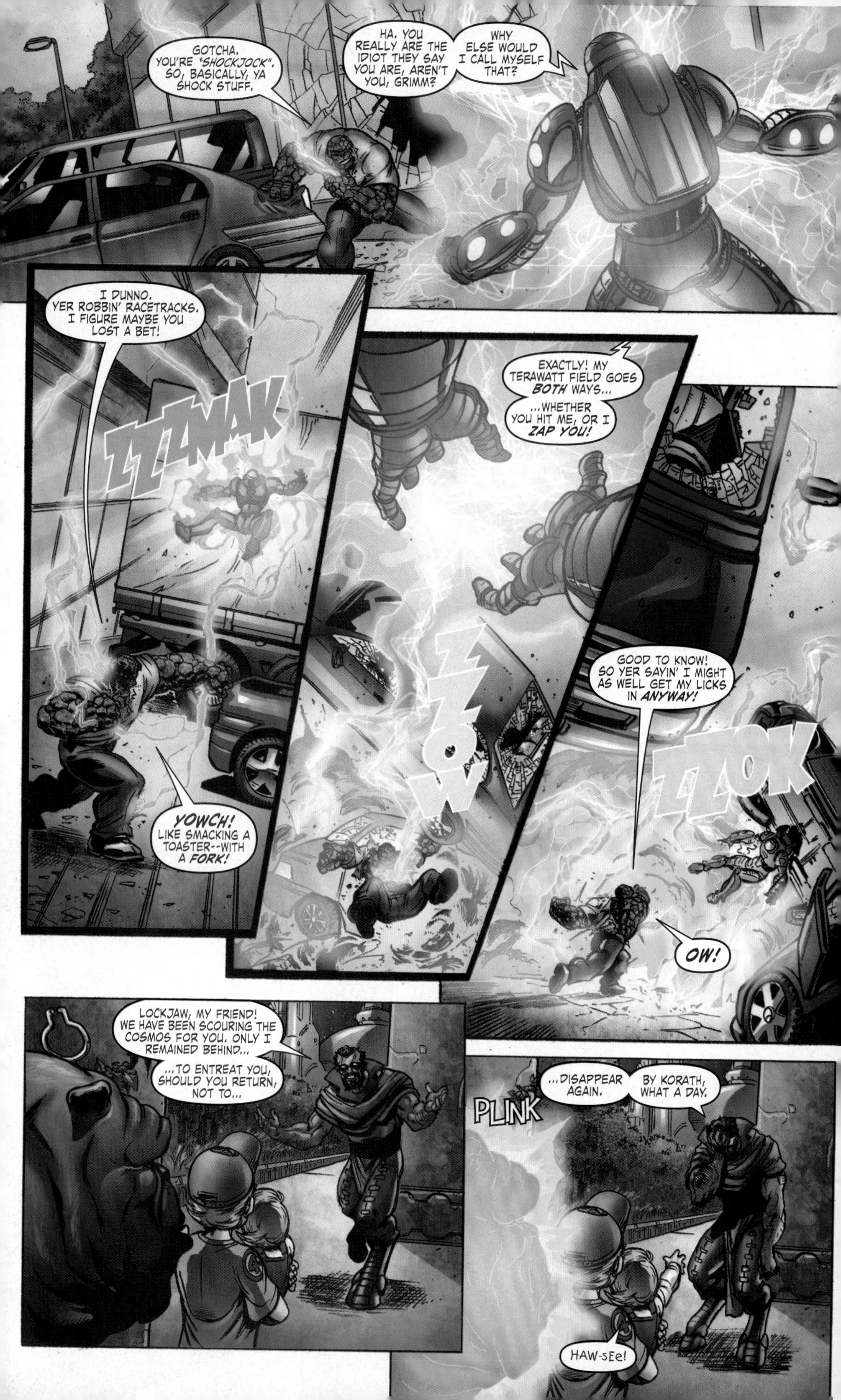
GOTCHA. YOU'RE "SHOCKJOCK". SO, BASICALLY, YA SHOCK STUFF.
HA. YOU REALLY ARE THE IDIOT THEY SAY YOU ARE, AREN'T YOU, GRIMM?
WHY ELSE WOULD I CALL MYSELF THAT?
I DUNNO. YER ROBBIN' RACETRACKS. I FIGURE MAYBE YOU LOST A BET!
TZZMAK
YOWCH! LIKE SMACKING A TOASTER--WITH A FORK!
EXACTLY! MY TERAWATT FIELD GOES BOTH WAYS...
...WHETHER YOU HIT ME, OR I ZAP YOU!
ZZOW
GOOD TO KNOW! SO YER SAYIN' I MIGHT AS WELL GET MY LICKS IN ANYWAY!
TZOK
OW!
LOCKJAW, MY FRIEND! WE HAVE BEEN SCOURING THE COSMOS FOR YOU. ONLY I REMAINED BEHIND...
...TO ENTREAT YOU, SHOULD YOU RETURN, NOT TO...
PLINK
...DISAPPEAR AGAIN.
BY KORATH, WHAT A DAY.
HAW-SEE!

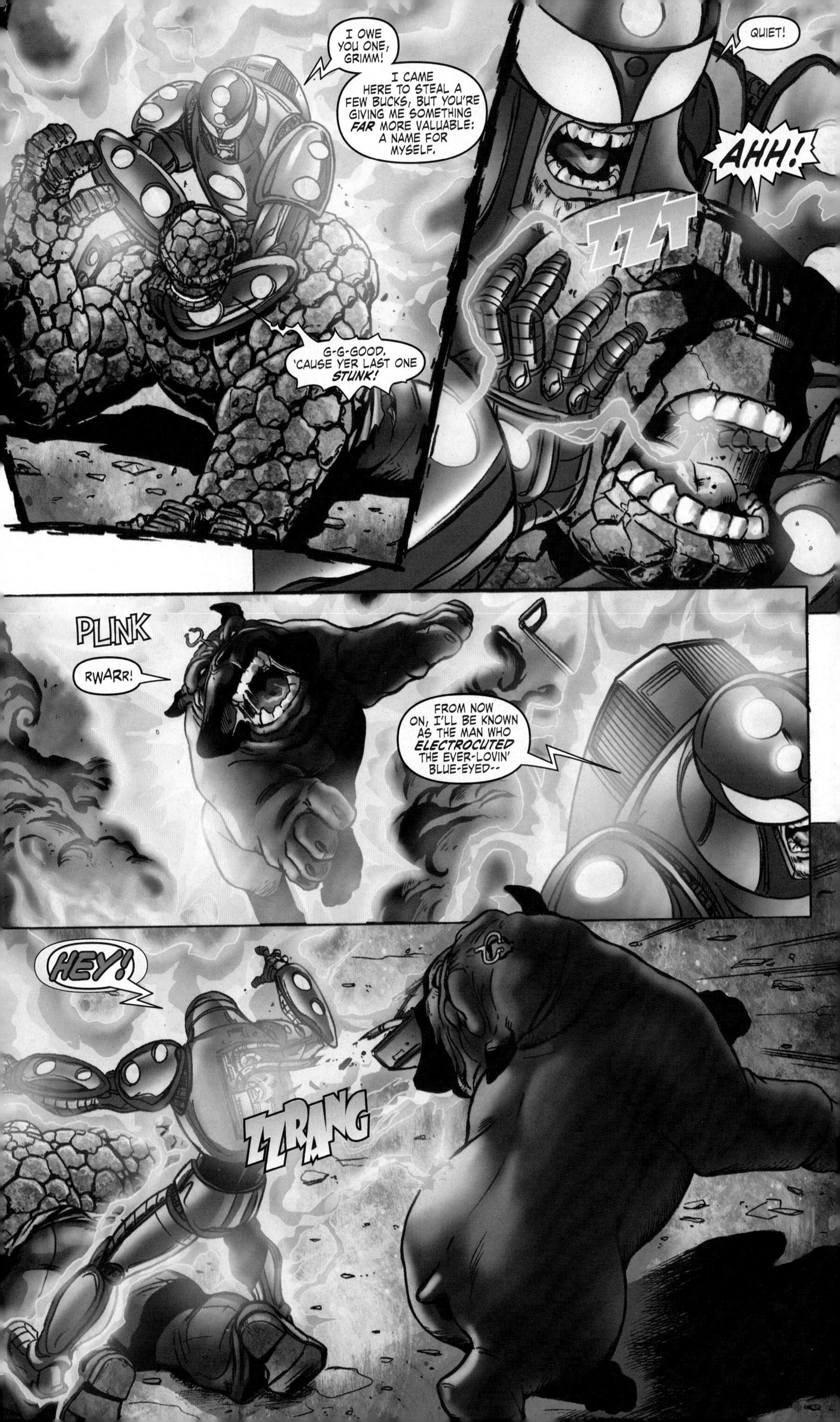

I OWE YOU ONE, GRIMM!
I CAME HERE TO STEAL A FEW BUCKS, BUT YOU'RE GIVING ME SOMETHING FAR MORE VALUABLE: A NAME FOR MYSELF.
G-G-GOOD. 'CAUSE YER LAST ONE STUNK!
QUIET!
AHH!
ZZT
PLINK
RWARR!
FROM NOW ON, I'LL BE KNOWN AS THE MAN WHO ELECTROCUTED THE EVER-LOVIN' BLUE-EYED--
HEY!
ZZRANG

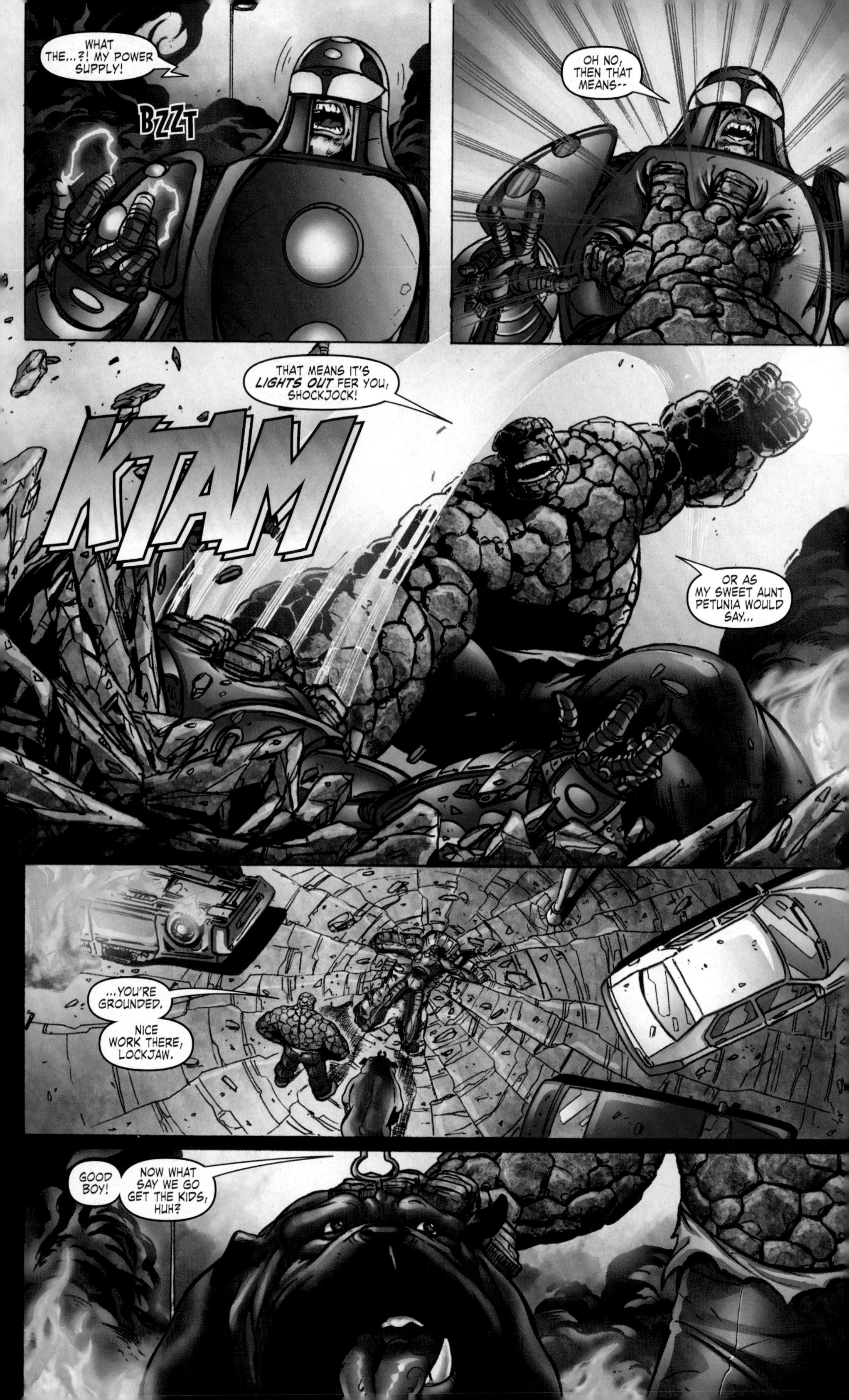
WHAT THE...?! MY POWER SUPPLY!
BZZT
OH NO, THEN THAT MEANS--
THAT MEANS IT'S *LIGHTS OUT* FER YOU, SHOCKJOCK!
KTAM
OR AS MY SWEET AUNT PETUNIA WOULD SAY...
...YOU'RE GROUNDED.
NICE WORK THERE, LOCKJAW.
GOOD BOY!
NOW WHAT SAY WE GO GET THE KIDS, HUH?

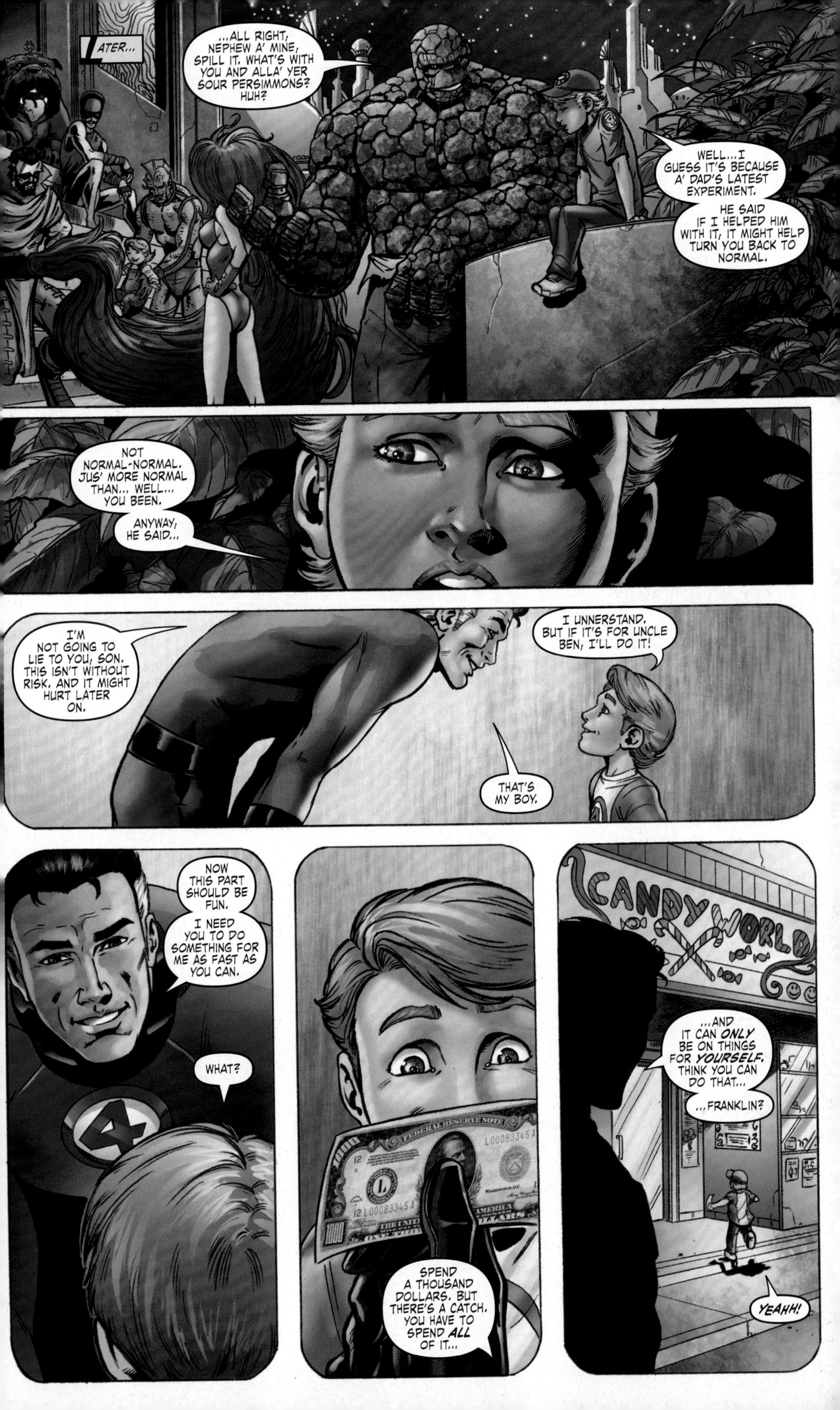
LATER...
...ALL RIGHT, NEPHEW A' MINE, SPILL IT. WHAT'S WITH YOU AND ALLA' YER SOUR PERSIMMONS? HUH?
WELL...I GUESS IT'S BECAUSE A' DAD'S LATEST EXPERIMENT.
HE SAID IF I HELPED HIM WITH IT, IT MIGHT HELP TURN YOU BACK TO NORMAL.
NOT NORMAL-NORMAL. JUS' MORE NORMAL THAN... WELL... YOU BEEN.
ANYWAY, HE SAID...
I'M NOT GOING TO LIE TO YOU, SON. THIS ISN'T WITHOUT RISK. AND IT MIGHT HURT LATER ON.
I UNNERSTAND. BUT IF IT'S FOR UNCLE BEN, I'LL DO IT!
THAT'S MY BOY.
NOW THIS PART SHOULD BE FUN.
I NEED YOU TO DO SOMETHING FOR ME AS FAST AS YOU CAN.
WHAT?
SPEND A THOUSAND DOLLARS. BUT THERE'S A CATCH. YOU HAVE TO SPEND ALL OF IT...
CANDY WORLD
...AND IT CAN ONLY BE ON THINGS FOR YOURSELF. THINK YOU CAN DO THAT...
...FRANKLIN?
YEAHH!

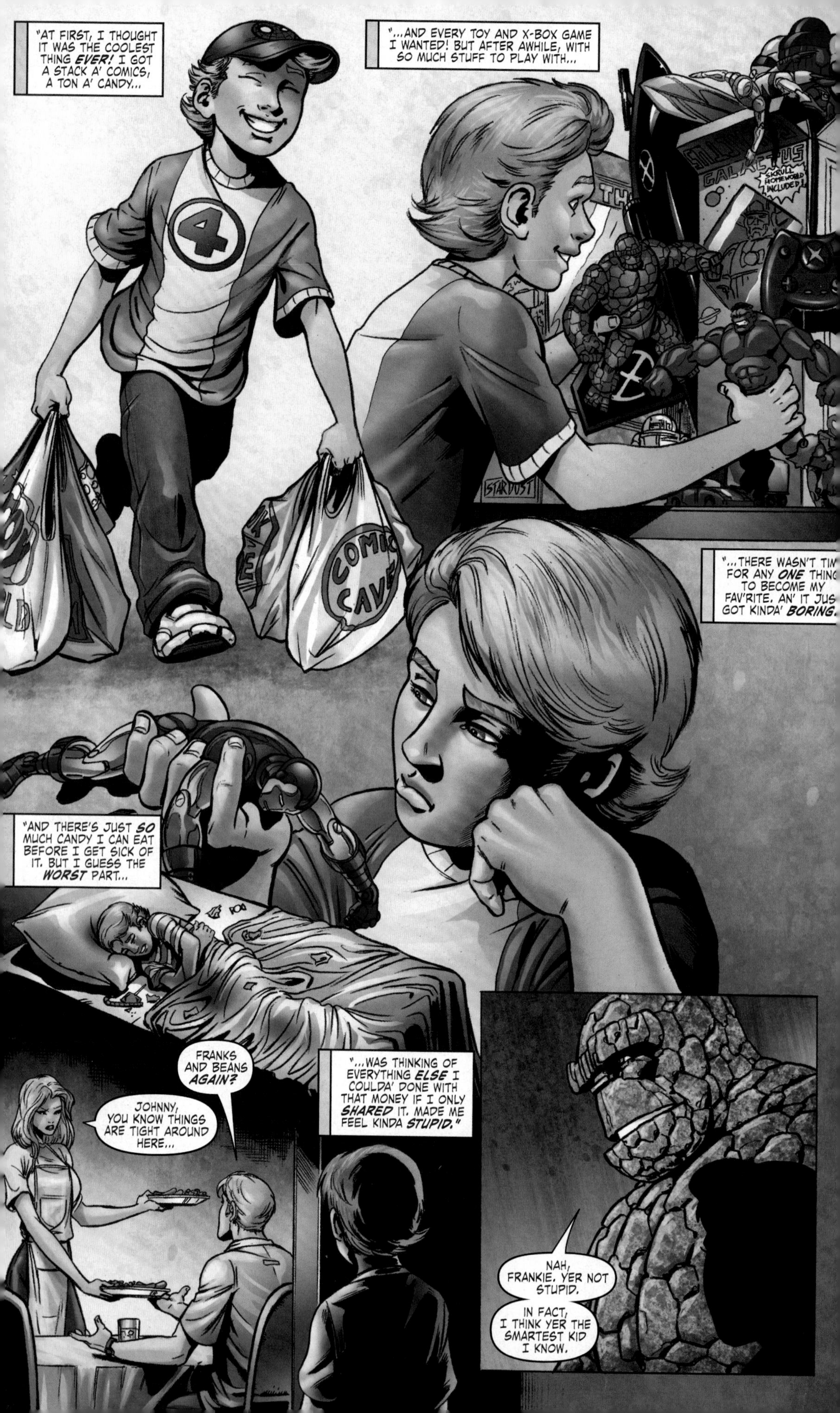
"AT FIRST, I THOUGHT IT WAS THE COOLEST THING EVER! I GOT A STACK A' COMICS, A TON A' CANDY...
"...AND EVERY TOY AND X-BOX GAME I WANTED! BUT AFTER AWHILE, WITH SO MUCH STUFF TO PLAY WITH...
GALACTUS
SKRULL HOMEWORLD INCLUDED!
STARDUST
COMIC CAVE
"...THERE WASN'T TIM FOR ANY ONE THING TO BECOME MY FAV'RITE. AN' IT JUS GOT KINDA' BORING.
"AND THERE'S JUST SO MUCH CANDY I CAN EAT BEFORE I GET SICK OF IT. BUT I GUESS THE WORST PART...
FRANKS AND BEANS AGAIN?
JOHNNY, YOU KNOW THINGS ARE TIGHT AROUND HERE...
"...WAS THINKING OF EVERYTHING ELSE I COULDA' DONE WITH THAT MONEY IF I ONLY SHARED IT. MADE ME FEEL KINDA STUPID."
NAH, FRANKIE. YER NOT STUPID.
IN FACT, I THINK YER THE SMARTEST KID I KNOW.

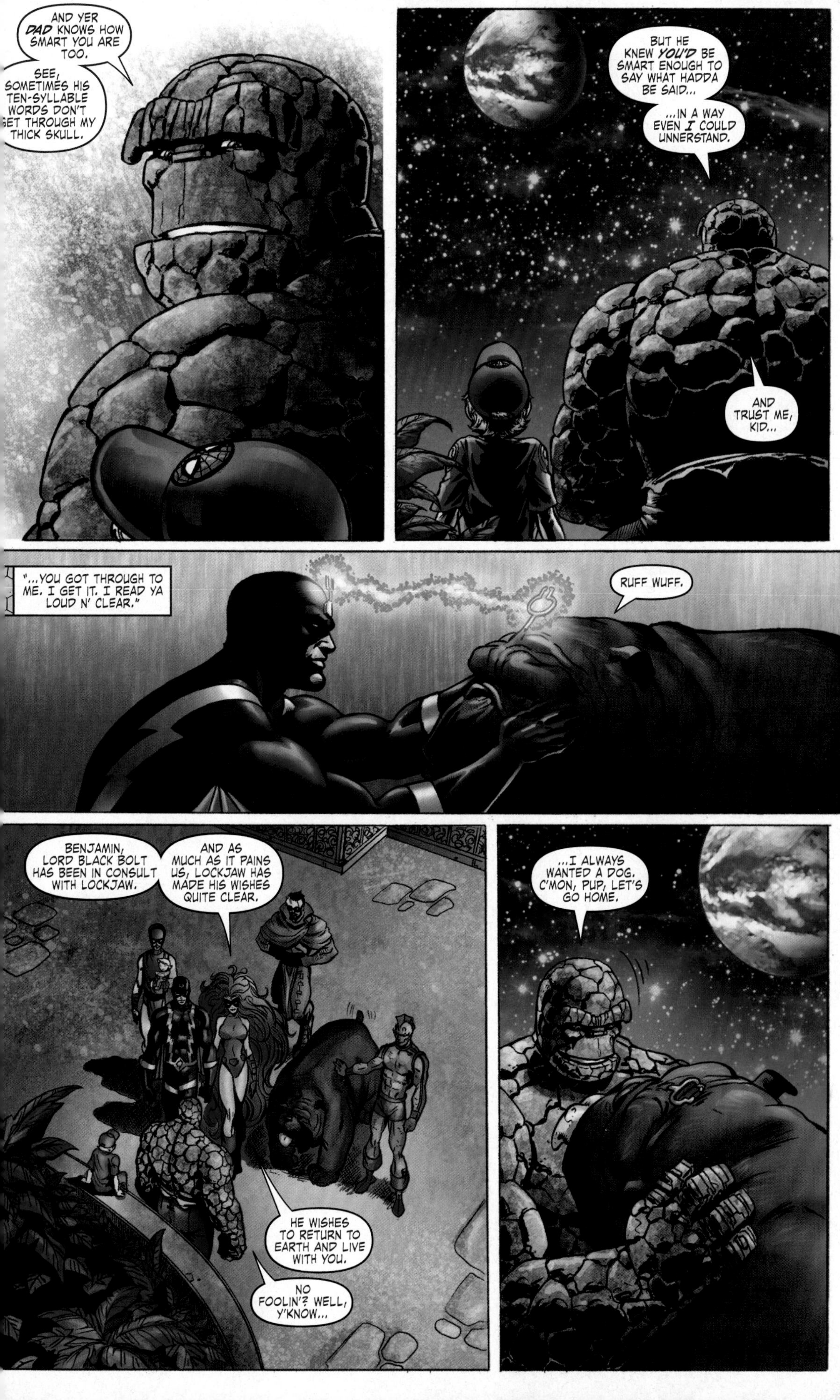
AND YER DAD KNOWS HOW SMART YOU ARE TOO.
SEE, SOMETIMES HIS TEN-SYLLABLE WORDS DON'T GET THROUGH MY THICK SKULL.
BUT HE KNEW YOU'D BE SMART ENOUGH TO SAY WHAT HADDA BE SAID...
...IN A WAY EVEN I COULD UNNERSTAND.
AND TRUST ME, KID...
"...YOU GOT THROUGH TO ME. I GET IT. I READ YA LOUD N' CLEAR."
RUFF WUFF.
BENJAMIN, LORD BLACK BOLT HAS BEEN IN CONSULT WITH LOCKJAW.
AND AS MUCH AS IT PAINS US, LOCKJAW HAS MADE HIS WISHES QUITE CLEAR.
HE WISHES TO RETURN TO EARTH AND LIVE WITH YOU.
NO FOOLIN'? WELL, Y'KNOW...
...I ALWAYS WANTED A DOG. C'MON, PUP, LET'S GO HOME.

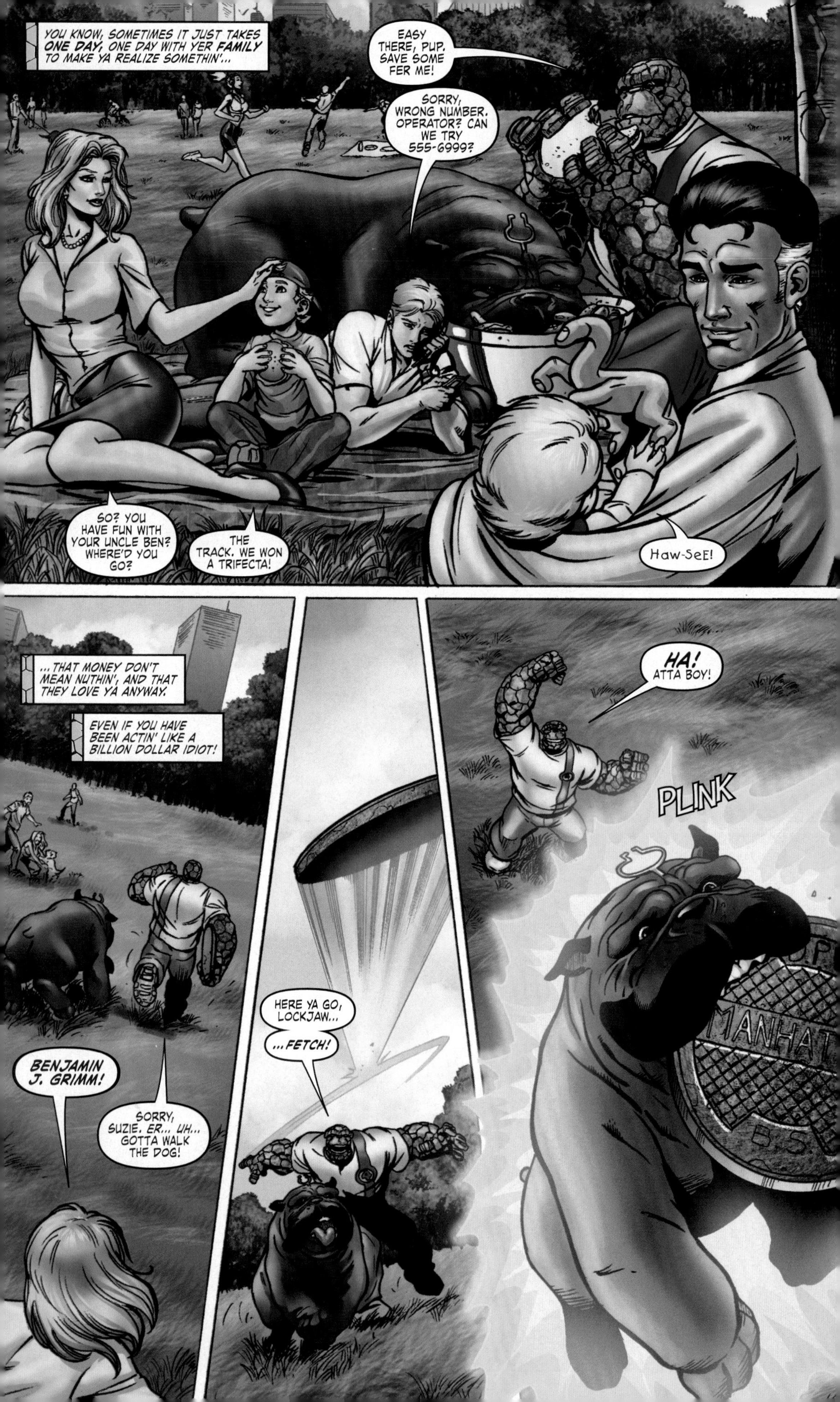

YOU KNOW, SOMETIMES IT JUST TAKES ONE DAY, ONE DAY WITH YER FAMILY TO MAKE YA REALIZE SOMETHIN'...
EASY THERE, PUP. SAVE SOME FER ME!
SORRY, WRONG NUMBER. OPERATOR? CAN WE TRY 555-6999?
SO? YOU HAVE FUN WITH YOUR UNCLE BEN? WHERE'D YOU GO?
THE TRACK. WE WON A TRIFECTA!
Haw-SeE!
...THAT MONEY DON'T MEAN NUTHIN', AND THAT THEY LOVE YA ANYWAY.
EVEN IF YOU HAVE BEEN ACTIN' LIKE A BILLION DOLLAR IDIOT!
BENJAMIN J. GRIMM!
SORRY, SUZIE. ER... UH... GOTTA WALK THE DOG!
HERE YA GO, LOCKJAW...
...FETCH!
HA! ATTA BOY!
PLINK

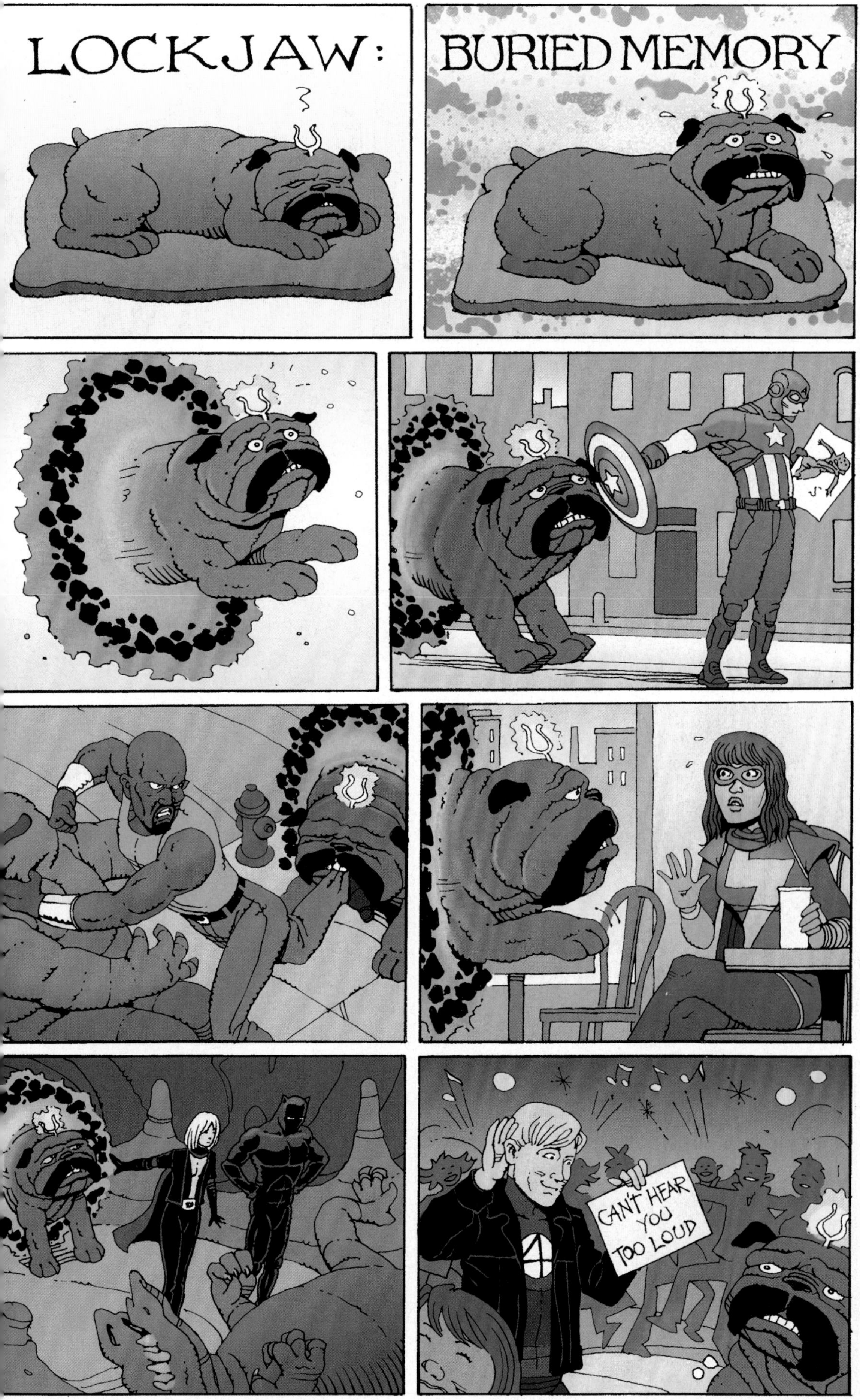
LOCKJAW: BURIED MEMORY
CAN'T HEAR
YOU
TOO LOUD

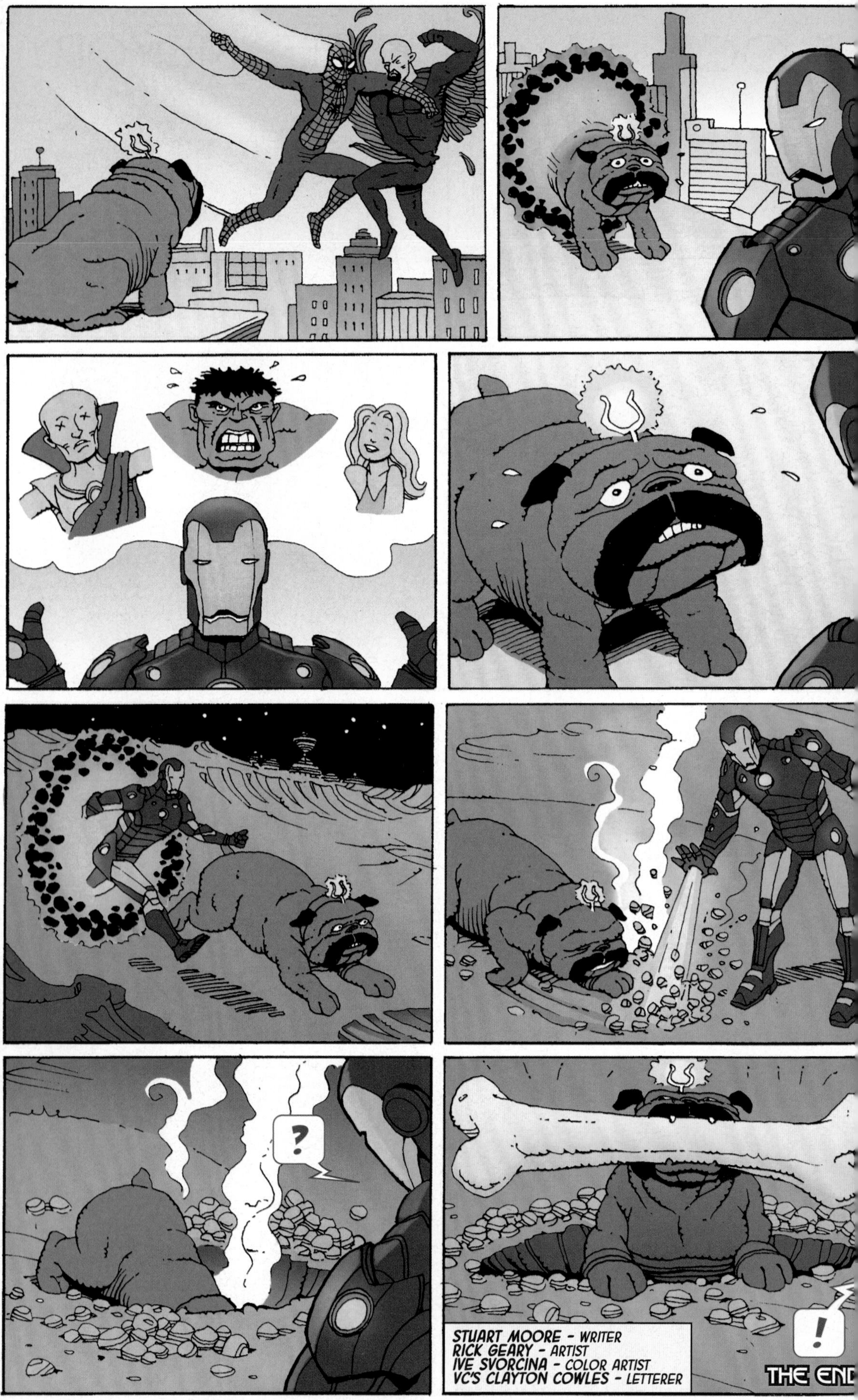
?
!
STUART MOORE - WRITER
RICK GEARY - ARTIST
IVE SVORCINA - COLOR ARTIST
VC'S CLAYTON COWLES - LETTERER
THE END

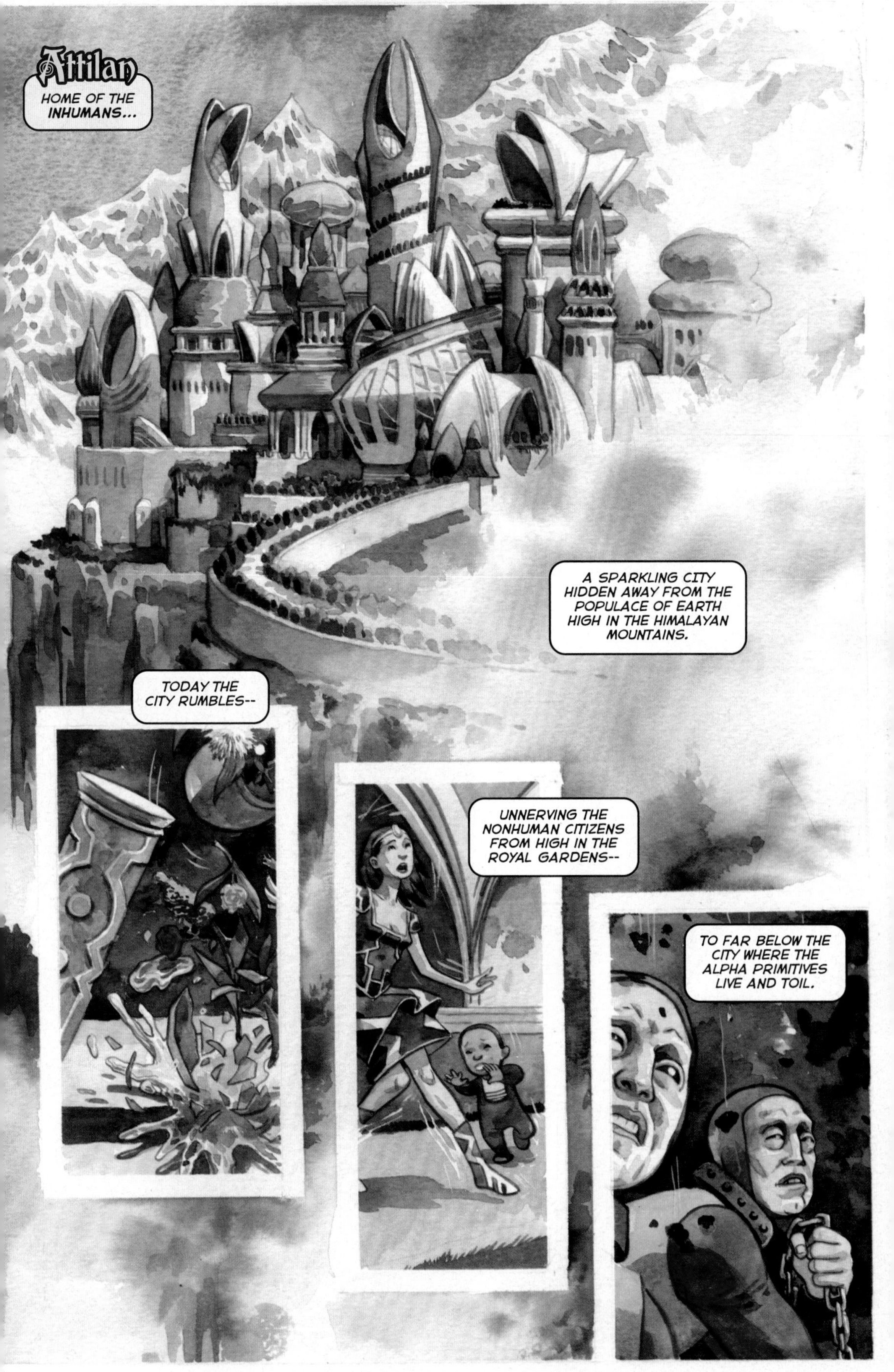
Attilan
HOME OF THE INHUMANS...
A SPARKLING CITY HIDDEN AWAY FROM THE POPULACE OF EARTH HIGH IN THE HIMALAYAN MOUNTAINS.
TODAY THE CITY RUMBLES--
UNNERVING THE NONHUMAN CITIZENS FROM HIGH IN THE ROYAL GARDENS--
TO FAR BELOW THE CITY WHERE THE ALPHA PRIMITIVES LIVE AND TOIL.

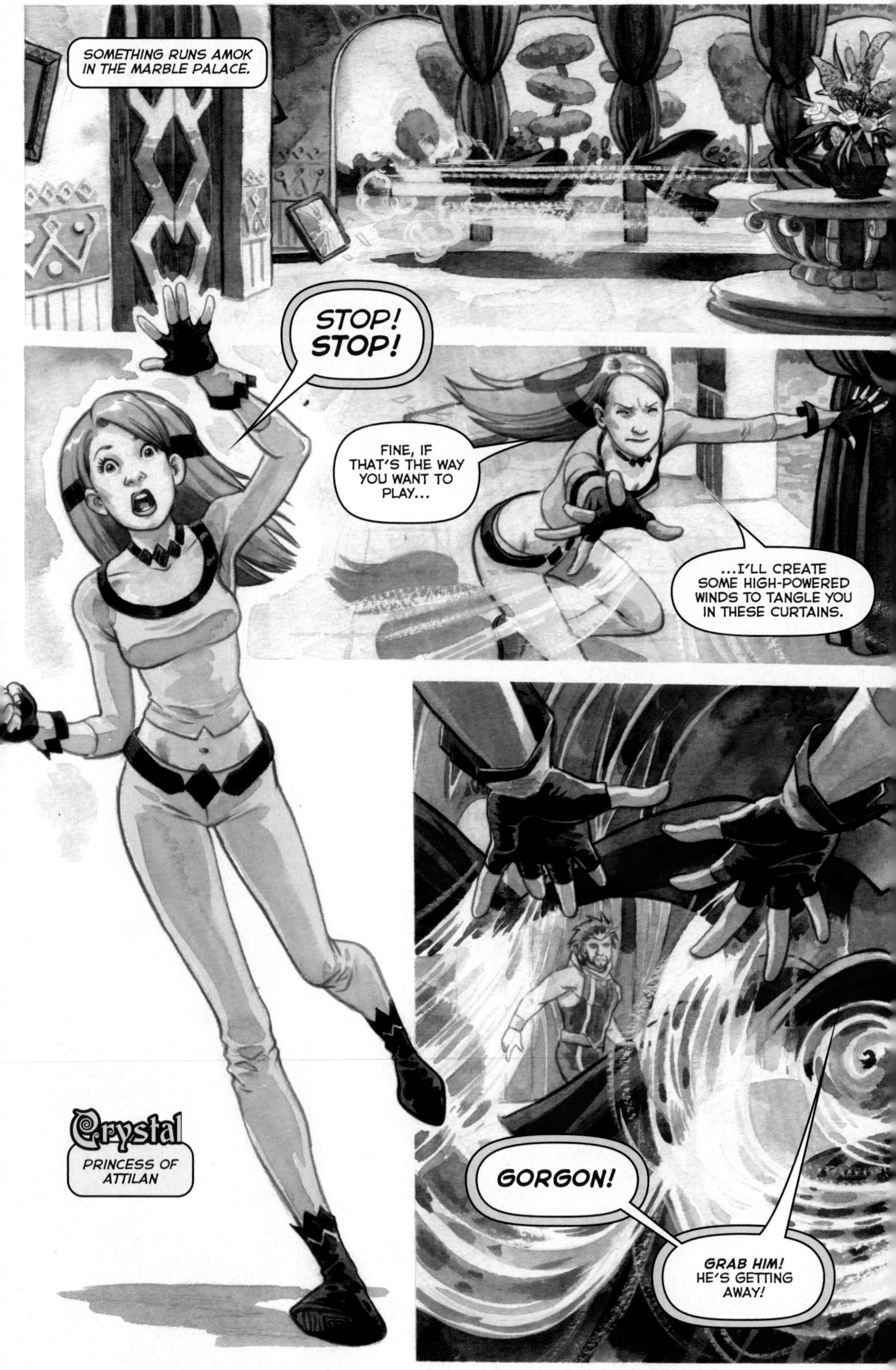
SOMETHING RUNS AMOK IN THE MARBLE PALACE.
STOP! STOP!
FINE, IF THAT'S THE WAY YOU WANT TO PLAY...
...I'LL CREATE SOME HIGH-POWERED WINDS TO TANGLE YOU IN THESE CURTAINS.
Crystal
PRINCESS OF ATTILAN
GORGON!
GRAB HIM! HE'S GETTING AWAY!

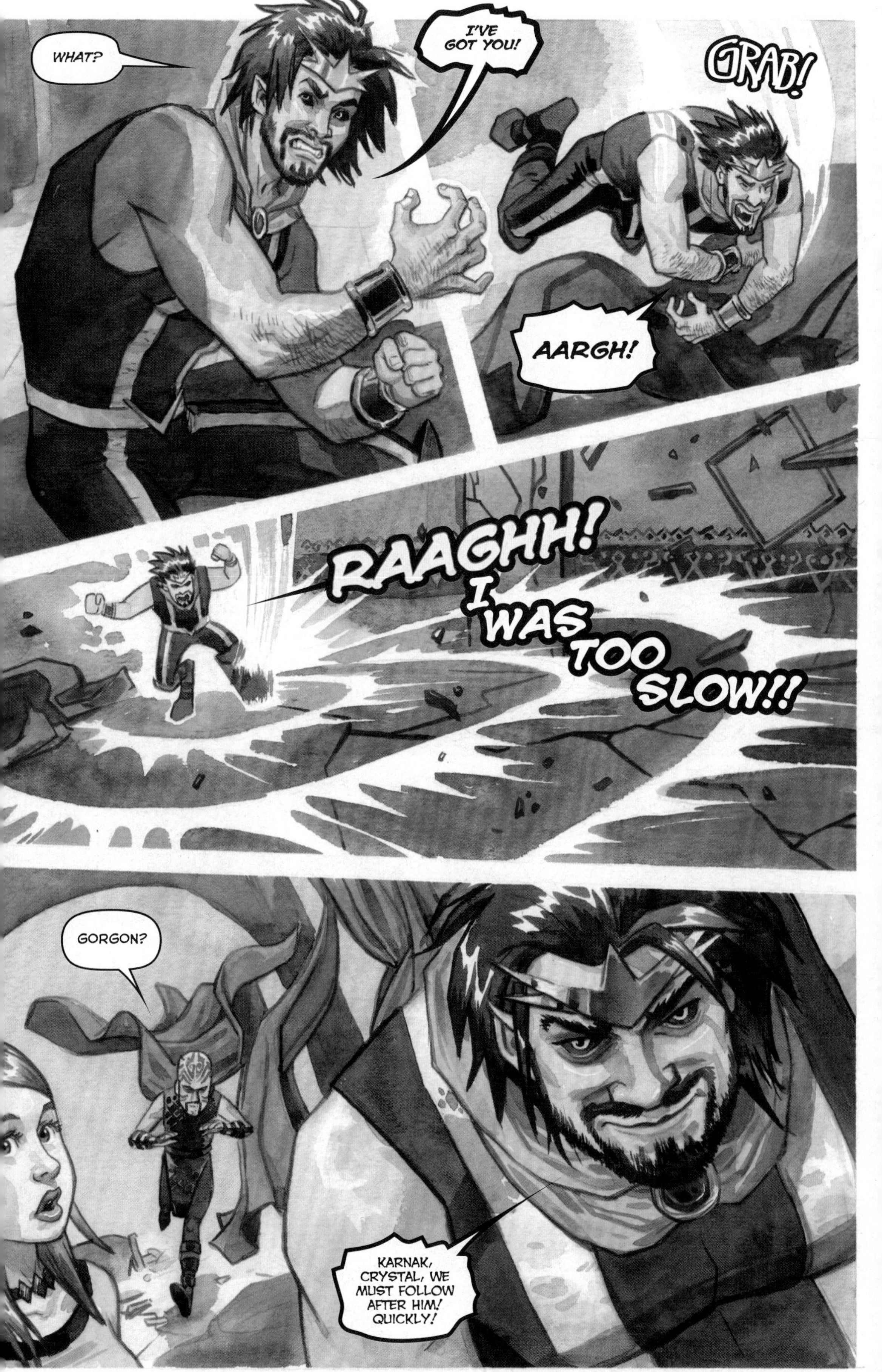
WHAT?
I'VE GOT YOU!
GRAB!
AARGH!
RAAGHH! I WAS TOO SLOW!!
GORGON?
KARNAK, CRYSTAL, WE MUST FOLLOW AFTER HIM! QUICKLY!

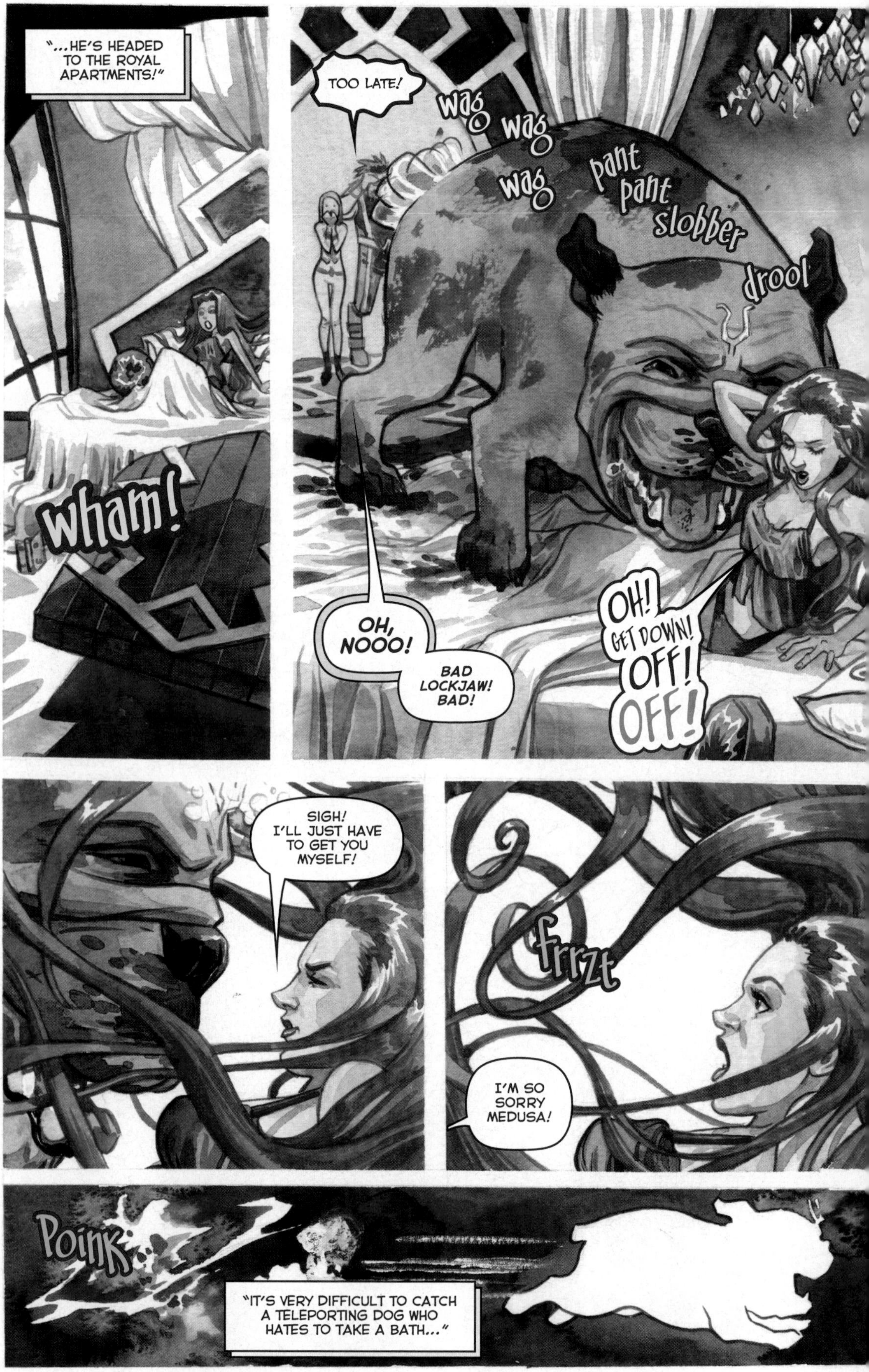
"...HE'S HEADED TO THE ROYAL APARTMENTS!"
wham!
TOO LATE!
wag wag wag
pant pant
slobber
drool
OH, NOOO!
BAD LOCKJAW! BAD!
OH! GET DOWN! OFF! OFF!
SIGH! I'LL JUST HAVE TO GET YOU MYSELF!
frrzt
I'M SO SORRY MEDUSA!
Poink
"IT'S VERY DIFFICULT TO CATCH A TELEPORTING DOG WHO HATES TO TAKE A BATH..."

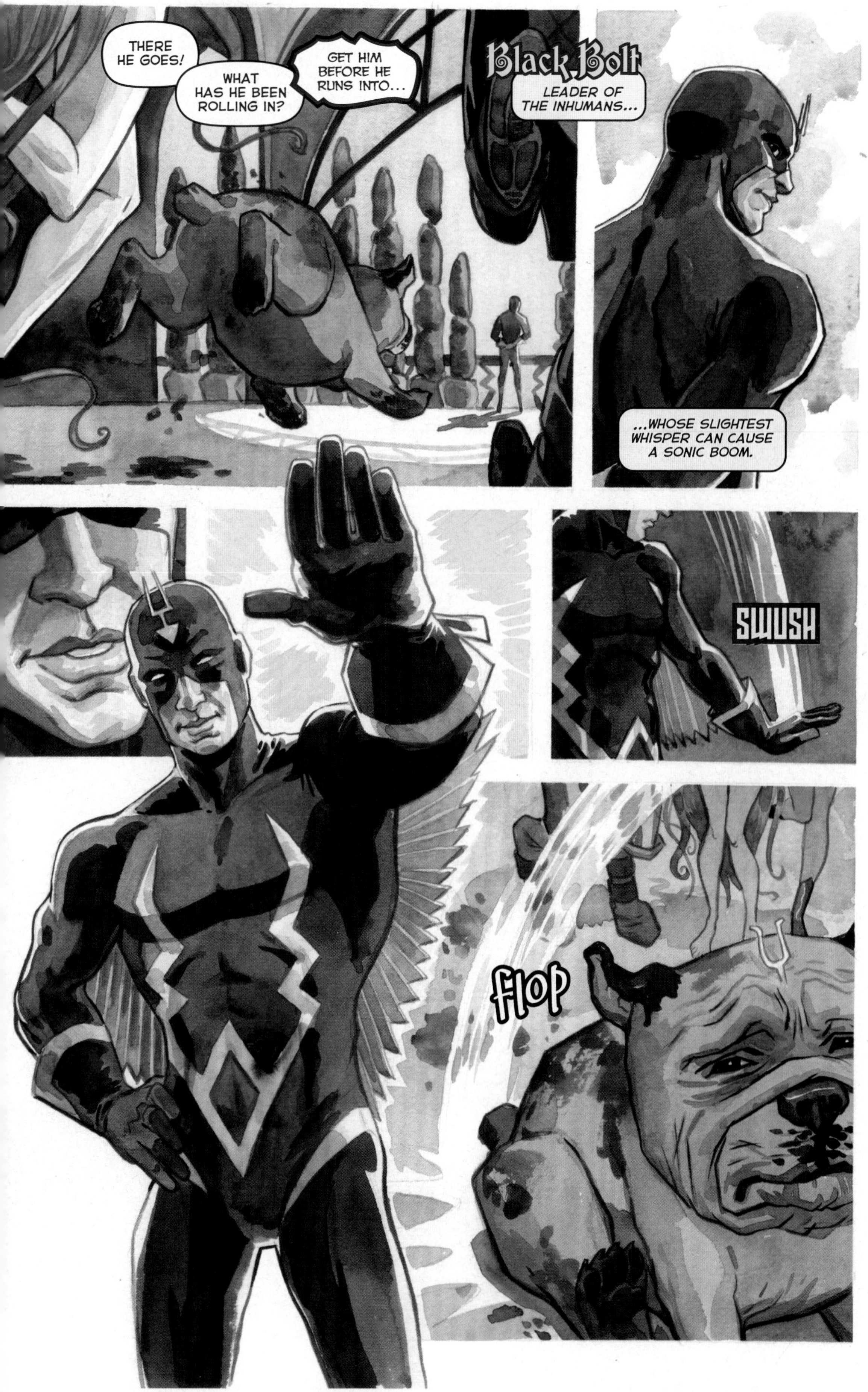

THERE HE GOES!
WHAT HAS HE BEEN ROLLING IN?
GET HIM BEFORE HE RUNS INTO...
Black Bolt
LEADER OF THE INHUMANS...
...WHOSE SLIGHTEST WHISPER CAN CAUSE A SONIC BOOM.
SWUSH
flop

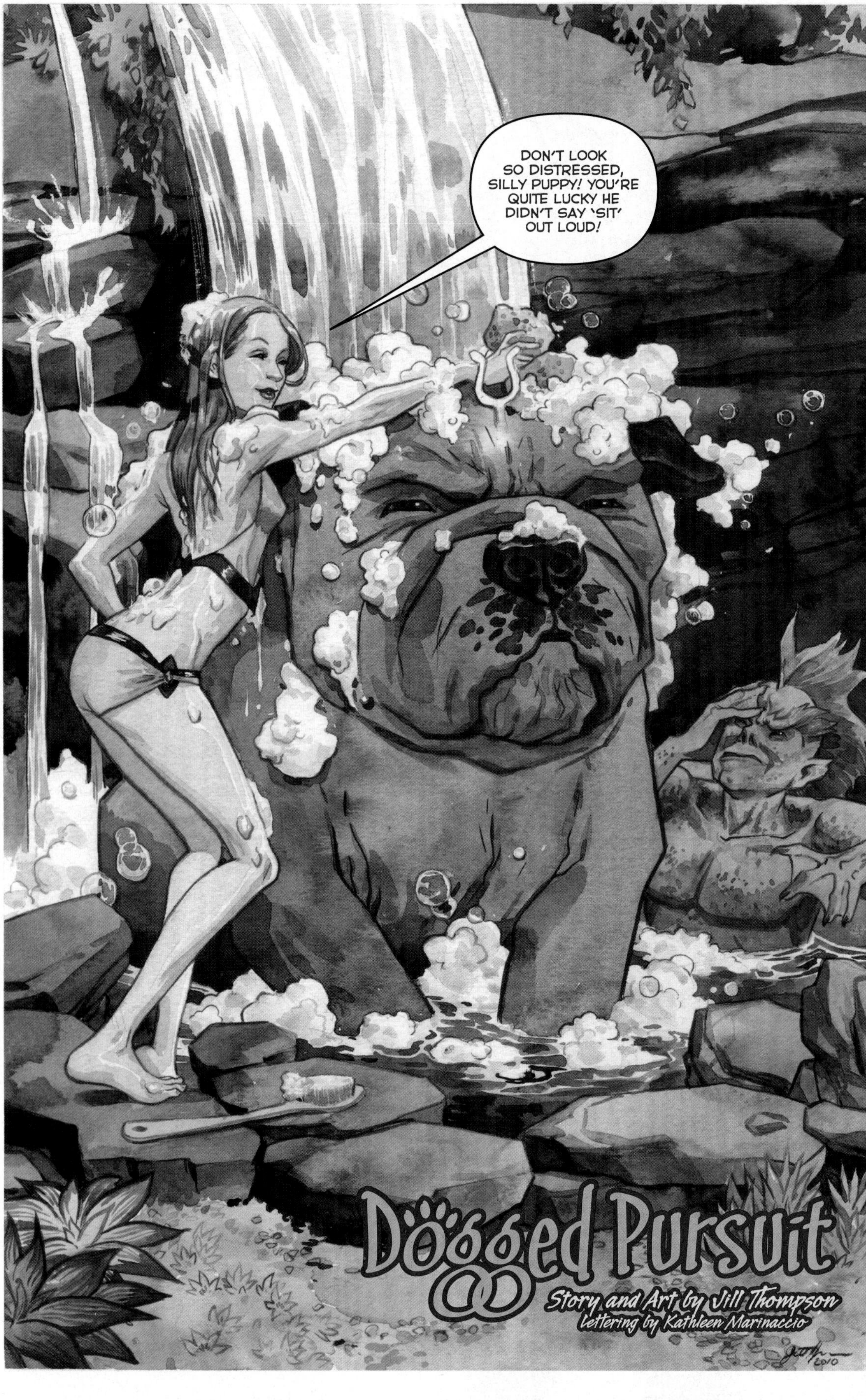

DON'T LOOK SO DISTRESSED, SILLY PUPPY! YOU'RE QUITE LUCKY HE DIDN'T SAY 'SIT' OUT LOUD!
Dogged Pursuit
Story and Art by Jill Thompson
lettering by Kathleen Marinaccio

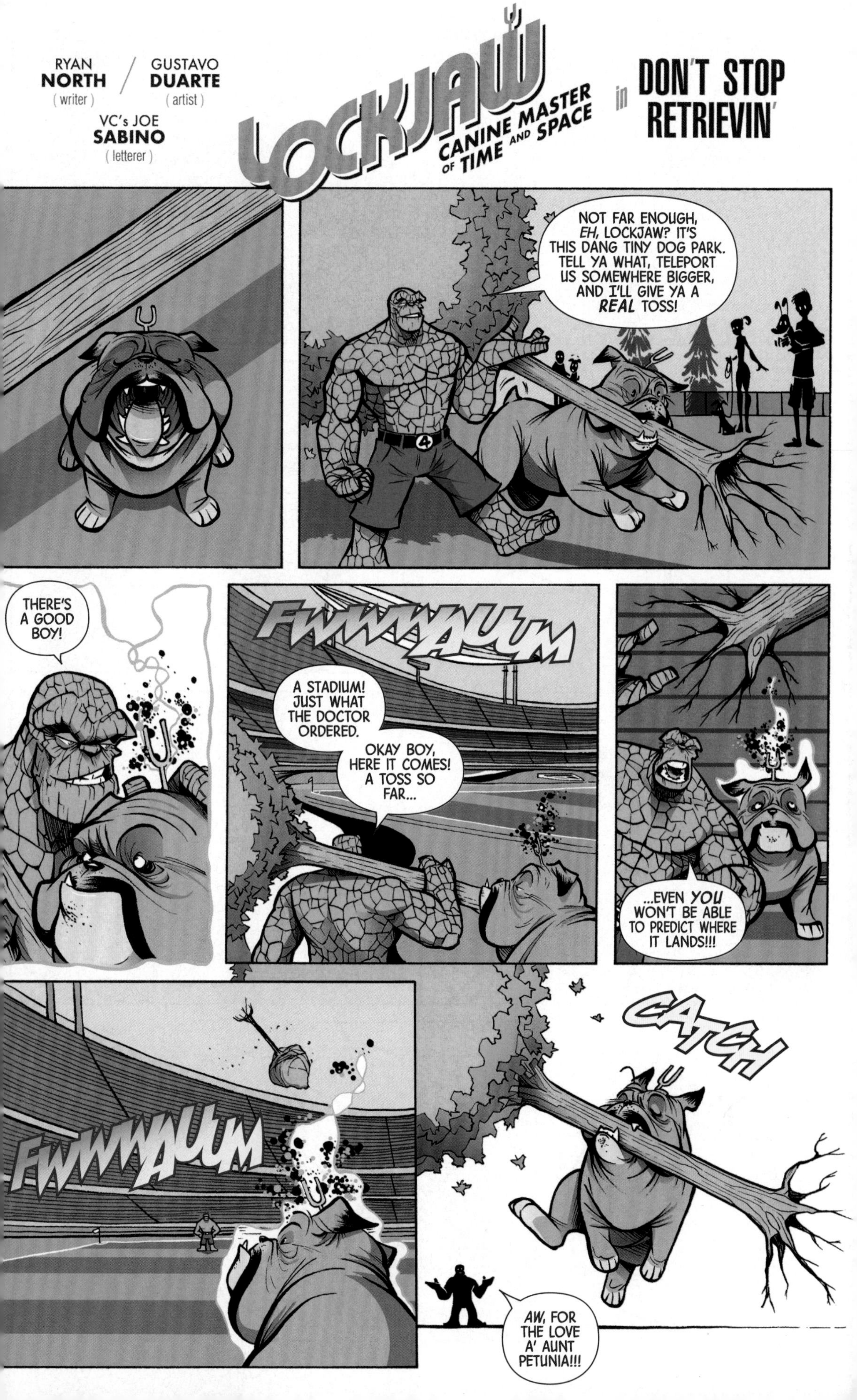

RYAN NORTH (writer) / GUSTAVO DUARTE (artist)
VC's JOE SABINO (letterer)
LOCKJAW CANINE MASTER OF TIME AND SPACE in DON'T STOP RETRIEVIN'
NOT FAR ENOUGH, EH, LOCKJAW? IT'S THIS DANG TINY DOG PARK. TELL YA WHAT, TELEPORT US SOMEWHERE BIGGER, AND I'LL GIVE YA A REAL TOSS!
THERE'S A GOOD BOY!
FWWWAUUM
A STADIUM! JUST WHAT THE DOCTOR ORDERED.
OKAY BOY, HERE IT COMES! A TOSS SO FAR...
...EVEN YOU WON'T BE ABLE TO PREDICT WHERE IT LANDS!!!
FWWWAUUM
CATCH
AW, FOR THE LOVE A' AUNT PETUNIA!!!

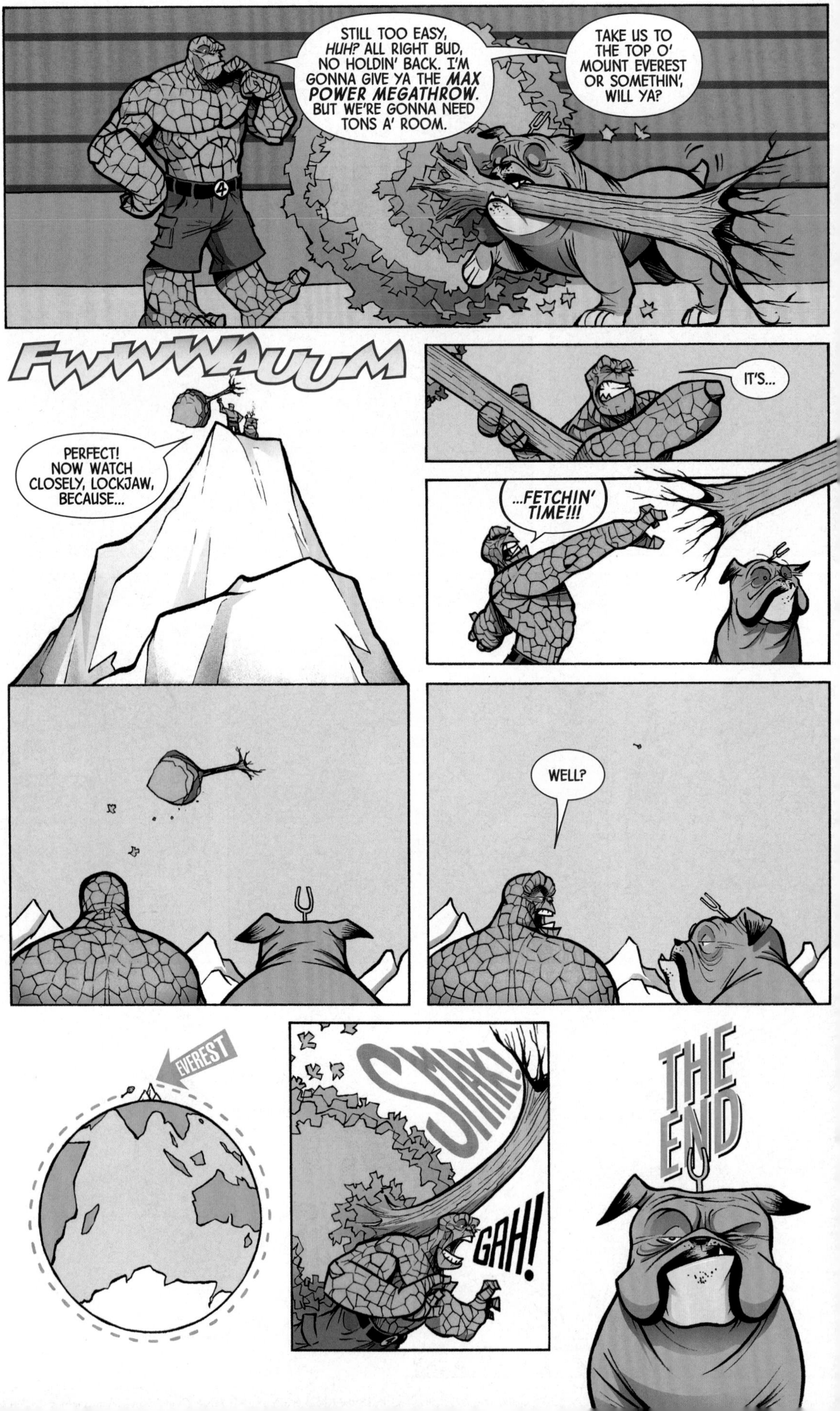
STILL TOO EASY, HUH? ALL RIGHT BUD, NO HOLDIN' BACK. I'M GONNA GIVE YA THE MAX POWER MEGATHROW. BUT WE'RE GONNA NEED TONS A' ROOM.
TAKE US TO THE TOP O' MOUNT EVEREST OR SOMETHIN', WILL YA?
FWWWAUUUM
PERFECT! NOW WATCH CLOSELY, LOCKJAW, BECAUSE...
IT'S...
...FETCHIN' TIME!!!
WELL?
EVEREST
SMAK!
GAH!
THE END

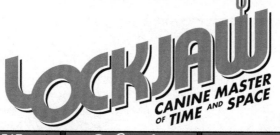

RYAN **NORTH**
(writer)
GUSTAVO **DUARTE**
(artist)
VC's JOE **SABINO**
(letterer)

LOCKJAW: CANINE MASTER OF TIME AND SPACE

in **ARE YOU KITTEN ME?**

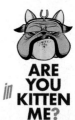

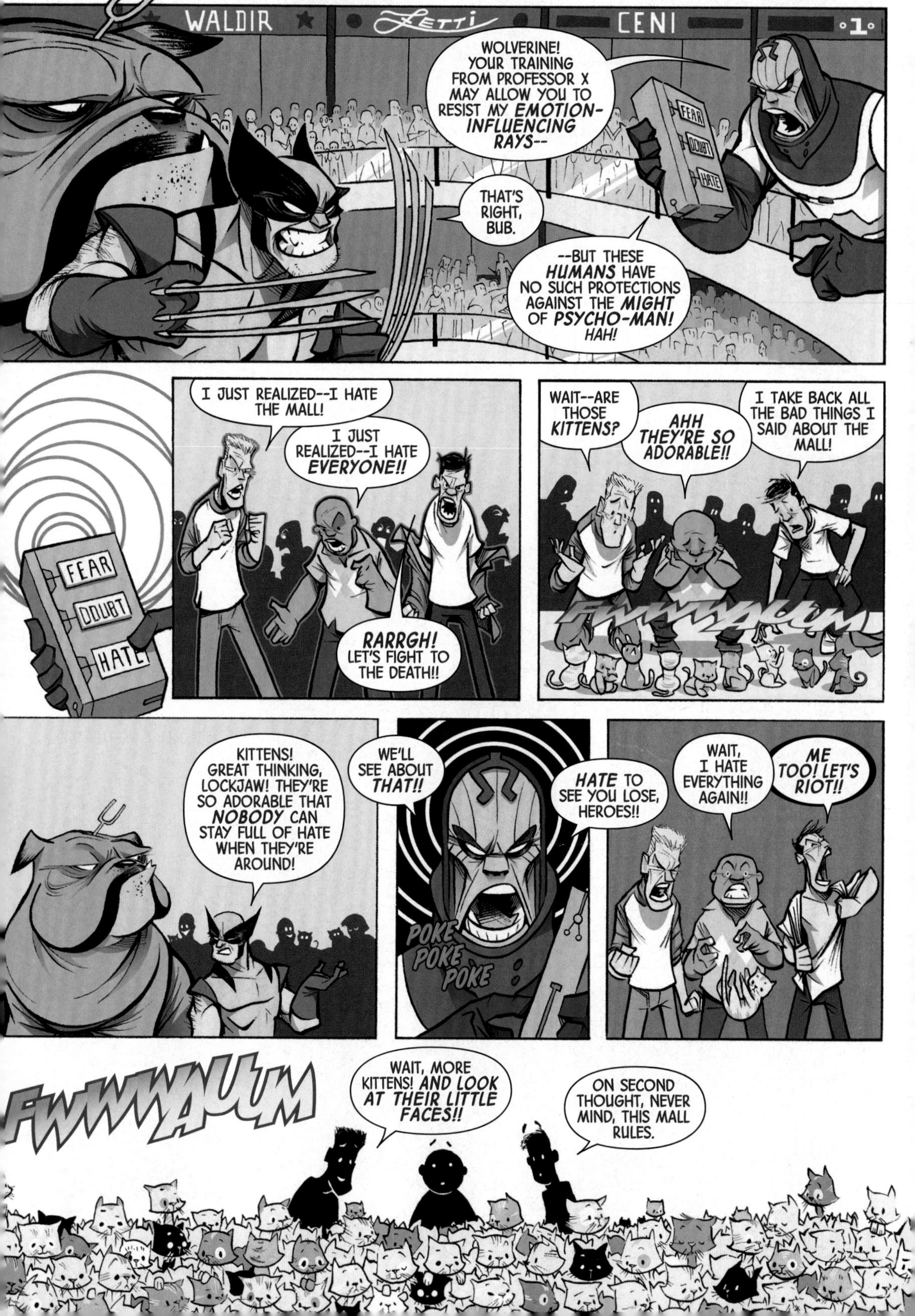
WALDIR
LETTI
CENI
1
WOLVERINE! YOUR TRAINING FROM PROFESSOR X MAY ALLOW YOU TO RESIST MY EMOTION-INFLUENCING RAYS--
THAT'S RIGHT, BUB.
--BUT THESE HUMANS HAVE NO SUCH PROTECTIONS AGAINST THE MIGHT OF PSYCHO-MAN! HAH!
FEAR
DOUBT
HATE
I JUST REALIZED--I HATE THE MALL!
I JUST REALIZED--I HATE EVERYONE!!
RARRGH! LET'S FIGHT TO THE DEATH!!
WAIT--ARE THOSE KITTENS?
AHH THEY'RE SO ADORABLE!!
I TAKE BACK ALL THE BAD THINGS I SAID ABOUT THE MALL!
FWWWAUUM
KITTENS! GREAT THINKING, LOCKJAW! THEY'RE SO ADORABLE THAT NOBODY CAN STAY FULL OF HATE WHEN THEY'RE AROUND!
WE'LL SEE ABOUT THAT!!
POKE POKE POKE
HATE TO SEE YOU LOSE, HEROES!!
WAIT, I HATE EVERYTHING AGAIN!!
ME TOO! LET'S RIOT!!
FWWWAUUM
WAIT, MORE KITTENS! AND LOOK AT THEIR LITTLE FACES!!
ON SECOND THOUGHT, NEVER MIND, THIS MALL RULES.

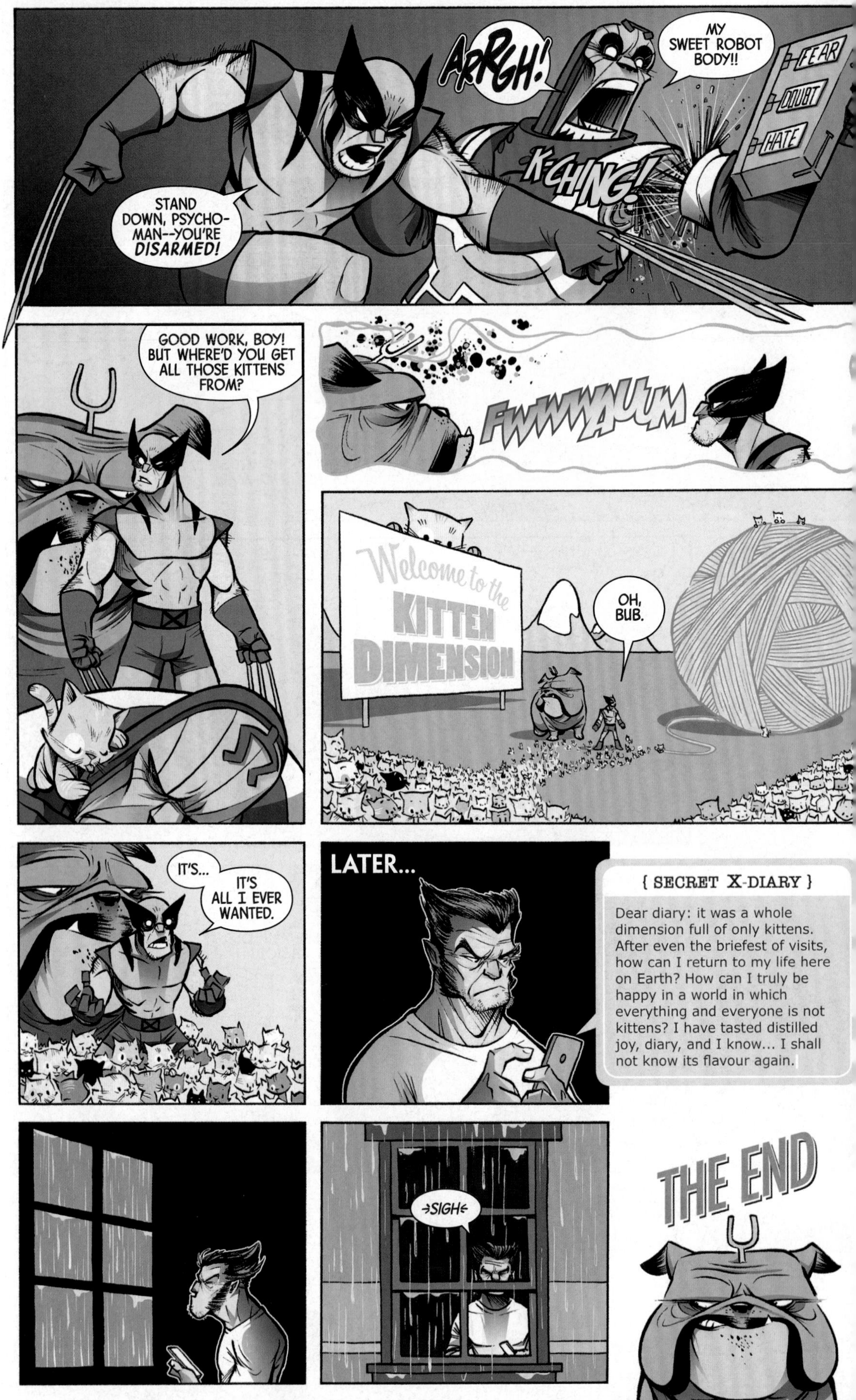

ARRGH!
MY SWEET ROBOT BODY!!
FEAR
DOUBT
HATE
K-CHING!
STAND DOWN, PSYCHO-MAN--YOU'RE DISARMED!
GOOD WORK, BOY! BUT WHERE'D YOU GET ALL THOSE KITTENS FROM?
FWWAUUM
Welcome to the KITTEN DIMENSION
OH, BUB.
IT'S...
IT'S ALL I EVER WANTED.
LATER...
{ SECRET X-DIARY }
Dear diary: it was a whole dimension full of only kittens. After even the briefest of visits, how can I return to my life here on Earth? How can I truly be happy in a world in which everything and everyone is not kittens? I have tasted distilled joy, diary, and I know... I shall not know its flavour again.
SIGH
THE END

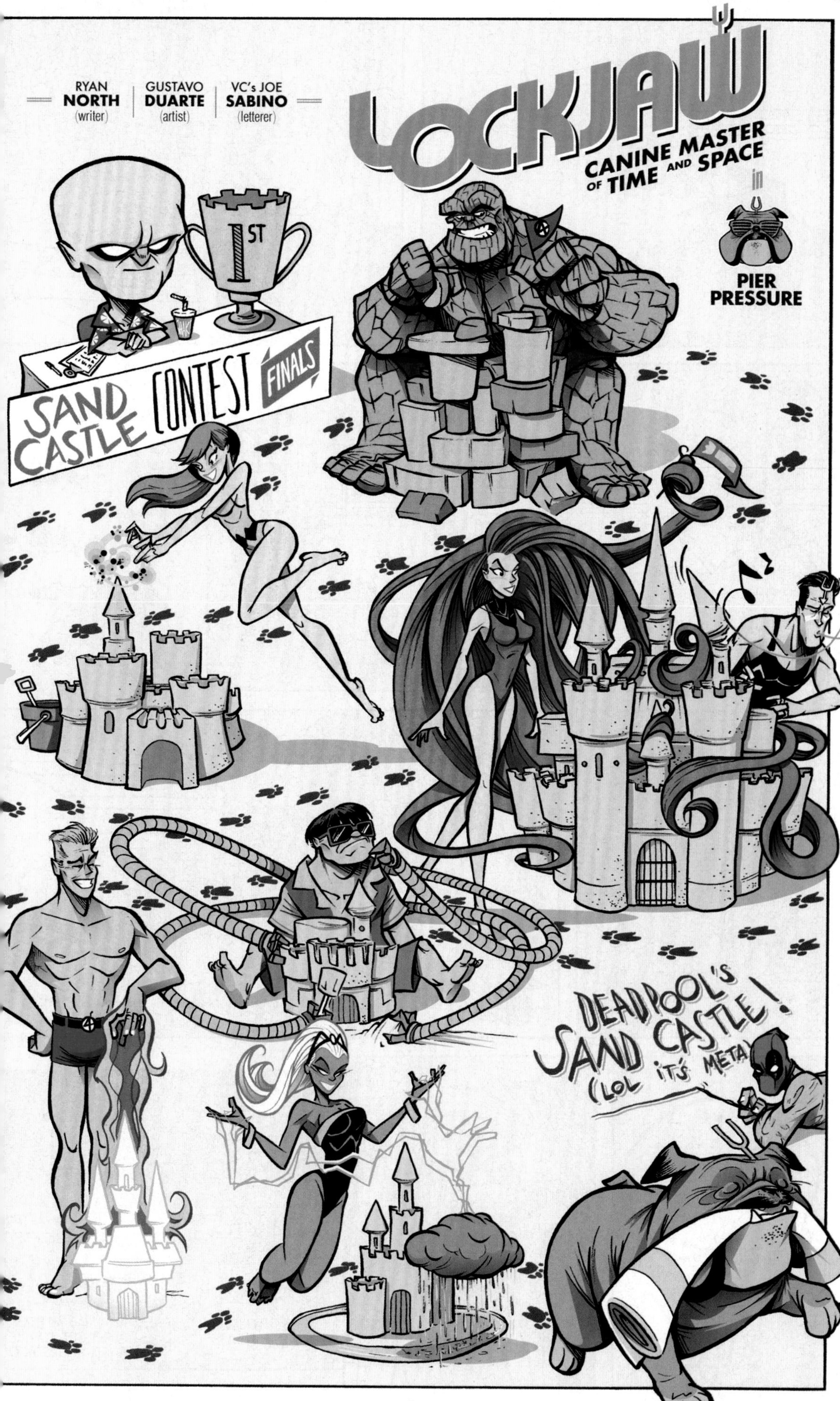

RYAN NORTH (writer)
GUSTAVO DUARTE (artist)
VC's JOE SABINO (letterer)
LOCKJAW
CANINE MASTER OF TIME AND SPACE
in
PIER PRESSURE
1ST
SAND CASTLE CONTEST FINALS
DEADPOOL'S SAND CASTLE! (LOL IT'S META)

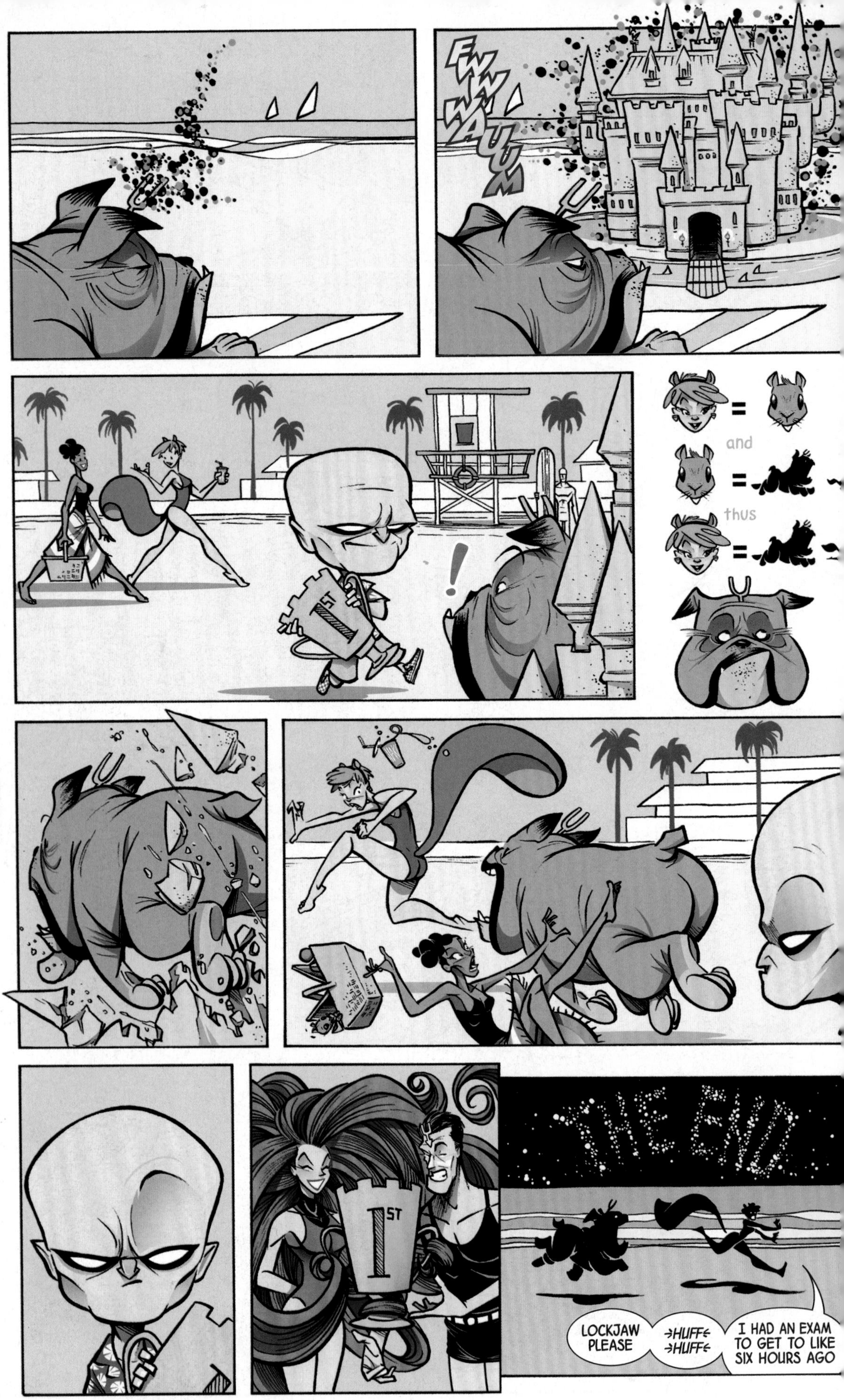
FWWAUUM
and
thus
1ST
THE END
LOCKJAW PLEASE
HUFF HUFF
I HAD AN EXAM TO GET TO LIKE SIX HOURS AGO

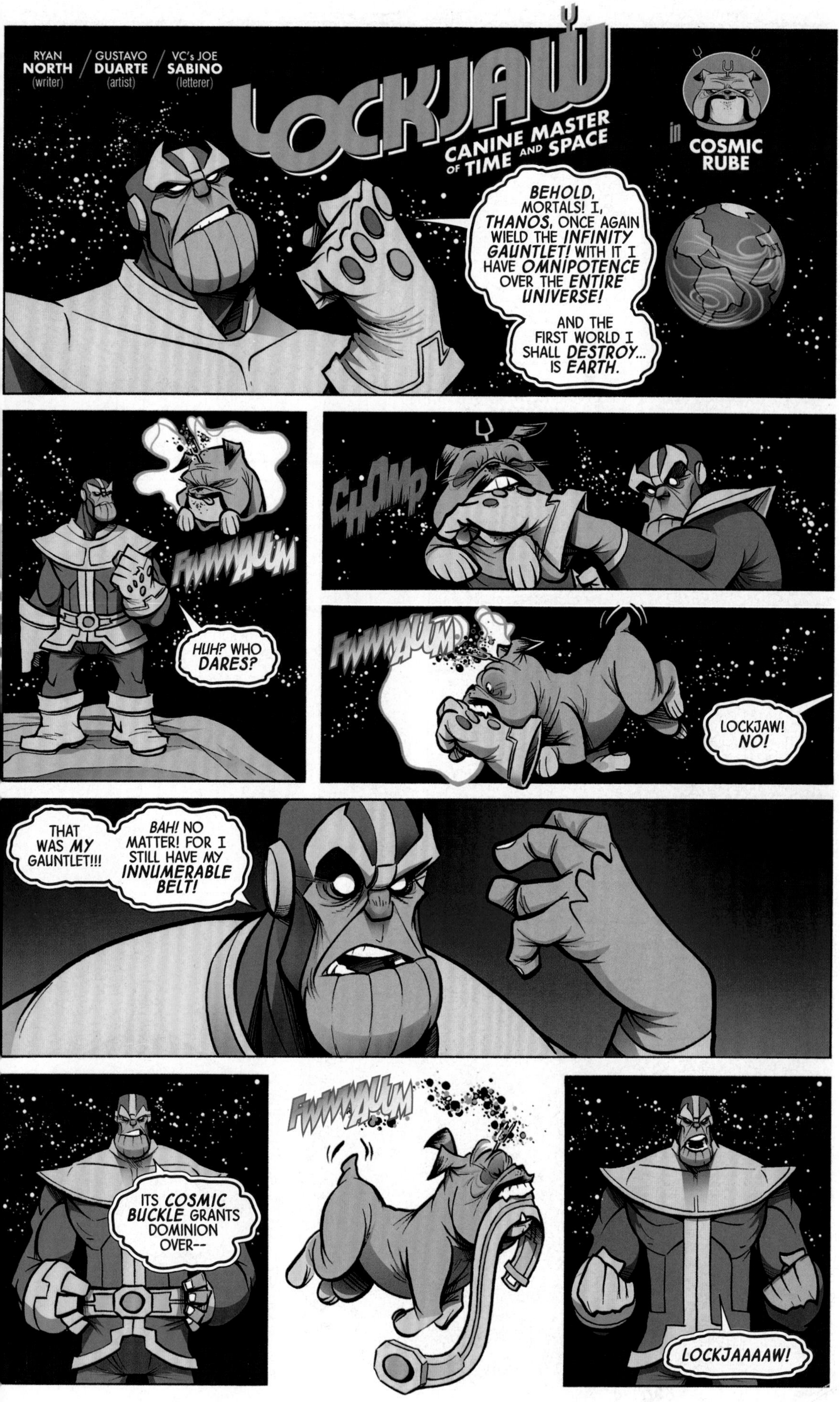
RYAN NORTH (writer) / GUSTAVO DUARTE (artist) / VC's JOE SABINO (letterer)
LOCKJAW CANINE MASTER OF TIME AND SPACE
in COSMIC RUBE
BEHOLD, MORTALS! I, THANOS, ONCE AGAIN WIELD THE INFINITY GAUNTLET! WITH IT I HAVE OMNIPOTENCE OVER THE ENTIRE UNIVERSE!
AND THE FIRST WORLD I SHALL DESTROY... IS EARTH.
FWMAUM
HUH? WHO DARES?
CHOMP
FWMAUM
LOCKJAW! NO!
THAT WAS MY GAUNTLET!!!
BAH! NO MATTER! FOR I STILL HAVE MY INNUMERABLE BELT!
ITS COSMIC BUCKLE GRANTS DOMINION OVER--
FWMAUM
LOCKJAAAAW!

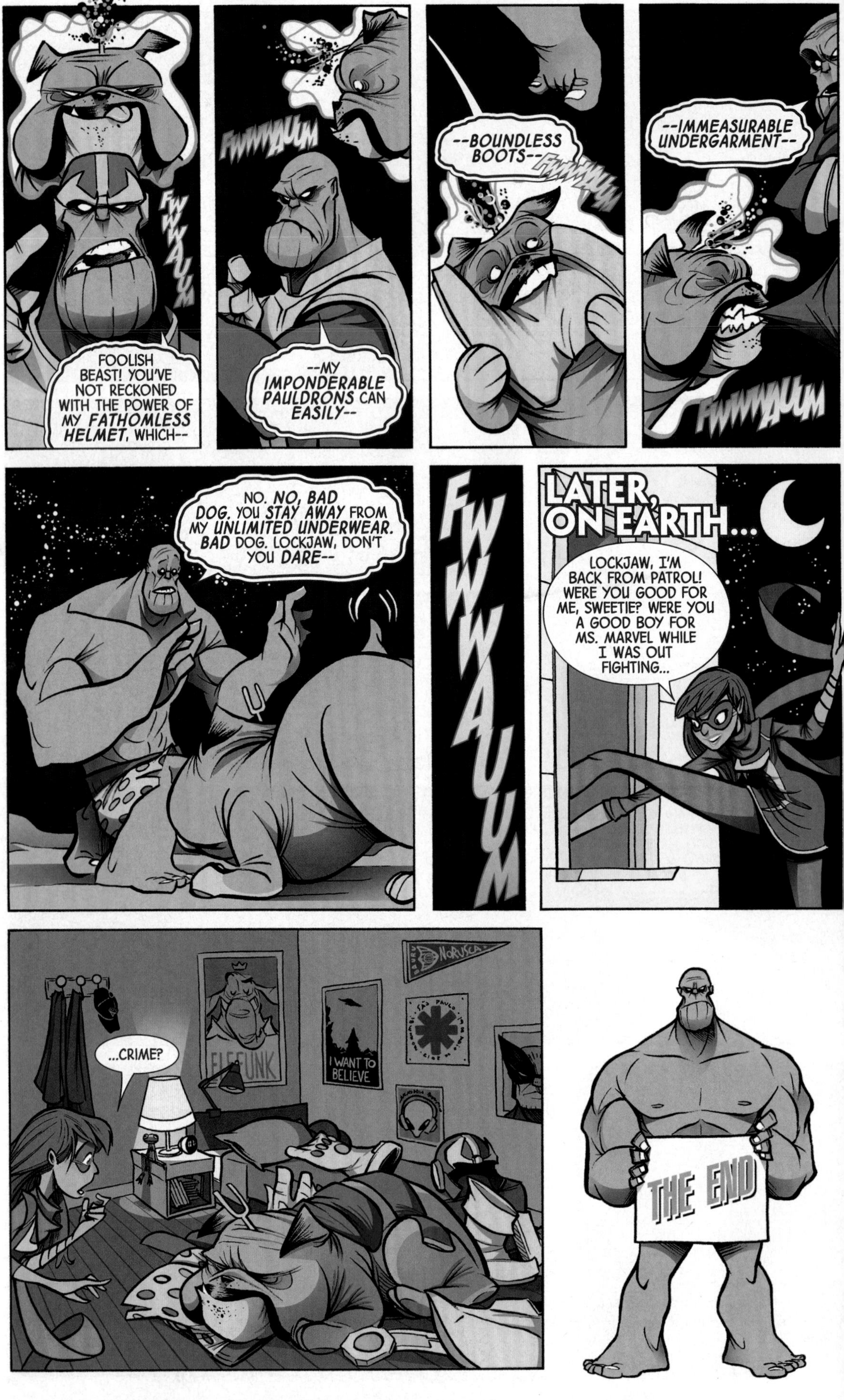

FOOLISH BEAST! YOU'VE NOT RECKONED WITH THE POWER OF MY FATHOMLESS HELMET, WHICH--
FWWAUUM
FWWAUUM
--MY IMPONDERABLE PAULDRONS CAN EASILY--
--BOUNDLESS BOOTS--
FWWAUUM
--IMMEASURABLE UNDERGARMENT--
FWWAUUM
NO. NO, BAD DOG. YOU STAY AWAY FROM MY UNLIMITED UNDERWEAR. BAD DOG. LOCKJAW, DON'T YOU DARE--
FWWAUUM
LATER, ON EARTH...
LOCKJAW, I'M BACK FROM PATROL! WERE YOU GOOD FOR ME, SWEETIE? WERE YOU A GOOD BOY FOR MS. MARVEL WHILE I WAS OUT FIGHTING...
...CRIME?
ELEFUNK
I WANT TO BELIEVE
THE END

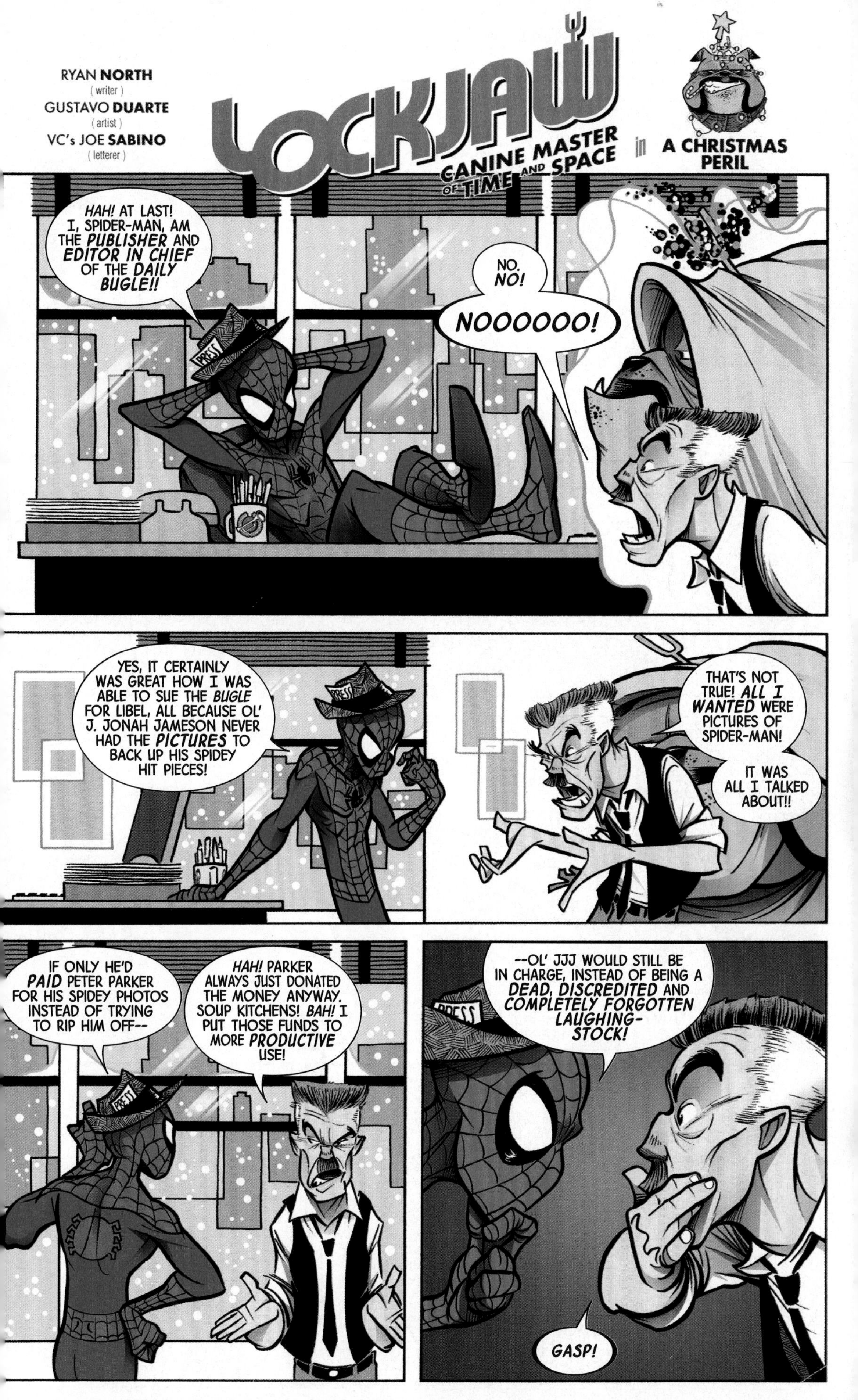

RYAN NORTH (writer)
GUSTAVO DUARTE (artist)
VC's JOE SABINO (letterer)
LOCKJAW CANINE MASTER OF TIME AND SPACE in A CHRISTMAS PERIL
HAH! AT LAST! I, SPIDER-MAN, AM THE PUBLISHER AND EDITOR IN CHIEF OF THE DAILY BUGLE!!
NO. NO!
NOOOOOO!
YES, IT CERTAINLY WAS GREAT HOW I WAS ABLE TO SUE THE BUGLE FOR LIBEL, ALL BECAUSE OL' J. JONAH JAMESON NEVER HAD THE PICTURES TO BACK UP HIS SPIDEY HIT PIECES!
THAT'S NOT TRUE! ALL I WANTED WERE PICTURES OF SPIDER-MAN!
IT WAS ALL I TALKED ABOUT!!
IF ONLY HE'D PAID PETER PARKER FOR HIS SPIDEY PHOTOS INSTEAD OF TRYING TO RIP HIM OFF--
HAH! PARKER ALWAYS JUST DONATED THE MONEY ANYWAY. SOUP KITCHENS! BAH! I PUT THOSE FUNDS TO MORE PRODUCTIVE USE!
--OL' JJJ WOULD STILL BE IN CHARGE, INSTEAD OF BEING A DEAD, DISCREDITED AND COMPLETELY FORGOTTEN LAUGHING-STOCK!
GASP!

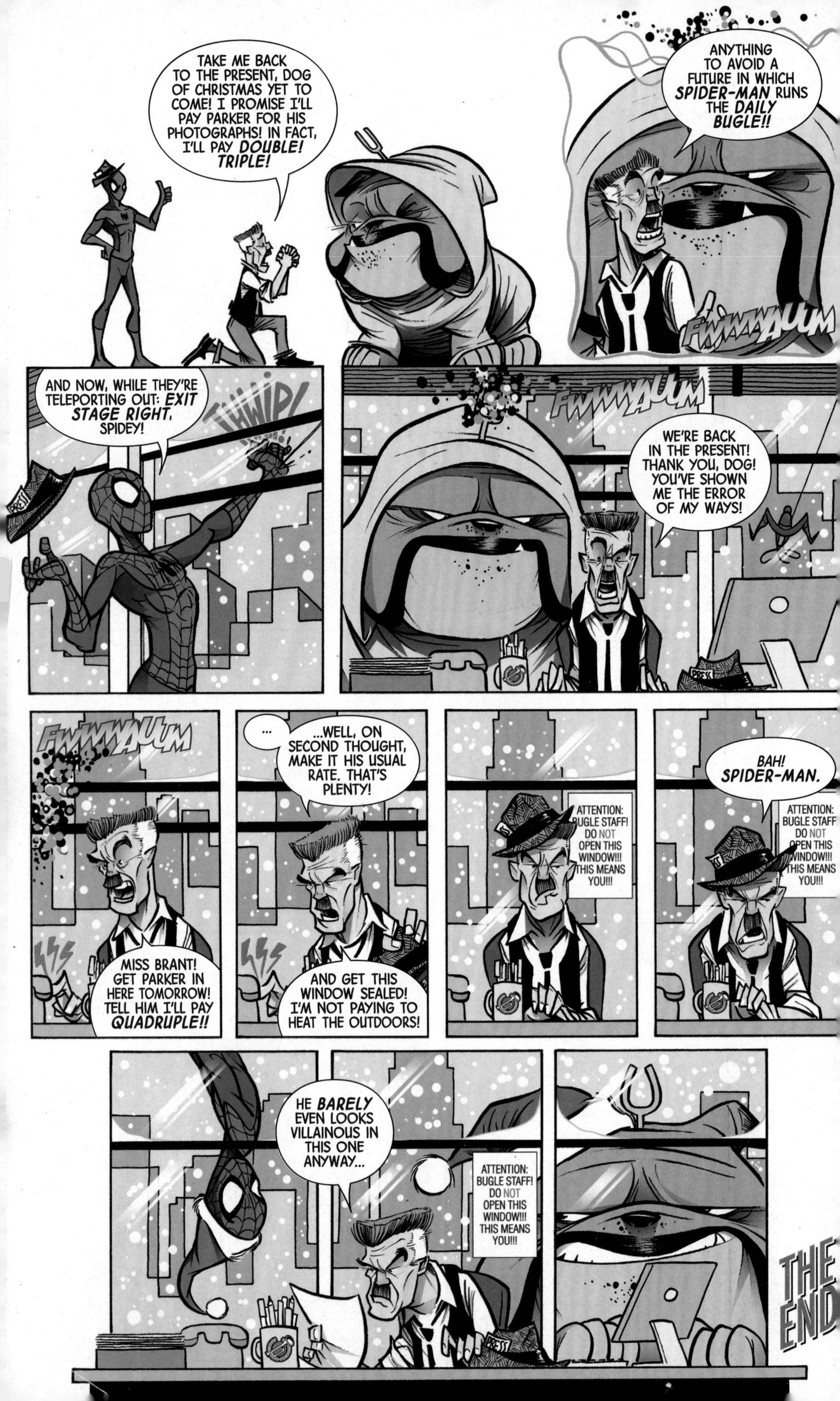

TAKE ME BACK TO THE PRESENT, DOG OF CHRISTMAS YET TO COME! I PROMISE I'LL PAY PARKER FOR HIS PHOTOGRAPHS! IN FACT, I'LL PAY DOUBLE! TRIPLE!
ANYTHING TO AVOID A FUTURE IN WHICH SPIDER-MAN RUNS THE DAILY BUGLE!!
FWWWAUUM
AND NOW, WHILE THEY'RE TELEPORTING OUT: EXIT STAGE RIGHT, SPIDEY!
THWIP!
FWWWAUUM
WE'RE BACK IN THE PRESENT! THANK YOU, DOG! YOU'VE SHOWN ME THE ERROR OF MY WAYS!
FWWWAUUM
MISS BRANT! GET PARKER IN HERE TOMORROW! TELL HIM I'LL PAY QUADRUPLE!!
...
...WELL, ON SECOND THOUGHT, MAKE IT HIS USUAL RATE. THAT'S PLENTY!
AND GET THIS WINDOW SEALED! I'M NOT PAYING TO HEAT THE OUTDOORS!
ATTENTION: BUGLE STAFF! DO NOT OPEN THIS WINDOW!!! THIS MEANS YOU!!!
BAH! SPIDER-MAN.
ATTENTION: BUGLE STAFF DO NOT OPEN THIS WINDOW!!! THIS MEANS YOU!!!
HE BARELY EVEN LOOKS VILLAINOUS IN THIS ONE ANYWAY...
ATTENTION: BUGLE STAFF! DO NOT OPEN THIS WINDOW!!! THIS MEANS YOU!!!
THE END